The Social Power of Algorithms

The vast circulations of mobile devices, sensors and data mean that the social world is now defined by a complex interweaving of human and machine agency. Key to this is the growing power of algorithms – the decision-making parts of code – in our software-dense and data-rich environments. Algorithms can shape how we are treated, what we know, who we connect with and what we encounter, and they present us with some important questions about how society operates and how we understand it.

This book offers a series of concepts, approaches and ideas for understanding the relations between algorithms and power. Each chapter provides a unique perspective on the integration of algorithms into the social world. As such, this book directly tackles some of the most important questions facing the social sciences today.

The chapters in this book were originally published as a special issue of *Information, Communication & Society*.

David Beer is Reader in Sociology at the University of York, UK. He is the author of *Metric Power* (2016), *Punk Sociology* (2014), *Popular Culture and New Media: The Politics of Circulation* (2013) and *New Media: The Key Concepts* (2008, with Nicholas Gane).

The Social Power of Algorithms

Edited by
David Beer

Routledge
Taylor & Francis Group

LONDON AND NEW YORK

First published 2018 by Routledge

2 Park Square, Milton Park, Abingdon, Oxfordshire OX14 4RN
52 Vanderbilt Avenue, New York, NY 10017

Routledge is an imprint of the Taylor & Francis Group, an informa business

First issued in paperback 2020

British Library Cataloguing in Publication Data
A catalogue record for this book is available from the British Library

ISBN 13: 978-0-8153-9183-8 (hbk)
ISBN 13: 978-0-367-59281-3 (pbk)

Typeset in MinionPro
by diacriTech, Chennai

Publisher's Note
The publisher accepts responsibility for any inconsistencies that may have arisen during
the conversion of this book from journal articles to book chapters, namely the possible
inclusion of journal terminology.

Disclaimer
Every effort has been made to contact copyright holders for their permission to reprint
material in this book. The publishers would be grateful to hear from any copyright holder
who is not here acknowledged and will undertake to rectify any errors or omissions in
future editions of this book.

Contents

CONTENTS

Citation Information

The chapters in this book were originally published in *Information, Communication & Society*, volume 20, issue 1 (January 2017). When citing this material, please use the original page numbering for each article, as follows:

Introduction
The social power of algorithms
David Beer
Information, Communication & Society, volume 20, issue 1 (January 2017) pp. 1–13

Chapter 1
Thinking critically about and researching algorithms
Rob Kitchin
Information, Communication & Society, volume 20, issue 1 (January 2017) pp. 14–29

Chapter 2
The algorithmic imaginary: exploring the ordinary affects of Facebook algorithms
Taina Bucher
Information, Communication & Society, volume 20, issue 1 (January 2017) pp. 30–44

Chapter 3
Algorithmic IF … THEN rules and the conditions and consequences of power
Daniel Neyland and Norma Möllers
Information, Communication & Society, volume 20, issue 1 (January 2017) pp. 45–62

Chapter 4
Algorithmically recognizable: Santorum's Google problem, and Google's Santorum problem
Tarleton Gillespie
Information, Communication & Society, volume 20, issue 1 (January 2017) pp. 63–80

Chapter 5
Computing brains: learning algorithms and neurocomputation in the smart city
Ben Williamson
Information, Communication & Society, volume 20, issue 1 (January 2017) pp. 81–99

Chapter 6

Scrutinizing an algorithmic technique: the Bayes classifier as interested reading of reality
Bernhard Rieder
Information, Communication & Society, volume 20, issue 1 (January 2017) pp. 100–117

Chapter 7

'Hypernudge': Big Data as a mode of regulation by design
Karen Yeung
Information, Communication & Society, volume 20, issue 1 (January 2017) pp. 118–136

Chapter 8

Algorithms (and the) everyday
Michele Willson
Information, Communication & Society, volume 20, issue 1 (January 2017) pp. 137–150

For any permission-related enquiries please visit:
http://www.tandfonline.com/page/help/permissions

Notes on Contributors

David Beer is Reader in Sociology at the University of York, UK. He is the author of *Metric Power* (2016), *Punk Sociology* (2014), *Popular Culture and New Media: The Politics of Circulation* (2013) and *New Media: The Key Concepts* (2008, with Nicholas Gane).

Taina Bucher is Associate Professor in Communication and IT at the University of Copenhagen, Denmark. Her research centres on social media, software studies, and the power and politics of algorithms in everyday life.

Tarleton Gillespie is a principal researcher at Microsoft Research, and an Adjunct Associate Professor in the Department of Communication and the Department of Information Science at Cornell University, USA. He is co-founder of the blog Culture Digitally, the author of *Wired Shut: Copyright and the Shape of Digital Culture* (2007) and co-editor of *Media Technologies: Essays on Communication, Materiality, and Society* (2014).

Rob Kitchin is Professor and ERC Advanced Investigator at the National University of Ireland Maynooth. He is currently a principal investigator on the Programmable City project, the Digital Repository of Ireland, the All-Island Research Observatory and the Dublin Dashboard.

Norma Möllers is Assistant Professor of Sociology at Queen's University at Kingston, Canada. She is interested in how governments enrol science and engineering in national security and surveillance strategies, and how this relates to broader shifts in knowledge production. Drawing on science and technology studies, she ethnographically investigates these issues with particular emphasis on the everyday politics of technoscientific work and labour.

Daniel Neyland is Professor of Sociology at Goldsmiths, University of London, UK. His research engages issues of governance, accountability, innovation and ethics in forms of science, technology and organisation. His substantive interests are focused on: algorithms, traffic management, waste, airports, biometrics, parking, signposts, malaria and the utility of social science, ideas of equivalence, parasitism, the mundane, market failures, problems and solutions, deleting, value and privacy.

NOTES ON CONTRIBUTORS

Bernhard Rieder is Associate Professor of New Media and Digital Culture at the Department of Media Studies at the University of Amsterdam, the Netherlands, and a researcher with the Digital Methods Initiative. His work is focused on the theory and history of software and on the development, application and critique of digital methods for Internet research.

Ben Williamson is a Lecturer in the School of Social Sciences at the University of Stirling, UK. His research focuses on digital data and algorithmic technologies in education, and has been published in *Big Data and Society*, *Critical Policy Studies* and the *Journal of Education Policy*.

Michele Willson is Associate Professor in Internet Studies, Curtin University, Australia. Her research interests converge around understanding our various relationships with and through technology. Her publications include *Social, Casual and Mobile Games*, *A New Theory of Information and the Internet* (2016) and *Technically Together* (2006).

Karen Yeung is Professor of Law and Director at the Centre for Technology, Ethics, Law and Society (TELOS), The Dickson Poon School of Law, King's College London, UK. She is also Distinguished Visiting Fellow, Melbourne Law School, Australia.

The social power of algorithms

David Beer

ABSTRACT
This article explores the questions associated with what might be
thought of as *the social power of algorithms*. The article, which
introduces a special issue on the same topic, begins by reflecting
on how we might approach algorithms from a social scientific
perspective. The article is then split into two sections. The first
deals with the issues that might be associated with an analysis of
the power of the algorithms themselves. This section outlines a
series of issues associated with the functionality of the algorithms
and how these functions are powerfully deployed within social
world. The second section then focuses upon the *notion* of the
algorithm. In this section, the article argues that we need to look
beyond the algorithms themselves, as a technical and material
presence, to explore how the notion or concept of the algorithm
is also an important feature of their potential power. In this
section, it is suggested that we look at the way that notions of the
algorithm are evoked as a part of broader rationalities and ways
of seeing the world. Exploring the notion of the algorithm may
enable us to see how algorithms also play a part in social ordering
processes, both in terms of how the algorithm is used to promote
certain visions of calculative objectivity and also in relation to
the wider governmentalities that this concept might be used to
open up.

The recent TV drama *Casual* (2016) introduced the viewer to Alex, a disenchanted internet entrepreneur who obsesses over his algorithm. Alex's algorithm, we discover, is the key
to the significant success of his online dating company Snooger. He already lives an apparently limitless if unfulfilling life of decadence and luxury. Yet, he keeps tweaking and playing with the algorithm, trying to perfect it, trying to hone and refine its powers. Alex, it
would seem, wants the algorithm to perfectly match couples and to predict successful part-
nerships – including for himself. With a nagging need to hone, he keeps fiddling and
working at the algorithm to try to perfect the outcomes. He knows how to play the algorithm to his advantage, as do other users of the site. They know what combination of profile
features will produce lots of matches, but Alex wants the algorithm to match profiles in
ways that cannot be played. When we return in the second season of *Casual*, we find
that Alex's co-directed company is now in trouble. The problem, we discover from the
venture capitalists who wish to purchase the company, is that the algorithm is just too

good. Its predictions are too precise. As a result, people are finding long-term matches and no longer need the site. The answer – to make the algorithm less predictive.

In *Casual*'s mise-en-scène we have the algorithm as a kind of intermittent, shadowy and powerful force, drawing Alex's pursuit of perfection but also active in shaping social connections and relations. A little like their presence in the social world, the algorithm is a part of the background or setting (see, for instance, Parisi, 2013, pp. 26–36). *Casual* reproduces the sense that algorithms are a powerful if largely unnoticed social presence. But we should hesitate. This is obviously an imagined sense of the power of algorithms; it is a vision in which an investment in coding can lead to uncanny and irresistible predictive powers of deduction. This example presents two things to consider. The first is that it provides an illustration of the type of embedded nature of algorithms and their potential role in social processes (amongst a range of examples, see, for instance, Kitchin & Dodge, 2011 or Manovich, 2013). I would add, however, that it is a very particular notion of how these algorithms work and the type of role that they play. More importantly, for the purpose of the arguments I wish to develop towards the end of this article, the TV show *Casual* is just one illustrative example of the way in which we have come to imagine the power of the algorithm today. That is to say that when thinking about the power of the algorithm, we need to think not just about the impact and consequences of code, we also need to think about the powerful ways in which notions and ideas about the algorithm circulate through the social world. Within these notions of the algorithm, we are likely to find broader rationalities, knowledge-making and norms – with the concept of the algorithm holding powerful and convincing sway in how things are done or how they should be done.

This takes us to the doors of a very famous garage. In 1998, working out of the inauspicious surroundings of their Menlo Park garage, Larry Page and Sergey Brin developed the well-known PageRank algorithm that drives Google Search results. The power of this algorithm, MacCormick (2012, p. 25) has explained, is in its ability to 'find needles in haystacks'. This power, as we know, is in the ability to sort and prioritise the media we encounter. Through its use of models of 'authority', this algorithm is able to use markers to assess importance in relation to the chosen search terms (see MacCormick, 2012, p. 36). As algorithms go, the PageRank algorithm is unusual in its fame (for a discussion, see both Gillespie and Willson's pieces in this issue). It is one of the more visible spikes in which the 'technological unconscious' (Thrift, 2006, p. 224) is momentarily pierced by the fame of one of the component parts of a complex media assemblage. As such, the PageRank algorithm is certainly atypical. It is an algorithm we know something about, allowing us the opportunity to reflect on its ability to shape our knowledge and to produce outcomes (see Bilić, 2016). It is far more common for algorithmic processes to pass us by without being noticed. Once we begin to reflect on the scale of these processes – with algorithms, sorting, filtering, searching, prioritising, recommending, deciding and so on – it is perhaps little wonder that a discussion of the social role of algorithms is picking up pace. There is a desire to try to understand how these algorithmic processes shape social and everyday life (see Willson, this issue). There is a desire to see how 'algorithmic culture' (Striphas, 2015) is experienced and how 'algorithmic life' (Amoore & Piotukh, 2016) is lived. This is to be expected, not least because the density of technological assemblages continues to escalate and so too, it would seem, algorithmic processes take on increasing weight and responsibility.

This suggests two preliminary problems. The first problem is understanding what an algorithm is. The second is understanding how different algorithms work. In other words, we will need descriptions to assist in the pursuit of a more detailed understanding of what we might call *the social power of algorothms*. That is to say that there is a sense that we need to understand what algorithms are and what they do in order to fully grasp their influence and consequences. This is where we can hit blockages in our understandings. It is quite hard to be versed in social theory and in the technical minutiae of coding. It is not that this combination is impossible, but it is more likely to require collaborative work than being within the scope of the lone scholar. Books such as MacCormick's (2012) *9 Algorithms that changed the future* are useful for giving a sense of the scale, but it is then hard to move towards the depth of what we are looking at – the scale, variation and design principles of the many algorithmic forms still reside largely in Thrift's (2006) 'technological unconscious'. Social scientists end up operating in one register and coders in another, with it being difficult to permeate the divide. There is plenty of work that is now uncovering the influence of particular algorithmic processes. Bucher's (2012) exemplary work on Facebook's EdgeRank algorithm is one such instance (and we can also point to the piece by Neyland and Möller in this issue). Bucher's work reveals a great deal about the nature of the news feed on that popular social media platform and how it makes certain things visible to the individual user. Indeed, we are now seeing a growing interest in treating algorithms as objects of study (see, for example, the collection edited by Ziewitz, 2016a).

As this would suggest, perhaps the biggest single issue we have to consider when attempting to research the social power of algorithms is the potential difficulty of fully appreciating the object of study. Uncertainty about the algorithm could lead us to misjudge their power, to overemphasise their importance, to misconceive of the algorithm as a lone detached actor, or to miss how power might actually be deployed through such technologies. This difficulty of comprehension, amongst other things, has led Pasquale (2015) to conclude that we are living in a 'black box society'. This is a society, he suggests, that is populated by 'enigmatic technologies' (Pasquale, 2015, p. 1). Pasquale's central point is that the 'values and prerogatives that the encoded rules enact are hidden within black boxes'. This matters, Pasquale (2015, p. 8) claims, because 'authority is increasingly expressed algorithmically'. Such a point opens up a series of questions about the role of algorithms in the deployment or expression of power. These questions would concern the nature of such an authority and whether an algorithm has the capability to express or enable authority. The association in Pasquale's work is between big data and algorithms, with algorithms giving those big data a purpose and direction. Thus, the algorithm becomes the source of political concern, with the data being operationalised through those algorithmic decisions. As Pasquale (2015, p. 21) puts it, 'critical decisions are made not on the basis of the data per se, but on the basis of data analyzed algorithmically'. Here, we see the role of algorithms, as decision-making parts of code (see Beer, 2013, p. 65), as being analytic and decisive (for a discussion of the role of algorithms in data analytics, see Kitchin, 2014, pp. 100–112). Indeed, it is often this ability to take decisions without (or with little) human intervention that is at the heart of discussions about algorithms potential power. Of course, again, this creates questions about the role of agency and the like (see, for instance, Pasquale, 2015, p. 38), but there is clearly something here that should be of interest to anyone who wishes to understand the ordering of the social world, especially where software may be taking on some constitutive or performative role in ordering that world on our behalf.

As this alludes, one key problem with attempting to explore the social power of algorithms is in how we approach those algorithms in the first place. Should we treat them as lines of code, as objects, or should we see them as social processes in which the social world is embodied in the substrate of the code? The problem comes if we try to detach the algorithm from the social world in order to analyse its properties and powers – seeing it as a technical and self-contained object that exists as a distinct presence is likely to be a mistake. Detaching the algorithm in order to ask what it does requires separating the algorithm from the social world in the first place and then to treat it as a separate entity to those social processes. Algorithms are inevitably modelled on visions of the social world, and with outcomes in mind, outcomes influenced by commercial or other interests and agendas (as discussed by Williamson, this issue). As well as being produced from a social context, the algorithms are lived with, they are an integral part of that social world; they are woven into practices and outcomes. And then, we have the recursive processes as those outcomes are modelled back into algorithm design (see Parisi, 2013). As algorithms afford data circulations, they can be tweaked and re-coded where the outcomes are seen to be in need of adjustment (see, for example, the discussion in Kitchin & Dodge, 2011, p. 30; or Gillespie's article in this issue). So, seeing the algorithm as a separate item of study outside of its social ecology is likely to be a mistake. Algorithms should not be understood as an object that exists outside of those social processes (as discussed in a range of places in this volume, especially in the contributions from Neyland and Möllers, Kitchin and Willson). Their existence and design are a product of social forces, as are their implementations and redesigns.

To set the scene for thinking broadly about the material ways in which power may operate through the algorithm, I intend to briefly outline a series points that we might think of as representing the areas in which algorithms are in some way implicated, involved or integrated into social power dynamics (noting also that a detailed discussion of how to approach algorithms can be found in Rob Kitchin's contribution to this issue). Emerging from the articles gathered in this volume, the below section outlines a series of issues that might be associated with the functionality of algorithms and how these functions can be seen to be a part of the deployment of power in social ordering.

Power and the algorithm

Over the last 10 years, algorithms have become a fairly well-established presence in social scientific work (as outlined by Kitchin in this volume; see also Ziewitz, 2016b). When we consider this work and the broader changes with which it is associated, we can begin to draw out some important analytical issues that we may wish to consider were we to be interested in understanding the social power of algorithms – or social power operating through the algorithm. A primary concern here might be the meshing of human and machine agency (see Beer, 2013, pp. 63–101; Crang & Graham, 2007, p. 792; Mackenzie, 2006; Ziewitz, 2016b, p. 7). Such observations have recently been placed into broader debates about the status of agency as processes of 'datafication' continue to expand and as data feeds-back into people's lives in different ways (Kennedy, Poell, & van Dijk, 2015).

We can link these broader issues to some specific questions that algorithms create for human discretion (see Amoore, 2013; Berry, 2014) or even link it to what Introna (2011, pp. 122–130) has called the 'encoding of human agency'. Such a concern could well take us back beyond these interests in the algorithm, to the type of work done on cybernetics, interfaced bodies and posthumanism by Haraway (1991), Hayles (1999) and Mitchell (2003). But with the emergence of algorithmic systems in the everyday (see Willson's piece in this volume), this interest has gained new momentum, especially where algorithms are seen to be taking decisions out of the hands of human actors or where discretion is eroded by algorithmic limitations to thought (see Berry, 2014, p. 11). This has led Crawford (2016) to reflect on the politics of such agency and to ask whether it is possible for algorithms to be agonistic. The questions around agency are complex, but the notion of algorithmic power is often premised on the idea that algorithms carry some form of agentic power. The role of cognition is discussed in Ben Williamson's contribution to this collection. He takes popular visions of the 'smart city' and explores how these then filter into the 'smarter classroom' and 'smarter education'. This focus enables Williamson to explore how the 'learning brain' is seen to interact with the 'learning algorithm'. His contribution explores how we have come to understand or represent such a set of interactions. This, as he puts it, is to explore how 'mental life is understood algorithmically'. This contribution provides us with a direct illustration of how we might explore the apparent meshing of human and machine agency, a theme that continues in relation to notions of 'distributed agency' in Neyland and Möllers' article. Of course, both Neyland and Möllers and Williamson's balanced and revealing analyses illustrate how easy it might be to get carried away with ideas that algorithms take over decision-making processes; instead, they indicate that there is a much more complex interweaving of types of agency going on that needs careful and critical understanding (see also Amoore, 2013; and Yeung's piece in this issue) – if indeed agency is even the right terminology for this. As Bolin and Schwarz (2015) have discussed elsewhere, algorithmic outcomes are often 'translated back' into 'traditional' social parameters. In broad terms, however, there is a sense of a need to explore how algorithms make choices or how they provide information that informs and shapes choice. And then, of course, we have the human agents who design the algorithms, whose designs then shape how these processes play out or how desired outcomes are modelled into those systems (see Mackenzie, 2006).

Given that algorithms are seen to be the decision-making parts of code, it is perhaps little surprise then that there is an interest in understanding how algorithms shape organisation, institutional, commercial and governmental decision-making. The second issue, which, related to the above, concerns the role of algorithms in such decision-making. This is to reflect on the role of algorithms in shaping how people are treated and judged. Or the way that algorithms shape outcomes and opportunities. This is to reflect on the way that algorithmic systems are built into organisational structures and to think about how they then shape decisions or become integrated into the choices that are made – and how those choices then become a part of people's lives. Karen Yeung's contribution explores the role of algorithms in regulation and governance. Yeung looks at the part played by algorithms and big data in 'design-based' regulation. Yeung explores the idea of the 'hypernudge' in exploring how algorithms shape choice, with big data-based nudges becoming a powerful presence in pre-empting behaviours. Elsewhere in this issue, Taina Bucher reflects on the other side of this process. As well as reflecting on the different ways that people think about algorithms, Bucher explores 'how algorithms make people feel' by focusing directly on the 'situations and spaces where people and algorithms meet' – fleshing out the details of these 'personal stories'. As such, Bucher's piece is an examination of everyday lived experiences of algorithms and their affects. This is a perspective on the algorithm that is also endorsed by Michele Willson's piece, which focuses on the embedded nature of algorithms as they frame everyday life. Such a perspective is also discussed as a potential analytical angle in Rob Kitchin's contribution. Similarly, Tarleton Gillespie's analysis illustrates how responding to algorithmic processes can facilitate the bending of the outcomes to particular agendas. Thus, those who understand the algorithms are able to render things 'algorithmically recognizable', as Gillespie puts it in his contribution to this issue. Here we see how algorithms are understood and potentially manipulated, particularly, as is made clear in Gillespie's case study, when the algorithm can be recoded to render certain things less visible. Taken together, these pieces provide insights and a range of perspectives on how algorithms are deployed to shape decision-making and behaviour, and then how these algorithmic processes are experienced and reacted to at the level of everyday experience. The articles here, when used in combination, afford the analysis of algorithms at a range of scales – incorporating anything from multi-national organisational structures to the individual body. We can bolster this multiscalar approach even further by looking at other resources. Cheney-Lippold (2011), for instance, has even written of the potential for an 'algorithmic identity' to be formed. On this point of scale, Bernhard Rieder's piece in this collection argues that we might explore some 'middle ground' that resides between the more conceptual theories of algorithms and their technical details. This, for Rieder, is a potentially rich analytical space that connects broader social understandings of algorithms with an understanding of their technical capacity and integration.

This brings us to the third set of issues, which might be understood as the politics of algorithmic sorting, ordering and prediction. This would include the capacity of the algorithm to create, maintain or cement norms and notions of abnormality (see Crandall, 2010, p. 83). Here, we might wonder how algorithms shape what is encountered, or how algorithms prioritise and make visible. This is to explore how the predictions of algorithmic systems feed into people's lives, shaping what they know, who they know, what they discover, and what they experience. The power of algorithms here is in their ability to make choices, to classify, to sort, to order and to rank. That is, to decide what matters and to decide what should be most visible. Again, the search result is one example, but so too is the social media news feed or the 'while you were away' list of Tweets and so on. Again, Rieder's piece makes a significant intervention in understanding such classification processes. Rieder reminds us that these algorithmic systems and, as he puts it, 'algorithmic techniques', do not come from nowhere, but are built upon existing classification means, ideas and categories. Mager's (2012) work on how capitalist ideologies are embedded in search engine processes is instructive here of how broader power structures might find their ways into algorithmic processes and designs. Similarly, Rob Kitchin's programmatic overview of the various approaches we might take to exploring algorithms picks up on this, with his emphasis upon the performative role of algorithms. Kitchin proposes that we expose how algorithms are constructed, how they work, and the performative part they then play in the world. His piece provides six methodological approaches for exploring this and for overcoming the difficulty of appreciating the performative role of algorithms in ordering processes. Grasping such performativity is placed alongside the problems of gaining access and managing the heterogeneous forms that algorithms take in Kitchin's piece. In relation to the above point, we also, of course, have the algorithmic sealing of life, or what has been referred to in Pariser's (2011) popular work as 'filter bubbles' (which is discussed by both Yeung and Rieder in this issue). This line or argument suggests that algorithmic sorting processes are likely to limit cultural experiences and social connections. This concerns the way that algorithms might narrow down or close off external influences, leaving people continually exposed to the same people, experiences, news, culture and so on. When thinking of how algorithms classify and order, we must, it is suggested, think of the way that algorithms repeat patterns and thus close down interactions to those that fit existing patterns. Extending these issues around ordering, Daniel Neyland and Norma Möllers use their piece to problematise the very notion of algorithmic power. They use a focus on the sorting and ordering dynamics of algorithms to open up questions about the difficulties of thinking of algorithms as holding some sort of power. They note that when attempting to understand power in relation to algorithms, we need to see this power as an 'effect and not a cause of events' (which returns us again to Yeung's vital discussion of the concept 'hypernudge'). That is to say that power is realised in the outcomes of algorithmic processes. Therefore, these processes such as algorithmic 'If … Then' processes, need careful attention. Their key point is that we need to see algorithms as being deeply relational and being a product of a set of associations. For Neyland and Möllers, the algorithms are 'tied to' various associations and situations in which they operate, rather than being entities in their own right. So, to understand the sorting power of algorithms, for instance, we need to understand the associations, dependencies and relations that facilitate those algorithmic processes and their outcomes – rather than seeing the algorithm as carrying social power.

All of this is by no means a fully populated list of all of the ways that algorithms might be seen to have some sort of social power (for more details, see the various papers in this collection or the overview provided by Kitchin in this issue). Rather, this is a cursory list of just a few of the most prominent issues as the functionality and performance of algorithms are considered alongside their social roles, implications and consequences. These points link directly and indirectly to a number of themes that emerge from this special issue. But the articles gathered in this volume are bursting with ideas and possibilities that stretch far beyond the cursory outline that I have provided. I have only really provided a whistle-stop tour of these far-reaching issues here.

The power of the notion of the algorithm

The previous section dealt with the issues that might be associated with an analysis of the power of the algorithms themselves. Before concluding, and to open up some further possibilities, this section focuses more directly upon the power of *the notion of the algorithm*. We need to look beyond the algorithms themselves to explore how the concept of the algorithm is also an important feature of their potential power. This is to suggest that we look at the way that notions of the algorithm are evoked as a part of broader rationalities and ways of seeing the world. The questions here would revolve around how the algorithm is envisioned to promote certain values and forms of calculative objectivity.

We can begin by linking this back to the previous section to argue that one way in which the power of algorithms might be explored is in relation to the production of truth. For Foucault, in the mid-1970s at least, the production of truth was placed centrally in understandings of the operation of power (see Foucault, 2004, 2014). Foucault (2004, p. 24) used a focus on truth to explore what he describes as the 'how' of power. In his 1976 lecture series, *Society must be defended*, he connects this interest in truth with his earlier interest in the connections between power and knowledge. In a lecture from the 14 January 1976, Foucault (2004, p. 24), reflecting on his approach to power in the previous years, argues that:

> multiple relations of power traverse, characterize, and constitute the social body; they are indissociable from a discourse of truth, and they can neither be established nor function unless a true discourse is produced, accumulated, put into circulation, and set to work. Power cannot be exercised unless a certain economy of discourses of truth functions in, on the basis of, and thanks to, that power.

Foucault, of course, could not have directly accounted for the power of these active algorithmic systems or how discourses might feed into algorithmic coding or be shaped by their outputs. However, at this point, reflecting on the role of truth in the 'how' of power, we might begin to reflect on how algorithms have the capacity to produce truths in two specific ways. First, through the material interventions that algorithms make. These are those things discussed above, as well as many other ways in which algorithms produce outcomes that become or reflect wider notions of truth. Power then is operationalised through the algorithm, in that the algorithmic output cements, maintains or produces certain truths. From this perspective, algorithms might be understood to create truths around things like riskiness, taste, choice, lifestyle, health and so on. The search for truth becomes then conflated with the perfect algorithmic design – which is to say the search for an algorithm that is seen to make the perfect material intervention. There is a truth to which the algorithm might adhere or a truth that its actions might produce. This first category is reflected in the above discussion and would be concerned with tracking the power plays of the algorithms themselves. Second, which leads into the point I would like to dedicate the remainder of this article to, we have the discursive interventions concerning algorithms. This is the type of truth making which is closer to that being proposed by Foucault. This is to do with the way that the term or notion of the algorithm is used, how it is framed and the type of truths that is wrapped up in. That is to say that algorithms are also a notional presence in discourse. We might look at how that term or notion is deployed to create or perpetuate certain truths about social orders and the like, or how certain truths are cultivated through discussions or evocations of the algorithm. This would be to suggest that the notion of the algorithm is itself doing some work in these discursive framings. It is a notion that carries some persuasive weight and is likely to be suggestive of wider power claims and rationalities. My cursory argument here, in this opening piece, is that the study of algorithms would be enriched even further were we to explore both these material and discursive interventions and the ways in which they combine to afford social power through the production and maintenance of certain truths.

We can turn to some of Foucault's other work to try to clarify what is meant here and how power might operate through a notion or concept of the algorithm. For instance, Foucault (1991, p. 60) also claims:

> I do not question discourses about their silently intended meanings, but about the fact and the conditions of their manifest appearance; not about the contents which they may conceal, but about the transformations which they have effected; not about the sense preserved within them like a perpetual origin, but about the field where they co-exist, reside and disappear. It is a question of the analysis of the discourses in the dimension of their exteriority.

In this passage, we see that Foucault's focus is not upon the connotations of discourse as such; rather, it is upon the conditions that afford that discourse, the transformations that the discourses afford and the potential for using such discursive framings to open up the fields in which they are deployed. This is helpful at least in beginning to see how we might be interested in the very concept or notion of the algorithm and the way that the discourse framing their material presences may themselves afford transformations, shape fields and reveal something of the conditions through which that discourse is elaborated. Elsewhere Foucault also claims that his approach aims 'to analyse the discourses themselves, that is, these discursive practices that are intermediary between words and things: these discursive practices starting from which one can define what are the things and mark out the usage of the word' (Foucault, 1989, p. 61). Again, we are only beginning to sketch out such an approach to algorithms, but this suggests an angle from which we might explore the relations and potential disconnects located in the discursive practices residing and inter-mediating between the algorithm as a *thing* and the algorithm as a *word*.

In a tentative mode, I would like to suggest that the term or notion of the algorithm should also be considered when attempting to understand the social power of algorithms. In some ways this power can potentially be detached from its technical and material form whilst still capturing something of the exteriority. As such, we would need to understand algorithms within their discursive practices and framings. The notion of the algorithm is evoked to influence and convince, to suggest things and to envision a certain approach, governmentality and way of ordering. Plus, the term is also part of wider rationalities and ways of thinking. Together then, this requires us to explore and illustrate the power of this term whilst also potentially using it as a focal point for opening up or reveal-ing these wider rationalities. The notion of the algorithm is part of a wider vocabulary, a vocabulary that we might see deployed to promote a certain rationality, a rationality based upon the virtues of calculation, competition, efficiency, objectivity and the need to be stra-tegic. As such, the notion of the algorithm can be powerful in shaping decisions, influen-cing behaviour and ushering in certain approaches and ideals. The algorithm's power may then not just be in the code, but in that way that it becomes part of a discursive under-standing of desirability and efficiency in which the mention of algorithms is part of 'a code of normalization' (Foucault, 2004, p. 38). The notion of the algorithm is part of the social power we should be exploring. The term algorithm carries something of this authority. Algorithms are, largely, trusted for their precision and objectivity. A certain rationality may well then be built into this perception of the algorithm. The discourse sur-rounding the algorithm might well reveal something of the wider political dynamics of which they are a part.

With this in mind, we might open up this dimension of the social power of algorithms. This would require us to reveal the life of the concept and how it circulates. It would require us to reveal the powers that are attached to or associated with the algorithm; these are promises and ideals that are then projected onto the code itself. The aim would be to reveal the type of trust placed in systems that are labelled algorithmic (i.e., the idea that these are neutral and trustworthy systems working beyond human capacity). And, finally, to reveal the way that algorithmic visions are then responsible for the expansion and integration of algorithmic systems. The way that those systems are spoken about is part of how they are incorporated into social and organisational structures and a part of how their implicit logic spreads. Notions of the algorithm might, for instance, to link this to the work of Cetina (1994, p. 5), become part of the fictions upon which organisation run.

We have then a two-pronged means for approaching the social power of algorithms emerging from this. In this regard, Foucault (2004, p. 34) made the following pertinent point:

> It is the actual instruments that form and accumulate knowledge, the observational methods, the recording techniques, the investigative research procedures, the verification mechanisms. That is, the delicate mechanisms of power cannot function unless knowledge, or rather knowledge apparatuses, are formed, organized, and put into circulation.

This would suggest that we need to think in terms of algorithms as part of this knowledge apparatus through which power is enacted. Yet, at the same time, there are linkages between 'discourse, concepts and institutions' in which, it is claimed, 'knowledge has an unconscious that has its own specific forms and rules' (Foucault, 2006, p. 578). With this in mind, we might also see the very notion of the algorithm as being a part of that knowledge apparatus as well. Especially as it is used to justify the expansion and integration of that technical apparatus by promoting the need for calculation and forms of knowledge-based governance.

There is obviously a good deal more to be said here; for the moment, I would like to simply suggest that the algorithm exists not just in code but it also exists in the social consciousness as a concept or term that is frequently used to stand for something (something that is not necessarily that code itself). To understand the social power of algorithms is to understand the power of algorithms as code whilst also attempting to understand how notions of the algorithm move out into the world, how they are framed by the discourse and what they are said to be able to achieve. Foucault's (2004, p. 25) point is that 'power constantly asks questions and questions us; it constantly investigates and records; it institutionalizes the search for truth, professionalizes it, and rewards it'. Part of that institutionalising of the search for truth is based upon the notions of these systems and their capacities along with the capillaries of these apparatuses and how discursive framings of their power are evoked to usher them in.

Concluding thoughts

In terms of future work on the social power of algorithms, we would, of course, point to the need to continue to look inside the black box – or inside the algorithmic workings of the 'black box society' (Pasquale, 2015). As has been argued before (see Graham, 2004), we need to look inside these systems. This will require us to understand the technicalities of the systems as well as their social ordering potentials. We will need to understand the code, but we will also need to examine the work that is done by those modelling and coding these various types of algorithms. This would need to be accompanied by studies of how those algorithms play out in practice, watching how algorithms mesh into organisations, routines, decision-making and so on. These would require us to analyse the materiality of the algorithms and the systems of which they are a part, to understand the work of coders, to see modelling processes in action, to understand how the algorithms then become part of everyday practices, to see the decisions made and to then see how people respond to those algorithmic processes. As I have outlined in this introduction, some of this work is well under way. I would like to suggest that we also develop an interest in algorithms that explores the discourse surrounding algorithmic processes. This would be to examine the way that algorithms are a part of broader rationalities, broader programmes of social change and development. This is to think about the notion of an algorithm as also being a part of power dynamics. This, I have suggested, can be thought of in terms of the two ways in which algorithmic power works by producing truths – both as outcomes or outputs of systems and as part of the discursive reinforcement of particular norms, approaches and modes of reasoning.

The notion of the 'algorithm' is now taking on its own force, as a kind of evocative shorthand for the power and potential of calculative systems that can think more quickly, more comprehensively and more accurately than humans. As well as understanding the integration of algorithms, we need to understand the way that this term is incorporated into organisational, institutional and everyday understandings. The discourse surrounding algorithms may then provide a focal point for analysing broader political rationalities and modes of governance. In this stream of work, the interest might not be in understanding the social powers of the technical systems, but in understanding how the notion of the algorithm itself has a kind of social power. The algorithm is now a cultural presence, perhaps even an iconic cultural presence, not just because of what they can do but also because of what the notion of the algorithm is used to project. This means that the algorithm can be part of the deployment of power, not just in terms of its function but also in terms of how it is understood as a phenomenon. Algorithmic decisions are depicted as neutral decisions, algorithmic decisions are understood to be efficient decisions, algorithmic decisions are presented as objective and trustworthy decisions, and so on. We certainly need to gain a greater view of the inside of the algorithmic systems in which we live, but we also need to develop an analysis of the cultural prominence of the notion of the algorithm, what this stands for, what it does and what it might reveal.

Admittedly, when I chose the title for this special issue (and for this article), I created myself something of a problem. My title suggests that algorithms have or hold some form of power. As such, it leads us to try to think about the power that they hold rather than thinking about how power might operate through them or be complicit in how those algorithms are designed, function and lead to outcomes. As Foucault (2002, p. 284) once put it, 'power is what needs to be explained, rather than being something that offers explanation'. The problem of conceptualising power in relation to algorithms is what I had hoped this issue might explore. It is easy to get caught up in a kind of sci-fi dystopia (or even utopia, depending on your perspective) of automated machines and the potent powers of intelligent environments. But the relations between power and algorithms require a broad conceptual and methodological palette from which the analysis might be developed. I have been fortunate in that the authors who have contributed to this issue have managed to skilfully sidestep any problems with the title of the issue and have used this as an opportunity to highlight exactly how we might rethink any blunt premises that the issue was built upon. I would like to thank them for engaging so carefully, thoughtfully and critically with the remit I set out. As the articles in this collection show, there are many other ways in which we might approach the questions that are suggested by thinking and questioning the social power of algorithms. It is at this point that I hand over to the articles contained in this collection in order for them to add the detail and nuance that is required. The themes I have set up in this introduction echo through the pieces, but these articles offer far more than I am able to fully summarise here.

Disclosure statement

No potential conflict of interest was reported by the author.

References

Amoore, L. (2013). *The politics of possibility*. Durham, NC: Duke University Press.

Amoore, L., & Piotukh, V. (Eds.). (2016). *Algorithmic life: Calculative devices in the age of big data*. London: Routledge.

Beer, D. (2013). *Popular culture and new media: The politics of circulation*. Basingstoke: Palgrave Macmillan.

Berry, D. (2014). *Critical theory and the digital*. London: Bloomsbury.

Bilić, P. (2016). Search algorithms, hidden labour and information control. *Big Data & Society, 3*, 1–9. doi:10.1177/2053951716652159

Bolin, G., & Schwarz, J. A. (2015). Heuristics of the algorithm: Big data, user interpretation and institutional translation. *Big Data & Society, 2*, 1–12. doi:10.1177/2053951715608406

Bucher, T. (2012). Want to be on top? Algorithmic power and the threat of invisibility on Facebook. *New Media & Society, 14*, 1164–1180. doi:10.1177/1461444812440159

Cetina, K. K. (1994). Primitive classification and postmodernity: Towards a sociological notion of fiction. *Theory, Culture & Society, 11*, 1–22. doi:10.1177/026327694011003001

Cheney-Lippold, J. (2011). A new algorithmic identity: Soft biopolitics and the modulation of control. *Theory, Culture & Society, 28*, 164–181. doi:10.1177/0263276411424420

Crandall, J. (2010). The geospatialization of calculative operations: Tracking, sensing and megacities. *Theory, Culture & Society, 27*, 68–90. doi:10.1177/0263276410382027

Crang, M., & Graham, S. (2007). Sentient cities: Ambient intelligence and the politics of urban space. *Information, Communication & Society, 10*, 789–817. doi:10.1080/13691180701750991

Crawford, K. (2016). Can an algorithm be agonistic? Ten scenes from life in calculated publics. *Science, Technology & Human Values, 41*, 77–92. doi:10.1177/0162243915589635

Foucault, M. (1989). *Foucault live: Collected interviews, 1961–1984*. New York: Semiotext[e].

Foucault, M. (1991). Politics and the study of discourse. In G. Burchell, C. Gordon, & P. Miller (Eds.), *The Foucault effect: Studies in governmentality* (pp. 53–72). Chicago, IL: The University of Chicago Press.

Foucault, M. (2002). *Power: Essential works of Foucault 1954–1984*, Volume 3. London: Penguin.

Foucault, M. (2004). *Society must be defended: Lectures at the collège de France, 1975–76*. London: Penguin.

Foucault, M. (2006). *History of madness*. London: Routledge.

Foucault, M. (2014). *On the government of the living: Lectures at the collège de France 1979–1980*. Basingstoke: Palgrave Macmillan.

Graham, S. (2004). Introduction: From dreams of transcendence to the remediation of urban life. In S. Graham (Ed.), *The cybercities reader* (pp. 1–30). London: Routledge.

Haraway, D. (1991). *Simians, cyborgs, and women: The reinvention of nature*. London: Free Association Books.

Hayles, N. K. (1999). *How we became posthuman: Virtual bodies in cybernetics, literature, and informatics*. Chicago, IL: The University of Chicago Press.

Introna, L. D. (2011). The enframing of code: Agency, originality and the plagiarist. *Theory, Culture & Society, 28*, 113–141. doi:10.1177/0263276411418131

Kennedy, H., Poell, T., & van Dijk, J. (2015). Data and agency. *Big Data & Society, 3*, 1–2. doi:10.1177/2053951715621569

Kitchin, R. (2014). *The data revolution: Big data, open data, data infrastructures & their consequences*. London: Sage.

Kitchin, R., & Dodge, M. (2011). *Code/space: Software and everyday life*. Cambridge: MIT Press.

MacCormick, J. (2012). *9 Algorithms that changed the future: The ingenious ideas that drive today's computers*. Princeton, NJ: Princeton University Press.

Mackenzie, A. (2006). *Cutting code: Software and sociality*. New York: Peter Lang.

Mager, A. (2012). Algorithmic ideology: How capitalist society shapes search engines. *Information, Communication & Society, 15*, 769–787. doi:10.1080/1369118X.2012.676056

Manovich, L. (2013). *Software takes command*. New York: Bloomsbury.

Mitchell, W. J. (2003). *Me++: The cyborg self and the networked city*. Cambridge: MIT Press.

Pariser, E. (2011). *The filter bubble: What the internet is hiding from You*. London: Viking.

Parisi, L. (2013). *Contagious architecture: Computation, aesthetics, and space*. Cambridge: MIT Press.

Pasquale, F. (2015). *The black Box society: The secret algorithms that control money and information*. Cambridge, MA: Harvard University Press.

Striphas, T. (2015). Algorithmic culture. *European Journal of Cultural Studies, 18*, 395–412. doi:10.1177/1367549415577392

Thrift, N. (2006). *Knowing capitalism*. London: Sage.

Ziewitz, M. (Ed.). (2016a). Governing algorithms. *Science, Technology & Human Values, 41*, 3–132.

Ziewitz, M. (2016b). Governing algorithms: Myth, mess, and methods. *Science, Technology & Human Values, 41*, 3–16. doi:10.1177/0162243915608948

Thinking critically about and researching algorithms

Rob Kitchin

ABSTRACT

More and more aspects of our everyday lives are being mediated, augmented, produced and regulated by software-enabled technologies. Software is fundamentally composed of algorithms: sets of defined steps structured to process instructions/data to produce an output. This paper synthesises and extends emerging critical thinking about algorithms and considers how best to research them in practice. Four main arguments are developed. First, there is a pressing need to focus critical and empirical attention on algorithms and the work that they do given their increasing importance in shaping social and economic life. Second, algorithms can be conceived in a number of ways – technically, computationally, mathematically, politically, culturally, economically, contextually, materially, philosophically, ethically – but are best understood as being contingent, ontogenetic and performative in nature, and embedded in wider socio-technical assemblages. Third, there are three main challenges that hinder research about algorithms (gaining access to their formulation; they are heterogeneous and embedded in wider systems; their work unfolds contextually and contingently), which require practical and epistemological attention. Fourth, the constitution and work of algorithms can be empirically studied in a number of ways, each of which has strengths and weaknesses that need to be systematically evaluated. Six methodological approaches designed to produce insights into the nature and work of algorithms are critically appraised. It is contended that these methods are best used in combination in order to help overcome epistemological and practical challenges.

Introduction: why study algorithms?

The era of ubiquitous computing and big data is now firmly established, with more and more aspects of our everyday lives – play, consumption, work, travel, communication, domestic tasks, security, etc. – being mediated, augmented, produced and regulated by digital devices and networked systems powered by software (Greenfield, 2006; Kitchin & Dodge, 2011; Manovich, 2013; Steiner, 2012). Software is fundamentally composed of algorithms – sets of defined steps structured to process instructions/data to produce an output – with all digital technologies thus constituting 'algorithm machines' (Gillespie, 2014a). These 'algorithm machines' enable extensive and complex tasks to be tackled that would be all but impossible by hand or analogue machines. They can perform millions of operations per second; minimise human error and bias in how a task is performed; and can significantly reduce costs and increase turnover and profit through automation and creating new services/products (Kitchin & Dodge, 2011). As such, dozens of key sets of algorithms are shaping everyday practices and tasks, including those that perform search, secure encrypted exchange, recommendation, pattern recognition, data compression, auto-correction, routing, predicting, profiling, simulation and optimisation (MacCormick, 2013).

As Diakopoulos (2013, p. 2) argues: 'We're living in a world now where algorithms adjudicate more and more consequential decisions in our lives. … Algorithms, driven by vast troves of data, are the new power brokers in society.' Steiner (2012, p. 214) thus contends:

> algorithms already have control of your money market funds, your stocks, and your retirement accounts. They'll soon decide who you talk to on phone calls; they will control the music that reaches your radio; they will decide your chances of getting lifesaving organs transplant; and for millions of people, algorithms will make perhaps the largest decision of in their life: choosing a spouse.

Similarly, Lenglet (2011), MacKenzie (2014), Arnoldi (2016), Pasquale (2015) document how algorithms have deeply and pervasively restructured how all aspects of the finance sector operate, from how funds are traded to how credit agencies assess risk and sort customers. Amoore (2006, 2009) details how algorithms are used to assess security risks in the 'war on terror' through the profiling passengers and citizens. With respect to the creation of Wikipedia, Geiger (2014, p. 345) notes how algorithms 'help create new articles, edit existing articles, enforce rules and standards, patrol for spam and vandalism, and generally work to support encyclopaedic or administrative work.' Likewise, Anderson (2011) details how algorithms are playing an increasingly important role in producing content and mediating the relationships between journalists, audiences, newsrooms and media products.

In whatever domain algorithms are deployed they appear to be having disruptive and transformative effect, both to how that domain is organised and operates, and to the labour market associated with it. Steiner (2012) provides numerous examples of how algorithms and computation have led to widespread job losses in some industries through automation. He concludes

> programmers now scout new industries for soft spots where algorithms might render old paradigms extinct, and in the process make mountains of money … Determining the next field to be invaded by bots [automated algorithms] is the sum of two simple functions: the potential to disrupt plus the reward for disruption. (Steiner, 2012, pp. 6, 119)

Such conclusions have led a number of commentators to argue that we are now entering an era of widespread algorithmic governance, wherein algorithms will play an ever-increasing role in the exercise of power, a means through which to automate the disciplining and controlling of societies and to increase the efficiency of capital accumulation. However, Diakopoulos (2013, p. 2, original emphasis) warns that: 'What we generally lack as a public is *clarity about how algorithms exercise their power over us*.' Such clarity is absent because although algorithms are imbued with the power to act upon data and make consequential decisions (such as to issue fines or block travel or approve a loan) they are largely black boxed and beyond query or question. What is at stake then with the rise of 'algorithm machines' is new forms of algorithmic power that are reshaping how social and economic systems work.

In response, over the past decade or so, a growing number of scholars have started to focus critical attention on software code and algorithms, drawing on and contributing to science and technology studies, new media studies and software studies, in order to unpack the nature of algorithms and their power and work. Their analyses typically take one of three forms: a detailed case study of a single algorithm, or class of algorithms, to examine the nature of algorithms more generally (e.g., Bucher, 2012; Geiger, 2014; Mackenzie, 2007; Montfort et al., 2012); a detailed examination of the use of algorithms in one domain, such as journalism (Anderson, 2011), security (Amoore, 2006, 2009) or finance (Pasquale, 2014, 2015); or a more general, critical account of algorithms, their nature and how they perform work (e.g., Cox, 2013; Gillespie, 2014a, 2014b; Seaver, 2013).

This paper synthesises, critiques and extends these studies. Divided into two main sections – thinking critically about and researching algorithms – the paper makes four key arguments. First, as already noted, there is a pressing need to focus critical and empirical attention on algorithms and the work that they do in the world. Second, it is most productive to conceive of algorithms as being contingent, ontogenetic, performative in nature and embedded in wider socio-technical assemblages. Third, there are three main challenges that hinder research about algorithms (gaining access to their formulation; they are heterogeneous and embedded in wider systems; their work unfolds contextually and contingently), which require practical and epistemological attention. Fourth, the constitution and work of algorithms can be empirically studied in a number of ways, each of which has strengths and weaknesses that need to be systematically evaluated. With respect to the latter, the paper provides a critical appraisal of six methodological approaches that might profitably be used to produce insights into the nature and work of algorithms.

Thinking critically about algorithms

While an algorithm is commonly understood as a set of defined steps to produce particular outputs it is important to note that this is somewhat of a simplification. What constitutes an algorithm has changed over time and they can be thought about in a number of ways: technically, computationally, mathematically, politically, culturally, economically, contextually, materially, philosophically, ethically and so on.

Miyazaki (2012) traces the term 'algorithm' to twelfth-century Spain when the scripts of the Arabian mathematician Muḥammad ibn Mūsā al-Khwārizmī were translated into Latin. These scripts describe methods of addition, subtraction, multiplication and division using numbers. Thereafter, 'algorism' meant 'the specific step-by-step method of performing written elementary arithmetic' (Miyazaki, 2012, p. 2) and 'came to describe any method of systematic or automatic calculation' (Steiner, 2012, p. 55). By the mid-twentieth century and the development of scientific computation and early high level programming languages, such as Algol 58 and its derivatives (short for ALGOrithmic Language), an algorithm was understood to be a set of defined steps that if followed in the correct order will computationally process input (instructions and/or data) to produce a desired outcome (Miyazaki, 2012).

From a computational and programming perspective an 'Algorithm = Logic + Control'; where the logic is the problem domain-specific component and specifies the abstract formulation and expression of a solution (what is to be done) and the control component is the problem-solving strategy and the instructions for processing the logic under different scenarios (how it should be done) (Kowalski, 1979). The efficiency of an algorithm can be enhanced by either refining the logic component or by improving the control over its use, including altering data structures (input) to improve efficiency (Kowalski, 1979). As reasoned logic, the formulation of an algorithm is, in theory at least, independent of programming languages and the machines that execute them; 'it has an autonomous existence independent of "implementation details"' (Goffey, 2008, p. 15).

Some ideas explicitly take the form of an algorithm. Mathematical formulae, for example, are expressed as precise algorithms in the form of equations. In other cases problems have to be abstracted and structured into a set of instructions (pseudo-code) which can then be coded (Goffey, 2008). A computer programme structures lots of relatively simple algorithms together to form large, often complex, recursive decision trees (Neyland, 2015; Steiner, 2012). The methods of guiding and calculating decisions are largely based on Boolean logic (e.g., if this, then that) and the mathematical formulae and equations of calculus, graph theory and probability theory. Coding thus consists of two key translation challenges centred on producing algorithms. The first is translating a task or problem into a structured formula with an appropriate rule set (pseudo-code). The second is translating this pseudo-code into source code that when compiled will perform the task or solve the problem. Both translations can be challenging, requiring the precise definition of what a task/problem is (logic), then breaking that down into a precise set of instructions, factoring in any contingencies such as how the algorithm should perform under different conditions (control). The consequences of mistranslating the problem and/or solution are erroneous outcomes and random uncertainties (Drucker, 2013).

The processes of translation are often portrayed as technical, benign and commonsensical. This is how algorithms are mostly presented by computer scientists and technology companies: that they are 'purely formal beings of reason' (Goffey, 2008, p. 16). Thus, as Seaver (2013) notes, in computer science texts the focus is centred on how to design an algorithm, determine its efficiency and prove its optimality from a purely technical perspective. If there is discussion of the work algorithms do in real-world contexts this concentrates on how algorithms function in practice to perform a specific task. In other words, algorithms are understood 'to be strictly rational concerns, marrying the certainties of mathematics with the objectivity of technology' (Seaver, 2013, p. 2). 'Other knowledge about algorithms – such as their applications, effects, and circulation – is strictly out of frame' (Seaver, 2013, pp. 1–2). As are the complex set of decision-making processes and practices, and the wider assemblage of systems of thought, finance, politics, legal codes and regulations, materialities and infrastructures, institutions, inter-personal relations, which shape their production (Kitchin, 2014).

Far from being objective, impartial, reliable and legitimate, critical scholars argue that algorithms possess none of these qualities except as carefully crafted fictions (Gillespie, 2014a). As Montfort et al. (2012, p. 3) note, '[c]ode is not purely abstract and mathematical; it has significant social, political, and aesthetic dimensions,' inherently framed and shaped by all kinds of decisions, politics, ideology and the materialities of hardware and infrastructure that enact its instruction. Whilst programmers might seek to maintain a high degree of mechanical objectivity – being distant, detached and impartial in how they work and thus acting independent of local customs, culture, knowledge and context (Porter, 1995) – in the process of translating a task or process or calculation into an algorithm they can never fully escape these. Nor can they escape factors such as available resources and the choice and quality of training data; requirements relating to standards, protocols and the law; and choices and conditionalities relating to hardware, platforms, bandwidth and languages (Diakopoulos, 2013; Drucker, 2013; Kitchin & Dodge, 2011; Neyland, 2015). In reality then, a great deal of expertise, judgement, choice and constraints are exercised in producing algorithms (Gillespie, 2014a). Moreover, algorithms are created for purposes that are often far from neutral: to create value and capital; to nudge behaviour and structure preferences in a certain way; and to identify, sort and classify people.

At the same time, 'programming is … a live process of engagement between thinking with and working on materials and the problem space that emerges' (Fuller, 2008, p. 10) and it 'is not a dry technical exercise but an exploration of aesthetic, material, and formal qualities' (Montfort et al., 2012, p. 266). In other words, creating an algorithm unfolds in context through processes such as trial and error, play, collaboration, discussion and negotiation. They are ontogenetic in nature (always in a state of becoming), teased into being: edited, revised, deleted and restarted, shared with others, passing through multiple iterations stretched out over time and space (Kitchin & Dodge, 2011). As a result, they are always somewhat uncertain, provisional and messy fragile accomplishments (Gillespie, 2014a; Neyland, 2015). And such practices are complemented by many others, such as researching the concept, selecting and cleaning data, tuning parameters, selling the idea and product, building coding teams, raising finance and so on. These practices are framed by systems of thought and forms of knowledge, modes of political economy, organisational and institutional cultures and politics, governmentalities and legalities, subjectivities and communities. As Seaver (2013, p. 10) notes, 'algorithmic systems are not standalone little boxes, but massive, networked ones with hundreds of hands reaching into them, tweaking and tuning, swapping out parts and experimenting with new arrangements.'

Creating algorithms thus sits at the 'intersection of dozens of … social and material practices' that are culturally, historically and institutionally situated (Montfort et al., 2012, p. 262; Napoli, 2013; Takhteyev, 2012). As such, as Mackenzie (2007, p. 93) argues treating algorithms simply 'as a general expression of mental effort, or, perhaps even more abstractly, as process of abstraction, is to lose track of proximities and relationalities that algorithms articulate.' Algorithms cannot be divorced from the conditions under which they are developed and deployed (Geiger, 2014). What this means is that algorithms need to be understood as relational, contingent, contextual in nature, framed within the wider context of their socio-technical assemblage. From this perspective, 'algorithm' is one element in a broader apparatus which means it can never be understood as a technical, objective, impartial form of knowledge or mode of operation.

Beyond thinking critically about the nature of algorithms, there is also a need to consider their work, effects and power. Just as algorithms are not neutral, impartial expressions of knowledge, their work is not impassive and apolitical. Algorithms search, collate, sort, categorise, group, match, analyse, profile, model, simulate, visualise and regulate people, processes and places. They shape how we understand the world and they do work in and make the world through their execution as software, with profound consequences (Kitchin & Dodge, 2011). In this sense, they are profoundly performative as they cause things to happen (Mackenzie & Vurdubakis, 2011). And while the creators of these algorithms might argue that they 'replace, displace, or reduce the role of biased or self-serving intermediaries' and remove subjectivity from decision-making, computation often deepens and accelerates processes of sorting, classifying and differentially treating, and reifying traditional pathologies, rather than reforming them (Pasquale, 2014, p. 5).

Far from being neutral in nature, algorithms construct and implement regimes of power and knowledge (Kushner, 2013) and their use has normative implications (Anderson, 2011). Algorithms are used to seduce, coerce, discipline, regulate and control: to guide and reshape how people, animals and objects interact with and pass through various systems. This is the same for systems designed to empower, entertain and enlighten, as they are also predicated on defined rule-sets about how a system behaves at any one time and situation. Algorithms thus claim and express algorithmic authority (Shirky, 2009) or algorithmic governance (Beer, 2009; Musiani, 2013), often through what Dodge and Kitchin (2007) term 'automated management' (decision-making processes that are automated, automatic and autonomous; outside of human oversight). The consequence for Lash (2007) is that society now has a new rule set to live by to complement constitutive and regulative rules: algorithmic, generative rules. He explains that such rules are embedded within computation, an expression of 'power through the algorithm'; they are 'virtuals that generate a whole variety of actuals. They are compressed and hidden and we do not encounter them in the way that we encounter constitutive and regulative rules. ... They are ... pathways through which capitalist power works' (Lash, 2007, p. 71).

It should be noted, however, that the effects of algorithms or their power is not always linear or always predictable for three reasons. First, algorithms act as part of a wider network of relations which mediate and refract their work, for example, poor input data will lead to weak outcomes (Goffey, 2008; Pasquale, 2014). Second, the performance of algorithms can have side effects and unintended consequences, and left unattended or unsupervised they can perform unanticipated acts (Steiner, 2012). Third, algorithms can have biases or make mistakes due to bugs or miscoding (Diakopoulos, 2013; Drucker, 2013). Moreover, once computation is made public it undergoes a process of domestication, with users embedding the technology in their lives in all kinds of alternative ways and using it for different means, or resisting, subverting and reworking the algorithms' intent (consider the ways in which users try to game Google's PageRank algorithm). In this sense, algorithms are not just what programmers create, or the effects they create based on certain input, they are also what users make of them on a daily basis (Gillespie, 2014a).

Steiner's (2012, p. 218) solution to living with the power of algorithms is to suggest that we '[g]et friendly with bots.' He argues that the way to thrive in the algorithmic future is to learn to 'build, maintain, and improve upon code and algorithms,' as if knowing how to produce algorithms protects oneself from their diverse and pernicious effects across multiple domains. Instead, I would argue, there is a need to focus more critical attention on the production, deployment and effects of algorithms in order to understand and contest the various ways that they can overtly and covertly shape life chances. However, such a programme of research is not as straightforward as one might hope, as the next section details.

Researching algorithms

The logical way to flesh out our understanding of algorithms and the work they do in the world is to conduct detailed empirical research centrally focused on algorithms. Such research could approach algorithms from a number of perspectives:

> a technical approach that studies algorithms as computer science; a sociological approach that studies algorithms as the product of interactions among programmers and designers; a legal approach that studies algorithms as a figure and agent in law; a philosophical approach that studies the ethics of algorithms, (Barocas, Hood, & Ziewitz, 2013, p. 3)

and a code/software studies' perspective that studies the politics and power embedded in algorithms, their framing within a wider socio-technical assemblage and how they reshape particular domains. There are a number of methodological approaches that can be used to operationalise such research, six of which are critically appraised below. Before doing so, however, it is important to acknowledge that there are three significant challenges to researching algorithms that require epistemological and practical attention.

Challenges

Access/black boxed

Many of the most important algorithms that people encounter on a regular basis and which (re)shape how they perform tasks or the services they receive are created in environments that are not open to scrutiny and their source code is hidden inside impenetrable executable files. Coding often happens in private settings, such as within companies or state agencies, and it can be difficult to negotiate access to coding teams to observe them work, interview programmers or analyse the source code they produce. This is unsurprising since it is often a company's algorithms that provide it with a competitive advantage and they are reluctant to expose their intellectual property even with non-disclosure agreements in place. They also want to limit the ability of users to game the algorithm to unfairly gain a competitive edge. Access is a little easier in the case of open-source programming teams and open-source programmes through repositories such as Github, but while they provide access to much code, this is limited in scope and does not include key proprietary algorithms that might be of more interest with respect to holding forms of algorithmic governance to account.

Heterogeneous and embedded

If access is gained, algorithms, as Seaver (2013) notes, are rarely straightforward to deconstruct. Within code algorithms are usually woven together with hundreds of other algorithms to create algorithmic systems. It is the workings of these algorithmic systems that we are mostly interested in, not specific algorithms, many of which are quite benign and procedural. Algorithmic systems are most often 'works of collective authorship, made, maintained, and revised by many people with different goals at different times' (Seaver, 2013, p. 10). They can consist of original formulations mashed together with those sourced from code libraries, including stock algorithms that are re-used in multiple instances. Moreover, they are embedded within complex socio-technical assemblages made up of a heterogeneous set of relations including potentially thousands of individuals, data sets, objects, apparatus, elements, protocols, standards, laws, etc. that frame their development.

Their construction, therefore, is often quite messy, full of 'flux, revisability, and nego-tiation' (p. 10), making unpacking the logic and rationality behind their formulation dif-ficult in practice. Indeed, it is unlikely that any one programmer has a complete understanding of a system, especially large, complex ones that are built by many teams of programmers, some of whom may be distributed all over the planet or may have only had sight of smaller outsourced segments. Getting access to a credit rating agency's algorithmic system then might give an insight into its formula for assessing and sorting individuals, its underlying logics and principles, and how it was created and works in practice, but will not necessarily provide full transparency as to its full reasoning, workings or the choices made in its construction (Bucher, 2012; Chun, 2011).

Ontogenetic, performative and contingent

As well as being heterogeneous and embedded, algorithms are rarely fixed in form and their work in practice unfolds in multifarious ways. As such, algorithms need to be recog-nised as being ontogenetic, performative and contingent: that is, they are never fixed in nature, but are emergent and constantly unfolding. In cases where an algorithm is static, for example, in firmware that is not patched, its work unfolds contextually, reactive to input, interaction and situation. In other cases, algorithms and their instantiation in code are often being refined, reworked, extended and patched, iterating through various versions (Miyazaki, 2012). Companies such as Google and Facebook might be live running dozens of different versions of an algorithm to assess their relative merits, with no guarantee that the version a user interacts with at one moment in time is the same as five seconds later. In some cases, the code has been programmed to evolve, re-writing its algorithms as it observes, experiments and learns independently of its crea-tors (Steiner, 2012).

Similarly, many algorithms are designed to be reactive and mutable to inputs. As Bucher (2012) notes, Facebook's EdgeRank algorithm (that determines what posts and in what order are fed into each users' timeline) does not act from above in a static, fixed manner, but rather works in concert with the each individual user, ordering posts dependent on how one interacts with 'friends.' Its parameters then are contextually weighted and fluid. In other cases, randomness might be built into an algorithm's design meaning its outcomes can never be perfectly predicted. What this means is that the outcomes for users inputting the same data might vary for contextual reasons (e.g., Mahnke and Uprichard (2014) examined Google's autocomplete search algorithm by typing in the same terms from two locations and comparing the results, finding differences in the suggestions the algorithm gave), and the same algorithms might be being used in quite varied and mutable ways (e.g., for work or for play). Examining one version of an algorithm will then provide a snapshot reading that fails to acknowledge or account for the mutable and often multiple natures of algorithms and their work (Bucher, 2012).

Algorithms then are often 'out of control' in the sense that their outcomes are some-times not easily anticipated, producing unexpected effects in terms of their work in the world (Mackenzie, 2005). As such, understanding the work and effects of algorithms needs to be sensitive to their contextual, contingent unfolding across situation, time and space. What this means in practice is that single or limited engagements with algor-ithms cannot be simply extrapolated to all cases and that a set of comparative case studies need to be employed, or a series of experiments performed with the same algorithm operating under different conditions.

Approaches

Keeping in mind these challenges, this final section critically appraises six methodological approaches for researching algorithms that I believe present the most promise for shedding light on the nature and workings of algorithms, their embedding in socio-technical systems, their effects and power, and dealing with and overcoming the difficulties of gaining access to source code. Each approach has its strengths and drawbacks and their use is not mutually exclusive. Indeed, I would argue that there would be much to be gained by using two or more of the approaches in combination to compensate for the drawbacks of employing them in isolation. Nor are they the only possible approaches, with ethnomethodologies, surveys and historical analysis using archives and oral histories offering other possible avenues of analysis and insight.

Examining pseudo-code/source code

Perhaps the most obvious way to try and understand an algorithm is to examine its pseudo-code (how a task or puzzle is translated into a model or recipe) and/or its construction in source code. There are three ways in which this can be undertaken in practice. The first is to carefully deconstruct the pseudo-code and/or source code, teasing apart the rule set to determine how the algorithm works to translate input to produce an outcome (Krysa & Sedek, 2008). In practice this means carefully sifting through documentation, code and programmer comments, tracing out how the algorithm works to process data and calculate outcomes, and decoding the translation process undertaken to construct the algorithm. The second is to map out a genealogy of how an algorithm mutates and evolves over time as it is tweaked and rewritten across different versions of code. For example, one might deconstruct how an algorithm is re-scripted in multiple instantiations of a programme within a code library such as github. Such a genealogy would reveal how thinking with respect to a problem is refined and transformed with respect to how the algorithm/code performs 'in the wild' and in relation to new technologies, situations and contexts (such as new platforms or regulations being introduced). The third is to examine how the same task is translated into various software languages and how it runs across different platforms. This is an approach used by Montfort et al. (2012) in their exploration of the '10 PRINT' algorithm, where they scripted code to perform the same task in multiple languages and ran it on different hardware, and also tweaked the parameters, to observe the specific contingencies and affordances this introduced.

While these methods do offer the promise of providing valuable insights into the ways in which algorithms are built, how power is vested in them through their various parameters and rules, and how they process data in abstract and material terms to complete a task, there are three significant issues with their deployment. First, as noted by Chandra (2013), deconstructing and tracing how an algorithm is constructed in code and mutates over time is not straightforward. Code often takes the form of a 'Big Ball of Mud': '[a] haphazardly structured, sprawling, sloppy, duct-tape and bailing wire, spaghetti code jungle' (Foote & Yoder, 1997; cited in Chandra, 2013, p. 126). Even those that have produced it can find it very difficult to unpack its algorithms and routines; those unfamiliar with its development can often find that the ball of mud remains just that. Second, it requires that the researcher is both an expert in the domain to which the algorithm refers and possesses sufficient skill and knowledge as a programmer that they can make sense of a 'Big Ball of Mud'; a pairing that few social scientists and humanities scholars possess. Third, these approaches largely decontextualise the algorithm from its wider socio-technical assemblage and its use.

Reflexively producing code

A related approach is to conduct auto-ethnographies of translating tasks into pseudo-code and the practices of producing algorithms in code. Here, rather than studying an algorithm created by others, a researcher reflects on and critically interrogates their own experiences of translating and formulating an algorithm. This would include an analysis of not only the practices of exploring and translating a task, originating and developing ideas, writing and revising code, but also how these practices are situated within and shaped by wider socio-technical factors such as regulatory and legal frameworks, form of knowledge, institutional arrangements, financial terms and conditions, and anticipated users and market. Ziewitz (2011) employed this kind of approach to reflect on producing a random routing algorithm for directing a walking path through a city, reflecting on the ontological uncertainty in the task itself (that there is often an ontological gerrymandering effect at work as the task itself is re-thought and re-defined while the process of producing an algorithm is undertaken), and the messy, contingent process of creating the rule set and parameters in practice and how these also kept shifting through deferred accountability. Similarly, Ullman (1997) uses such an approach to consider the practices of developing software and how this changed over her career.

While this approach will provide useful insights into how algorithms are created, it also has a couple of limitations. The first is the inherent subjectivities involved in doing an auto-ethnography and the difficulties of detaching oneself and gaining critical distance to be able to give clear insight into what is unfolding. Moreover, there is the possibility that in seeking to be reflexive what would usually take place is inflected in unknown ways. Further, it excludes any non-representational, unconscious acts from analysis. Second, one generally wants to study algorithms and code that have real concrete effects on peoples' everyday lives, such as those used in algorithmic governance. One way to try and achieve this is to contribute to open-source projects where the code is incorporated into products that others use, or to seek access to a commercial project as a programmer (on an overt, approved basis with non-disclosure agreements in place). The benefit here is that the method can be complemented with the sixth approach set out below, examining and reflecting on the relationship between the production of an algorithm and any associated ambitions and expectations vis-à-vis how it actually does work in the world.

Reverse engineering

In cases where the code remains black boxed, a researcher interested in the algorithm at the heart of its workings is left with the option of trying to reverse engineer the compiled software. Diakopoulos (2013, p. 13) explains that '[r]everse engineering is the process of articulating the specifications of a system through a rigorous examination drawing on domain knowledge, observation, and deduction to unearth a model of how that system works.' While software producers might desire their products to remain opaque, each pro-gramme inherently has two openings that enable lines of enquiry: input and output. By examining what data are fed into an algorithm and what output is produced it is possible to start to reverse engineer how the recipe of the algorithm is composed (how it weights and preferences some criteria) and what it does.

The main way this is attempted is by using carefully selected dummy data and seeing what is outputted under different scenarios. For example, researchers might search Google using the same terms on multiple computers in multiple jurisdictions to get a sense of how its PageRank algorithm is constructed and works in practice (Mahnke & Uprichard, 2014), or they might experiment with posting and interacting with posts on Facebook to try and determine how its EdgeRank algorithm positions and prioritises posts in user time lines (Bucher, 2012), or they might use proxy servers and feed dummy user profiles into e-commerce systems to see how prices might vary across users and locales (*Wall Street Journal*, detailed in Diakopoulos, 2013). One can also get a sense of an algorithm by 'looking closely at how information must be oriented to face them, how it is made algorithm-ready'; how the input data are delineated in terms of what input variables are sought and structured, and the associated meta-data (Gillespie, 2014a). Another possibility is to follow debates on online forums by users about how they perceive an algorithm works or has changed, or interview marketers, media strategists, and public relations firms that seek to game an algorithm to optimise an outcome for a client (Bucher, 2012).

While reverse engineering can give some indication of the factors and conditions embedded into an algorithm, they generally cannot do so with any specificity (Seaver, 2013). As such, they usually only provide fuzzy glimpses of how an algorithm works in practice but not its actual constitution (Diakopoulos, 2013). One solution to try and enhance clarity has been to employ bots, which posing as users, can more systematically engage with a system, running dummy data and interactions. However, as Seaver (2013) notes, many proprietary systems are aware that many people are seeking to determine and game their algorithm, and thus seek to identify and block bot users.

Interviewing designers or conducting an ethnography of a coding team

While deconstructing or reverse engineering code might provide some insights into the workings of an algorithm, they provide little more than conjecture as to the intent of the algorithm designers, and examining that and how and why an algorithm was produced requires a different approach. Interviewing designers and coders, or conducting an ethnography of a coding team, provides a means of uncovering the story behind the production of an algorithm and to interrogate its purpose and assumptions.

In the first case, respondents are questioned as to how they framed objectives, created pseudo-code and translated this into code, and quizzed about design decisions and choices with respect to languages and technologies, practices, influences, constraints, debates within a team or with clients, institutional politics and major changes in direction over time (Diakopoulos, 2013; MacKenzie, 2014; Mager, 2012). In the second case, a researcher seeks to spend time within a coding team, either observing the work of the coders, discussing it with them, and attending associated events such as team meetings, or working in situ as part of the team, taking an active role in producing code. An example of the former is Rosenberg's (2007) study of one company's attempt to produce a new product conducted over a three-year period in which he was given full access to the company, including observing and talking to coders, and having access to team chat rooms and phone confer- ences. An example of the latter is Takhteyev's (2012) study of an open-source coding project in Rio de Janeiro where he actively worked on developing the code, as well as taking part in the social life of the team. In both cases, Rosenberg and Takhteyev generate much insight into the contingent, relational and contextual way in which algorithms and software are produced, though in neither case are the specificities of algorithms and their work unpacked and detailed.

Unpacking the full socio-technical assemblage of algorithms

As already noted, algorithms are not formulated or do not work in isolation, but form part of a technological stack that includes infrastructure/hardware, code platforms, data and interfaces, and are framed and conditions by forms of knowledge, legalities, governmen- talities, institutions, marketplaces, finance and so on. A wider understanding of algorithms then requires their full socio-technical assemblage to be examined, including an analysis of the reasons for subjecting the system to the logic of computation in the first place. Exam- ining algorithms without considering their wider assemblage is, as Geiger (2014) argues, like considering a law without reference to the debate for its introduction, legal insti- tutions, infrastructures such as courts, implementers such as the police, and the operating and business practices of the legal profession. It also risks fetishising the algorithm and code at the expense of the rest of the assemblage (Chun, 2011).

Interviews and ethnographies of coding projects, and the wider institutional apparatus surrounding them (e.g., management and institutional collaboration), start to produce such knowledge, but they need to supplemented with other approaches, such as a discur- sive analysis of company documents, promotional/industry material, procurement tenders and legal and standards frameworks; attending trade fairs and other inter-company inter- actions; examining the practices, structures and behaviour of institutions; and document- ing the biographies of key actors and the histories of projects (Montfort et al., 2012; Napoli, 2013). Such a discursive analysis will also help to reveal how algorithms are ima- gined and narrated, illuminate the discourses surrounding and promoting them, and how they are understood by those that create and promote them. Gaining access to such a wider range of elements, and being able to gather data and interlink them to be able to unpack a socio-technical assemblage, is no easy task but it is manageable as a large case study, especially if undertaken by a research team rather than a single individual.

Examining how algorithms do work in the world

Given that algorithms do active work in the world it is important not only to focus on the construction of algorithms, and their production within a wider assemblage, but also to examine how they are deployed within different domains to perform a multitude of tasks. This cannot be simply denoted from an examination of the algorithm/code alone for two reasons. First, what an algorithm is designed to do in theory and what it actually does in practice do not always correspond due to a lack of refinement, miscodings, errors and bugs. Second, algorithms perform in context – in collaboration with data, technol- ogies, people, etc. under varying conditions – and therefore their effects unfold in contin- gent and relational ways, producing localised and situated outcomes. When users employ an algorithm, say for play or work, they are not simply playing or working in conjunction with the algorithm, rather they are 'learning, internalizing, and becoming intimate with' it

(Galloway, 2006, p. 90); how they behave is subtly reshaped through the engagement, but at the same time what the algorithm does is conditional on the input it receives from the user. We can therefore only know how algorithms make a different to everyday life by observing their work in the world under different conditions.

One way to undertake such research is to conduct ethnographies of how people engage with and are conditioned by algorithmic systems and how such systems reshape how organisations conduct their endeavours and are structured (e.g., Lenglet, 2011). It would also explore the ways in which people resist, subvert and transgress against the work of algorithms, and re-purpose and re-deploy them for purposes they were not originally intended. For example, examining the ways in which various mobile and web applications were re-purposed in the aftermath of the Haiti earthquake to coordinate disaster response, remap the nation and provide donations (Al-Akkad et al., 2013). Such research requires detailed observation and interviews focused on the use of particular systems and technologies by different populations and within different scenarios, and how individuals interfaced with the algorithm through software, including their assessments as to their intentions, sense of what is occurring and associated consequences, tactics of engagement, feelings, concerns and so on. In cases where an algorithm is black boxed, such research is also likely to shed some light on the constitution of the algorithm itself.

Conclusion

On an average day, people around the world come into contact with hundreds of algorithms embedded into the software that operates communications, utilities and transport infrastructure, and powers all kinds of digital devices used for work, play and consumption. These algorithms have disruptive and transformative effect, reconfiguring how systems operate, enacting new forms of algorithmic governance and enabling new forms of capital accumulation. Yet, despite their increasing pervasiveness, utility and the power vested in them to act in autonomous, automatic and automated ways, to date there has been limited critical attention paid to algorithms in contrast to the vast literature that approaches algorithms from a more technical perspective. This imbalance in how algorithms are thought about and intellectually engaged with is perhaps somewhat surprising given what is at stake in a computationally rich world. As such, there is a pressing need for critical attention across the social sciences and humanities to be focused on algorithms and forms of algorithmic governance. The contribution of this paper to this endeavour has been to: advance an understanding of algorithms as contingent, ontogenetic, performative in nature and embedded in wider socio-technical assemblages; to detail the epistemological and practical challenges facing algorithm scholars; and to critically appraise six promising methodological options to empirically research and make sense of algorithms. It is apparent from the studies conducted to date that there is a range of different ways of making sense of algorithms and the intention of the paper has not been to foreclose this diversity, but rather to encourage synthesis, comparison and evaluation of different positions and to create new ones. Indeed, the more angles taken to uncover and debate the nature and work of algorithms the better we will come to know them.

Likewise, the six approaches appraised were selected because I believe they hold the most promise in exposing how algorithms are constructed, how they work within socio-technical assemblages and how they perform actions and make a difference in particular domains, but they are by no means the only approaches that might be profitably pursued. My contention is, given each approach's varying strengths and weaknesses, that how they reveal the nature and work of algorithms needs to be systematically evaluated through methodologically focused research. Studies that have access to the pseudo-code, code and coders may well be the most illuminating, though they still face a number of challenges, such as deciphering how the algorithm works in practice. Moreover, there is a need to assess: (1) how they might be profitably used in conjunction with each other to overcome epistemological and practical challenges; (2) what other methods might be beneficially deployed in order to better understand the nature, production and use of algorithms? With respect to the latter, such methods might include ethnomethodologies, surveys, historical analysis using archives and oral histories, and comparative case studies. As such, while the approaches and foci I have detailed provide a useful starting set that others can apply, critique, refine and extend, there are others that can potentially emerge as critical research and thinking on algorithms develops and matures.

Acknowledgements

Many thanks to Tracey Lauriault, Sung-Yueh Perng and the referees for comments on earlier versions of this paper.

Disclosure statement

No potential conflict of interest was reported by the author.

Funding

The research for this paper was funded by a European Research Council Advanced Investigator award [ERC-2012-AdG-323636-SOFTCITY].

References

Al-Akkad, A., Ramirez, L., Denef, S., Boden, A., Wood, L., Buscher, M., & Zimmermann, A. (2013). *'Reconstructing normality': The use of infrastructure leftovers in crisis situations as inspiration for the design of resilient technology.* Proceedings of the 25th Australian Computer-Human Interaction Conference: Augmentation, Application, Innovation, Collaboration (pp. 457–466). New York, NY: ACM. Retrieved October 16, 2014, from http://dl.acm.org/citation.cfm?doid= 2541016.2541051

Amoore, L. (2006). Biometric borders: Governing mobilities in the war on terror. *Political Geography, 25*, 336–351.

Amoore, L. (2009). Algorithmic war: Everyday geographies of the war on terror. *Antipode, 41*, 49–69.

Anderson C. W. (2011). Deliberative, agonistic, and algorithmic audiences: Journalism's vision of its public in an age of audience. *Journal of Communication, 5*, 529–547.

Arnoldi, J. (2016). Computer algorithms, market manipulation and the institutionalization of high frequency trading. *Theory, Culture & Society, 33*(1), 29–52.

Barocas, S., Hood, S., & Ziewitz, M. (2013). Governing algorithms: A provocation piece. Retrieved October 16, 2014, from http://papers.ssrn.com/sol3/papers.cfm?abstract_id=2245322

Beer, D. (2009). Power through the algorithm? Participatory Web cultures and the technological unconscious. *New Media and Society, 11*(6), 985–1002.

Bucher, T. (2012). 'Want to be on the top?' Algorithmic power and the threat of invisibility on Facebook. *New Media and Society, 14*(7), 1164–1180.

Chandra, V. (2013). *Geek sublime: Writing fiction, coding software.* London: Faber.

Chun, W. H. K. (2011). *Programmed visions.* Cambridge: MIT Press.

Cox, G. (2013). *Speaking code: Coding as aesthetic and political expression.* Cambridge: MIT Press.

Diakopoulos, N. (2013). *Algorithmic accountability reporting: On the investigation of black boxes.* A Tow/Knight Brief. Tow Center for Digital Journalism, Columbia Journalism School. Retrieved August 21, 2014, from http://towcenter.org/algorithmic-accountability-2/

Dodge, M., & Kitchin, R. (2007). The automatic management of drivers and driving spaces. *Geoforum, 38*(2), 264–275.

Drucker, J. (2013). Performative materiality and theoretical approaches to interface. *Digital Humanities Quarterly, 7*(1). Retrieved June 5, 2014, from http://www.digitalhumanities.org/dhq/vol/7/1/000143/000143.html

Foote, B., & Yoder, J. (1997). Big Ball of Mud. *Pattern Languages of Program Design, 4*, 654–692.

Fuller, M. (2008). Introduction. In M. Fuller (Ed.), *Software studies – A lexicon* (pp. 1–14). Cambridge: MIT Press.

Galloway, A. R. (2006). *Gaming: Essays on algorithmic culture.* Minneapolis: University of Minnesota Press.

Geiger, S. R. (2014). Bots, bespoke, code and the materiality of software platforms. *Information, Communication & Society, 17*(3), 342–356.

Gillespie, T. (2014a). The relevance of algorithms. In T. Gillespie, P. J. Boczkowski, & K. A. Foot (Eds.), *Media technologies: Essays on communication, materiality, and society* (pp. 167–193). Cambridge: MIT Press.

Gillespie, T. (2014b, June 25). Algorithm [draft] [#digitalkeyword]. *Culture Digitally.* Retrieved October 16, 2014, from http://culturedigitally.org/2014/06/algorithm-draft-digitalkeyword/

Goffey, A. (2008). Algorithm. In M. Fuller (Ed.), *Software studies – A lexicon* (pp. 15–20). Cambridge: MIT Press.

Greenfield, A. (2006). *Everyware: The dawning age of ubiquitous computing.* Boston, MA: New Riders.

Kitchin, R. (2014). *The data revolution: Big data, open data, data infrastructures and their consequences.* London: Sage.

Kitchin, R., & Dodge, M. (2011). *Code/space: Software and everyday life.* Cambridge: MIT Press.

Kowalski, R. (1979). Algorithm = Logic + Control. *Communications of the ACM, 22*(7), 424–436.

Krysa, J., & Sedek, G. (2008). Source code. In M. Fuller (Ed.), *Software studies – A lexicon* (pp. 236–242). Cambridge: MIT Press.

Kushner, S. (2013). The freelance translation machine: Algorithmic culture and the invisible industry. *New Media & Society, 15*(8), 1241–1258.

Lash, S. (2007). Power after hegemony: Cultural studies in mutation. *Theory, Culture & Society, 24*(3), 55–78.

Lenglet, M. (2011). Conflicting codes and codings: How algorithmic trading is reshaping financial regulation. *Theory, Culture & Society, 28*(6), 44–66.

MacCormick, J. (2013). *Nine algorithms that changed the future: The ingenious ideas that drive today's computers.* Princeton, NJ: Princeton University Press.

Mackenzie, A. (2005). The performativity of code: Software and cultures of circulation. *Theory, Culture & Society, 22*(1), 71–92.

Mackenzie, A. (2007). Protocols and the irreducible traces of embodiment: The Viterbi algorithm and the mosaic of machine time. In R. Hassan & R. E. Purser (Eds.), *24/7: Time and temporality in the network society* (pp. 89–106). Stanford, CA: Stanford University Press.

Mackenzie, A., & Vurdubakis, T. (2011). Code and codings in Crisis: Signification, performativity and excess. *Theory, Culture & Society, 28*(6), 3–23.

MacKenzie, D. (2014). *A sociology of algorithms: High-frequency trading and the shaping of markets.* Working paper, University of Edinburgh. Retrieved July 6, 2015, from http://www.sps.ed.ac.uk/__data/assets/pdf_file/0004/156298/Algorithms25.pdf

Mager, A. (2012). Algorithmic ideology: How capitalist society shapes search engines. *Information, Communication, & Society, 15*(5), 769–787.

Mahnke, M., & Uprichard, E. (2014). Algorithming the algorithm. In R. König & M. Rasch (Eds.), *Society of the query reader: Reflections on web search* (pp. 256–270). Amsterdam: Institute of Network Cultures.

Manovich, L. (2013). *Software takes control.* New York, NY: Bloomsbury.

Miyazaki, S. (2012). Algorhythmics: Understanding micro-temporality in computational cultures. *Computational Culture,* Issue 2. Retrieved June 25, 2014, from http://computationalculture.net/article/algorhythmics-understanding-micro-temporality-in-computational-cultures

Montfort, N., Baudoin, P., Bell, J., Bogost, I., Douglass, J., Marino, M. C., … Vawter, N. (2012). *10 PRINT CHR$ (205.5 + RND (1)): GOTO 10.* Cambridge: MIT Press.

Musiani, F. (2013). Governance by algorithms. *Internet Policy Review, 2*(3). Retrieved October 7, 2014, from http://policyreview.info/articles/analysis/governance-algorithms

Napoli, P. M. (2013, May). *The algorithm as institution: Toward a theoretical framework for automated media production and consumption.* Paper presented at the Media in Transition Conference, Massachusetts Institute of Technology, Cambridge, MA. Retrieved from ssrn.com/abstract = 2260923

Neyland, D. (2015). On organizing algorithms. *Theory, Culture & Society, 32*(1), 119–132.

Pasquale, F. (2014). *The emperor's new codes: Reputation and search algorithms in the finance sector.* Draft for discussion at the NYU 'Governing Algorithms' conference. Retrieved October 16, 2014, from http://governingalgorithms.org/wp-content/uploads/2013/05/2-paper-pasquale.pdf

Pasquale, F. (2015). *The black box society: The secret algorithms that control money and information.* Cambridge, MA: Harvard University Press.

Porter, T. M. (1995). *Trust in numbers: The pursuit of objectivity in science and public life.* Princeton, NJ: Princeton University Press.

Rosenberg, S. (2007). *Dreaming in code: Two dozen programmers, three years, 4,732 bugs, and one quest for transcendent software.* New York: Three Rivers Press.

Seaver, N. (2013). *Knowing Algorithms.* Media in Transition 8, Cambridge, MA. Retrieved August 21, 2014, from http://nickseaver.net/papers/seaverMiT8.pdf

Shirky, C. (2009). *A speculative post on the idea of algorithmic authority.* Shirky.com. Retrieved October 7, 2014, from http://www.shirky.com/weblog/2009/11/a-speculative-post-on-the-idea-of-algorithmic-authority/

Steiner, C. (2012). *Automate this: How algorithms took over our markets, our jobs, and the world.* New York, NY: Portfolio.

Takhteyev, Y. (2012). *Coding places: Software practice in a South American City.* Cambridge: MIT Press.

Ullman, E. (1997). *Close to the machine.* San Francisco, CA: City Lights Books.

Ziewitz, M. (2011, September 29). *How to think about an algorithm? Notes from a not quite random walk.* Discussion paper for Symposium on 'Knowledge Machines between Freedom and Control'. Retrieved August 21, 2014, from http://ziewitz.org/papers/ziewitz_algorithm.pdf

The algorithmic imaginary: exploring the ordinary affects of Facebook algorithms

Taina Bucher

ABSTRACT

This article reflects the kinds of situations and spaces where people and algorithms meet. In what situations do people become aware of algorithms? How do they experience and make sense of these algorithms, given their often hidden and invisible nature? To what extent does an awareness of algorithms affect people's use of these platforms, if at all? To help answer these questions, this article examines people's personal stories about the Facebook algorithm through tweets and interviews with 25 ordinary users. To understand the spaces where people and algorithms meet, this article develops the notion of the algorithmic imaginary. It is argued that the algorithmic imaginary – ways of thinking about what algorithms are, what they should be and how they function – is not just productive of different moods and sensations but plays a generative role in moulding the Facebook algorithm itself. Examining how algorithms make people feel, then, seems crucial if we want to understand their social power.

Meet Jessa. She and her boyfriend, both in their mid-20s, recently moved to New York City for work. The couple has been subletting an apartment for one and a half months, sleeping on an air mattress that seems to be deflating gradually ever faster. They regularly talk about how much they look forward to sleeping on a real mattress. While Jessa trawls Craigslist for new apartments, her boyfriend looks at mattresses on Amazon. Then, one morning while Jessa scrolls through her Facebook news feed, there it is – an ad for air mattresses. Jessa is so perplexed she tweets about it: 'How on earth did the Facebook algorithm know she was sleeping on an air mattress?' Although the connection may have been coincidental, the effects are not incidental. While Jessa understands that clicks and browser behaviour are routinely tracked and used to tailor ads online, there is something 'wonderfully creepy' (Chun, in press) about the ways in which these ads function, as they call into question the clean separation between publicity and privacy.

This article reflects on the kinds of situations experienced by Jessa and other social media users like her as they encounter the workings of algorithms in their everyday life. When computer scientists speak of software, they generally refer to machine-readable instructions that direct the computer to perform a specific task. The algorithm, simply put, is just another term for those carefully planned instructions that follow a sequential order (Knuth, 1998). However, when social scientists speak about algorithms, they tend to be less concerned with the mechanical term, and more with the ways in which 'software conditions our very existence' (Kitchin & Dodge, 2011, p. ix). While media and communication scholars have started to take notice of algorithms – writing about their power (Beer, 2013), relevance (Gillespie, 2014) and accountability (Diakopoulos, 2015) – little is yet known about the ways in which users know and perceive that algorithms are part of their 'media life' (Deuze, 2012). The focus of this article is thus on users' understanding and experiences of algorithms in everyday life. In what situations do people become aware of algorithms? How do they experience and make sense of these algorithms, given their hidden and invisible nature? To what extent does an awareness of algorithms affect people's use of these platforms, if at all? To help answer these questions, this article examines people's personal algorithm stories – stories about situations and disparate scenes that draw algorithms and people together. The aim is to help provide an understanding of the cultural imaginaries and ordinary affects of algorithms by developing the notion of the algorithmic imaginary.

The algorithmic imaginary is not to be understood as a false belief or fetish of sorts but, rather, as the way in which people imagine, perceive and experience algorithms and what these imaginations make possible. Using the theoretical lens of affect, understood as mood and intensity corresponding to 'forces of encounter' (Gregg & Seigworth, 2010), the aim is to understand how algorithms have the capacity 'to affect and be affected' (Deleuze & Guattari, 1987). Methodologically, this article examines situations involving 'failed relays' and 'jumpy moves' (Stewart, 2007). It takes as its starting point tweets by ordinary users that express a thought, opinion, feeling, statement or question about the Facebook algorithm. Taking my lead from Berlant's book *Cruel optimism* (2011), I examine the affective dimensions of algorithms by attending to the situation, the episode, the interruption, that gives rise to these statements. A situation, as Berlant (2011) defines it, 'is a state of things in which something that will perhaps matter is unfolding amid the usual activity of life. It is a state of animated and animating suspension', one 'that forces itself on consciousness, that produces a sense of the emergence of something in the present' (p. 5). Algorithms, I suggest, may be productive of such an emerging presence.

Making sense of algorithms

While there is not much existing research on the ways in which people experience and perceive algorithms as part of their everyday life and media use, a few studies have recently emerged examining 'algorithm awareness', the extent to which people are aware that 'our daily digital life is full of algorithmically selected content' (Eslami et al., 2015). In their study of 40 Facebook users, Eslami et al. (2015) found that 'more than half of the participants (62.5%) were not aware of the News Feed curation' (p. 1). This, they argue, is worrisome as 'ignorance of the algorithm had serious consequences', leading some participants to attribute wrongly 'the composition of their feeds to the habits or intent of their friends and family' (Eslami et al., 2015, p. 9). By contrast, Rader and Gray (2015) found that most Facebook users were, in fact, aware that they were not seeing every post created by their friends. Analysing survey results from 464 respondents, Rader and Gray (2015) found that the clear majority (75%) did not think they were seeing everything. Only 8% answered yes. While users' beliefs about the Facebook systems varied a great deal, most survey respondents demonstrated 'a fairly sophisticated understanding of the system' (Rader & Gray, 2015, p. 7). Despite somewhat contradictory findings, these studies raise some interesting questions with regard to the power of algorithms, affecting not just *what* people think about the systems with which they are interacting on a daily basis but, perhaps more profoundly, how different ways of thinking about what algorithms are and do may affect how these systems are used.

While existing research has primarily been concerned with algorithm awareness – the extent to which users are aware of what is happening as part of Facebook's news feed, this paper considers the kinds of situations through which people become aware of and encounter algorithms. Building on phenomenological and ethnographically inspired approaches, the question is how do people experience and perceive algorithms as part of their everyday life? As the phenomenologist Merleau-Ponty (1962) suggests, people usually encounter the world through invisibilities. When we meet other people, they appear to us by virtue of their habits, experiences and personalities. We do not merely perceive people through their clothing, language or general demeanour. Phenomenologists (who do not, of course, make up a homogeneous group) would suggest that invisible moods, affects and values are key to the constitution of what appears to us in the first place. This implies that people do not necessarily need access to the precise instructions that tell the computer what to do in order to experience an algorithm. As the opening sequence describing Jessa's everyday encounter with an algorithm suggests, what people experience is not the mathematical recipe as such but, rather, the moods, affects and sensations that the algorithm helps to generate.

If we follow the phenomenological line of thinking discussed above, we do not necessarily need access to the thing itself (whatever that may be) in order to perceive it. Accordingly, phenomena of all sorts – including algorithms – can be 'accessed' via experience and the ways in which they make people feel. This is closely related to the notion of affect but not exactly the same. As Papacharissi (2014) points out, affect is what permits feelings to be felt; it is the movement that may lead to a particular feeling. Affect, she suggests, can be thought of as the 'rhythm of our pace as we walk' (p. 21). For example, a fast-paced rhythm may lead to and amplify feelings of stress; a slow and light-paced rhythm may make us calm. In the context of this study, the question is where we might find the force of movement in algorithms, 'the reason to react', as Stewart (2007) puts it (p. 16).

Encountering algorithms

Method

In order to investigate the affective dimensions and perceptions of algorithms, this article takes its methodological leads from Berlant's (2011) notion of the situation and Stewart's (2007) cultural analysis of emotional experience. Accessing people's personal stories and experiences with data and algorithms can be tricky. Where do you go to gather stories about things algorithmic? It turns out that one particularly useful place is the microblogging service Twitter. The public nature of Twitter, with millions of public profiles and text-based short statements in no more than 140 characters and the ability to search for tweets using a platform-specific search engine, provides a great tool for accessing ideas, sentiments and statements about almost anything, including algorithms.

During a nine-month period stretching from October 2014 to June 2015, I searched Twitter regularly for keywords and combinations of keywords, including: 'Facebook algorithm', 'algorithm AND Facebook', 'algorithm AND weird', 'algorithm AND creepy', 'algorithm AND great', etc. The aim was to understand how ordinary users experience encounters with algorithms by taking their own accounts as the starting point. It should be noted that this article focuses specifically on users' encounters with the algorithms of the Facebook platform. The decision was made to limit discussion of findings to one platform for reasons of consistency and comparability. Facebook is taken as a particularly interesting case in point, due to its widespread use, experienced long-time users and an increase in public attention towards its algorithms, in part due to considerable media coverage in the wake of the so-called Facebook emotion contagion experiment. Querying Twitter every few weeks, I manually scrolled down the stream of tweets and took screenshots of the ones that seemed to be more personal rather than marketing-oriented. Using a research profile I had set up on Twitter, I occasionally contacted people who had recently tweeted about the Facebook algorithm to ask whether they would be willing to answer a few questions related to that tweet. Out of 47 people that I contacted, 25 people got back to me with a positive reply. I then contacted these individuals via email, providing more background information about the project, along with an informed consent statement and 3–4 questions. As the primary concern was to inquire about the tweets in question, the decision was made to opt for email interviews in order to get quick feedback on the scenes, stories and sentiments contained in those tweets in order to validate the participants' memory about the events in question. Questions included: 'What is the context of this tweet? What led you to write this?', 'In your opinion, how does the FB algorithm work?', 'Has your awareness of the algorithm affected your use of Facebook in any way?'

The answers were coded for information about the kinds of situations that provided the informants a 'reason to react', the beliefs and mental models informants had about the workings of the Facebook algorithms, the extent to which their awareness of the algorithm affected their use of the platform, what kinds of tactics and strategies they developed in response to the algorithm (if any), and the kinds of issues and concerns they voiced about the algorithm. All 25 participants are pseudonymised, whereas their real age, country of residence and occupation are disclosed (see Appendix 1). Despite the study being limited to data from 25 users and to Facebook's algorithm only, the findings provide novel insights into the ways in which people experience algorithms. If we want to understand the social power of algorithms, it is important to understand how users encounter and make sense of algorithms, and how these experiences, in turn, not only shape the expectations users have towards computational systems, but also help shape the algorithms themselves.

Sites and scenes of ordinary affects

Using people's tweets as an entry point to a better understanding of people's perceptions and personal experiences with algorithms, the following section reports on some of the scenes and situations prompting people to tweet about the Facebook algorithm. Stewart's

Ordinary affects (2007) serves as a model for the presentation of these scenes and situations, although the presentation of findings in this article makes no claim or attempt to match Stewart's poetic prose. Not meant as an exhaustive account of the kinds of situations that generate algorithm awareness, the scenes described below serve as exemplary cases that find resonance in the sample as a whole. Just like the kinds of ordinary affects described by Stewart (2007), the following accounts experiment with the style of writing, paying attention to pressure the points and the forms of attachments that the tweets and stories people tell may help to reveal about the social power of algorithms. The presentation of the findings is written in the form of brief scenes, reiterating the participants' stories and accounts of the situations that moved them to tweet about Facebook's algorithms. When relevant, these scenes include the tweet itself and select quotations. The exact wording of the tweets – if directly quoted – has been slightly altered in order to ensure the privacy of the participants. What, then, were some of the pressing situations and observations that made people reach out on social media to tweet about the Facebook algorithm?

Profiling identity

In the past, Kayla has posted on Facebook about being broke and single. She had to cancel her gym membership (Facebook seems to constantly remind her of this) and she has used dating apps to find a potential partner. Recently, Kayla has been looking at nursery decorations online for a baby shower gift. As she scrolls down her news feed, she notices how the algorithm for suggested apps shows her multiple dating sites and multiple pregnancy-related apps in the same set of suggestions. How bizarre. On Twitter, she notes how Facebook seems to think that she is 'pregnant, single, broke and should lose weight'. Tellingly, Kayla adds, 'the Facebook algorithm confuses me'.

Like Jessa and the air mattress ad described in the beginning of the article, Kayla, a 23-year-old student from New York, intuitively understands that the Facebook algorithm makes connections between her online activity and the kinds of apps and ads that are shown to her. She knows she is being tracked, but this understanding does not take away from the strange feeling of being classified and profiled by algorithms in a certain way. Such is the work of 'profiling machines' (Elmer, 2004) that produce detailed consumer profiles to anticipate future needs. These forms of algorithmic profiling thrive on the continuous reconfiguration of identification and personalised forms of surveillance (De Vries, 2010; Fuchs, Boersma, Albrechtslund, & Sandoval, 2012). While the inferences that Facebook makes about Jessa and Kayla might seem right, the point is that they *feel* wrong. As Kayla suggests, no one likes to be reminded of being broke and overweight.

At other times, the connections that Facebook makes are simply wrong, as when Shannon, a career counsellor in her 40s who blogged about Taylor Swift, all of a sudden gets Facebook ads for products that younger people might like, quite possibly because the typical Taylor Swift fan falls into a different demographic classifier. Shannon notes that she usually gets 'ads for wrinkle cream and fat loss', which reflects stereotypical assumptions about what the typical middle-aged woman is like. While Shannon thinks that the Taylor Swift incident is rather amusing, she often finds Facebook ads to be 'slightly offensive as they make assumptions about me, which I don't like to think are true'. The question is not just whether the categories and classifications that algorithms rely on match our own sense of self, but to what extent we come to see and identify ourselves through the 'eyes' of the algorithm?

'Whoa' moment

Sat down and opened up Facebook this morning while having my coffee, and there they were two ads for Nespresso. Kind of a 'whoa' moment when the product you're drinking pops up on the screen in front of you.

Just like algorithms track behaviour in order to profile identity, they can be productive of what Jessa calls 'whoa' moments – events in which the intimate power of algorithms reveals itself in strange sensations. Even for a tech-savvy journalist like Jessa, there is something peculiarly unexplainable about these whoa moments. While the Nespresso ads are likely an effect of contextual advertising based on the time of the day and other information, Jessa's encounter more importantly describes how algorithms 'function as a means of directing and disciplining attention' (Amoore, 2009, p. 22). As Beer (2013) suggests, algorithms define 'what "finds us", and so have a powerful place in the circulation of data and how these are filtered and directed' (p. 82). Whoa moments arise when people become aware of being found.

Faulty prediction

Scrolling through and reading the Facebook news feed has become a sensory habit. Lena does it several times a day. She is not particularly impressed by what she sees. A majority of the content in her news feed seems to come from people with political views opposite to hers, and the trending topics all have to do with celebrity gossip. Facebook suggests she should 'poke' her ex-boyfriend (Yes! People still do that). She has hidden his posts from her news feed, but Facebook seems to ignore this fact dutifully. Lena is annoyed. She is annoyed that her 'own social network is so out of sync' with her interests and beliefs. Maybe it is because she added most of her Facebook friends while she still attended high school in rural Texas. She now lives in New York City and feels at home there. She goes to grad school, and she votes for the Democrats. As Lena sarcastically notes in her tweet: 'Either the Facebook algorithm is crappy or I really do want to learn about celebrities, read conservative news, and interact with my ex'. The algorithm 'must be incorrectly assessing my social networking desires', she says.

While 'whoa' moments are generated by the sometimes uncanny ways in which algorithms seem to know what we are up to in the present, Lena's annoyance stems from the fact that she cannot seem to overcome her past. While 'real' life allows the past to be the past, algorithmic systems make it difficult to 'move on'. Algorithms and the databases with which they are intertwined make it hard to forget the past. Herein lies the politics of the archive. Beer (2013) notes that the archive not only records, but also works to shape memory by defining what is relatable and retrievable. For Lena the Facebook algorithm is at odds with how she sees her life. Lena is no longer the person she used to be, nor is she simply a reflection of her friends. Algorithms have a hard time picking up on such existential and social nuances, which raises the question of possibilities for escape. What happens when the world algorithms create is not in sync (as Lena says) with how people experience themselves in the present? To what extent do existing social networking profiles remain forever muddied by past lives and experiences?

A recurrent theme among the participants was the normative dimension of algorithms, the ways in which people expect algorithms to behave in a certain way. Quite often these expectations were not made intelligible until the algorithm did something to upset them, throw people off guard or frustrate. People generally started to notice the Facebook algorithm in moments of perceived breakdown. For Lena, it was clear that the Facebook algorithm did a poor job in assessing her life and social desires. Although she admitted to thinking that it was not solely the algorithms fault – after all, she did add those people as friends herself – she also thought the algorithm should be able to do better than that.

When algorithms do not behave in the way people expect, they tend to describe the system as broken. Like Lena, several of the other participants described situations reflecting this. Lucas, a 25-year-old quality assurance engineer, tweeted that he was 'pretty sure the Facebook algorithm is getting worse. I'm getting even less variety than usual lately'. He later explained the context of his tweet by saying that he had become increasingly frustrated by the algorithm's insistence on displaying the same 5–6 stories at the top of his news feed for many consecutive hours. As he said, having 'absolutely no new content show up agitated me, so I tweeted about my feelings on the algorithm'. Like the agitated feelings Lucas described, other participants stated how much they 'hated the algorithm' (Jolene), calling the algorithm a 'joke' (Sarah) or describing its workings as 'sheer mockery' (Jacob).

Popularity game

He presses the post button and waits. Normally, it should take no longer than 5 minutes before the 'likes' or 'comments' start ticking in. Nothing happens. Instead, Michael tweets: 'The whole Facebook algorithm thing is super frustrating'. As an independent musician, Michael has to find ways of spreading the word about his music and reaching an audience. Facebook seems like the perfect platform for self-promotion. Except only for those who have learned to play by its algorithmic drum. Michael says he has gotten better at 'playing Facebook's game'. For example, 'statuses do better based on what night you post it, the words you choose to use, and how much buzz it initially builds'. He knows from previous experience that 'if the status doesn't build buzz (likes, comments, shares) within the first 10 minutes or so, it immediately starts moving down the news feed and eventually gets lost'. He has just released a new album and needs to get the word out. He had picked the perfect day of the week, carefully crafted the words of the update, deliberately used phrases like 'wow!' and 'this is amazing!' Or so he thought. 0 downloads and 'only' 35 plays. 'Pure frustration', Michael notes.

While Facebook offers a tool for the performance of 'microcelebrity' (Marwick & Boyd, 2011), understood as the creation of online status and audiences by amateurs through social media, the business models and underlying algorithmic logic of the platform restrict how these practices can play out. Being a student and independent musician, Michael is frustrated by having his professional life at the mercy of the Facebook algorithm. Although Michael thinks he has become better at playing 'Facebook's game', he also suspects that Facebook will 'only showcase the statuses that people have paid to promote'.

Popularity, of course, is the gist of social networking platforms. While Facebook goes to great length to emphasise the 'notion of sharing in user-to-user traffic', while de-emphasising its 'interest in commercial exploitation' (Van Dijck, 2013, p. 61), sharing does not carry equal weight. As Bucher has argued, the Facebook algorithm tends to only reward the 'right' kind of sharing, giving certain kinds of posts more visibility at the expense of others (Bucher, 2012). Nora, another participant and a Canadian student, worries that the popularity bias of social media algorithms potentially diminishes the kinds of posts people get to see on their news feed. She says Facebook makes her uncomfortable because of its 'catch-up with friends' angle. Nora worries that the algorithmic bias towards 'likes' and 'shares' makes viral videos like the 'ice bucket challenge' much more prominent, hiding more important but less 'liked' current events such as the racial conflicts in Ferguson. As Nora says, 'I don't like having an algorithm or editor or curator or whatever controlling too much of what I say – if they're trying to go for more "trending topics", will my posts on "non-trending topics" get shuttered away?'

When I asked Nora to describe what caused her to write that there was 'definitely something strange going on with the Facebook algorithm', she said the tweet was meant as a comment on the perceived performance of one of her Facebook posts. She often posts about Canadian current affairs and regularly compares how well her posts are received in terms of gathering 'likes', 'comments' and so on. 'As much as I hate to say it, I dislike it when not a lot of people like my posts or statuses', she says. The amounts of 'likes' fuel the popularity game supported by Facebook, in which algorithms feed off on the social disposition towards interaction. Agger (2012) suggests that social media platforms like Facebook have created 'a generalized anxiety' that requires users to attend to their profiles in hopes of not being ignored (p. 44). For Nora, however, gathering likes is not a 'narcissistic cry for help' (Agger, 2012, p. 45). Rather, it is a necessary strategy that users need to deploy if they want to impact the algorithm's willingness to show the posts more prominently.

Interestingly, the majority of participants had experimented or played around with the system and algorithmic workings in one way or another. Kate, a former school teacher who now runs a Facebook page for parents in her neighbourhood, said she posts consciously, using multiple pictures instead of one, always trying to choose the right words and the right time of the day for 'maximum reach'. As a page owner, Kate says, 'I have completely changed how I share information to make it work best for the algorithm'. Nora, too, orients her updates and Facebook use towards the algorithm, and she shares Michael's observations about timeliness and the importance of building buzz. As Nora explains, 'if I post things and they receive no likes within the first 5 minutes, or very sparse likes (1–2 in the first minute), then they'll drop off and not get many comments or likes at all'. Over the years, Nora has developed different strategies for making her 'posts more frequently recognized' by the algorithm. These strategies include: posting at a certain time ('usually around late evening on a weekday that's not Friday'), structuring the post in specific ways, making sure that other people are *not* shown in her profile pictures (otherwise they are 'likely to get fewer likes') and making sure to avoid or include certain keywords in her updates. As Gillespie (2014) has usefully pointed out, adapting online behaviour to social media platforms and their operational logics can be seen as a form of optimisation, whereby content producers make their posts 'algorithmically recognizable'. When users wait until a certain day of the week and for a particular time of day, use multiple pictures instead of one, carefully choose their words and deliberately use positive sounding phrasing, they are not just strategically updating their social media profiles or hoping to be seen by others. Consistent with Gillespie's (2014) argument about using hashtags as a means of optimising for the algorithm, the personal algorithm stories shared as part of this study suggest that many of the participants are redesigning their expressions so as to be better recognised and distributed by Facebook's news feed algorithm.

Cruel connections

Memory is a powerful thing. It lives in the flash of a second, and the duration of a lifetime, it emerges in lifelike dreams and the drowsiness of mornings. Memories can be recalled at will or wilfully withdrawn. A memory is an event that connects us to the past and makes it possible to project a path for the future. Memory is an encounter, a distraction, an opportunity, daydream, or denial. In the digital age, memories can be made, encouraged, and programmed by the machine. Engineered to make people connect and participate, apps do the memory lane. Memories materialized in 'look back' videos and 'year in review' features giving people the impression of having a life. Except, in some cases, that good life is long lost. Features and apps do not just remind people about their friends' birthdays, they may also linger as a painful reminder of the tragedies of life. Emerging at odd moments, memories flash across the screen. Software apps that make you 'raise your head in surprise or alarm at the uncanny sensation of a half-known influence'. (Stewart, 2007, p. 60)

Such was the case for Eric Meyer, who did not go for grief that day but which found him anyway – on Facebook. 'Eric, here's what your year looked like'. A picture of his daughter, who died that year. On Twitter, a stranger ponders 'just maybe, there isn't an algorithm capable of capturing human experience'.

Albert – the stranger's name – lives in Massachusetts and works in advertising. While an algorithm might not be good at capturing human experience, Albert's tweet nicely captures the oddness of machines intercepting emotions. The story of Eric Meyer and the 'cruel algorithm' serving up a picture of his recently deceased daughter as part of the 'year in review' went all over the news when it happened in December 2014. For Albert, as for some of the other participants, the incident constituted a forceful encounter with the power of algorithms, giving him a 'reason to react' (Stewart, 2007). While Richard, another participant, decided to leave Facebook because of it, the incident sparked for Albert some fundamental questions about human nature and machines. 'While algorithms might (or might not) be a good tool for effectively serving up the right ad to the right user', Albert contemplated, 'they might not be the best way to create emotional content or connect on a human level'. In many ways, these sentiments point to what David Hill, drawing on Lyotard's (2012) work on *The inhuman*, describes as the 'inhuman functioning of new technologies' (p. 107). As Beer (2012) points out, algorithmic systems 'judge individuals against a set of contrasting norms, without human discretion intervening or altering decisions' (p. 77). Indeed, the year-in-review fiasco shows how computers and humans 'think' nothing alike. For Albert, this incident pointed him 'to the most obvious thing about algorithms – they're just machines'. What was obviously missing, says Albert, was the 'human judgment that says, "You know, this guy probably doesn't want to be reminded that his daughter died this year, so even though the post got tons of attention, I'll leave it out"'.

For both Richard and Albert, algorithms are not just capable of misjudging humans; they might not even be able to judge humans at all. While Albert is not sure 'what the algorithm in this case *should* have done', what seems clear to him is that 'an algorithm can only be as smart as the human who builds it'. However, human developers are not a guarantee for a *humane* working of software. The problem, as Hill (2012) suggests, 'is the rigidity of the algorithmic mode of processing data compared with the human's ability to ascertain contextual differences' (p. 113).

Ruined friendships

The tweet is short and concise: 'The Facebook algorithm wrecks friendship'. No more, no less. Rachel has been observing the algorithm for a while. She learned about the Facebook algorithm through an article in the Washington Post. She is a journalist herself. The algorithm makes her curious. What is it, how does it behave, what effect does it have? She has been monitoring her 'feed more closely to find signs of it'. There! A friend from high school just liked one of her posts. Rachel had 'totally forgotten she was even on Facebook'. 'I'm constantly taken aback by all the info and people Facebook hides from my feed on a daily basis'.

Facebook is all about friendship. From the moment people log in, create a profile and start using the site, they are encouraged to find, add, maintain and communicate with their friends. Facebook does not just mediate friendships. As Rachel's story suggests, Facebook also does something *to* friendships. In Rachel's experience, friendships on Facebook are filtered and curated. In her mind, the algorithm ruins friendship by making certain people disappear from view, only to emerge into awareness by chance. As Rachel elaborates, 'it does feel as if there is only a select group of friends I interact with on the social network, while I've practically forgotten about the hundreds of others I have on there'. Just as Facebook programmatically reminds people through various features and functionalities including the above-mentioned memory apps, Facebook also makes people forget. While it 'can feel almost like a relief', Rachel says, 'that Facebook chooses to not bombard me with updates' on the lives of people she does not care about, there is also the sense in which she has lost control of her own life and relationships. 'As far as "forgetting people" goes', she says, 'I do feel that the algorithm is trying to make decisions on my behalf, which angers me'.

This is a fairly common Facebook experience. Several of the participants said they felt uncomfortable and uneasy about the ways in which they perceive the Facebook algorithm to make decisions on their behalf, controlling what they see and do not get to see. Anthony, a Canadian art professor in his 60s, says it makes him 'think that there are intentional manipulations being experimented by the Facebook administration'. He finds the ways in which 'irregular people show up' on the newsfeed to be 'slightly creepy'. Not unlike Jessa's notion of a 'whoa' moment Anthony says the Facebook algorithm tends 'to place me into the "who are these people who suddenly show up?" state'. Like a ghost in the machine, the algorithm reminds people about their own lives and relationships, whether they like it or not. These reminders may feel uncanny, as Anthony put it, precisely because they should not be. When friends we have not talked to in a while, or have forgotten we even knew, all of a sudden appear on the news feed, the sensation of discomfort felt at the sudden surprise speaks to the specific affective dimension of Facebook friendships.

The algorithmic imaginary

The Facebook algorithm seizes the social imaginary through the various affective encounters it generates. As the many different personal algorithm stories analysed in this article attest to, Facebook's algorithms become part of 'force-relations' and are generative of different experiences, moods and sensations. The different scenes and situations can be understood as forming part of what might be called an algorithmic imaginary – ways of thinking about what algorithms are, what they should be, how they function and what these imaginations in turn make possible. While, as Steven suggests, 'nobody outside Facebook really knows' how the algorithm works, the personal algorithm stories illuminate how knowing algorithms might involve other forms of registers besides code. This is to say that what the algorithm does is not necessarily 'in' the algorithm as such (Introna, 2016). Rather, we may begin to understand the performance of algorithms through the ways in which they are being articulated, experienced and contested in the public domain. This is not to suggest that people's experiences and encounters with algorithms are somehow imaginary. Quite the opposite, they are 'real'. Algorithms are not just abstract computational processes; they also have the power to enact material realities by shaping social life to various degrees (Beer, 2013; Kitchin & Dodge, 2011). When Rachel finds herself 'clicking consciously everyday' to influence what will subsequently show up in her news feed, the algorithm is not merely an abstract 'unreal' thing that she thinks about but something that influences the ways in which she uses Facebook. Similarly, Lucas says his awareness of the Facebook algorithm has affected not just how he posts but also how he responds to others. As Lucas explains:

> I know that, if a friend of mine posts something they are passionate about, I will go out of my way to 'like' and 'comment' because I know that will programmatically 'support' them and hopefully put them into more people's feeds because EdgeRank will give them more points for my participation.

Lucas' willingness to go out of his way to like his friends' posts to enhance their visibility echoes some of the findings in recent work on social media surveillance. As Trottier and Lyon (2012) have shown, Facebook users engage in 'collaborative identity construction' augmenting each other's visibility through practices of tagging, commenting and liking.

Users' perceptions about what the algorithm is and how it works shape their orientation towards it. Several of the participants reported having changed their information-sharing behaviour 'to make it work best for the algorithm', as Kate put it. This seemed particularly true of the users whose responses indicated that they were avid and long-time Facebook users. These responses made apparent how engagement with Facebook as a publishing platform implies developing tacit knowledge about the underlying logic of the system. While most technologies are designed in such a way that people do *not* have to know exactly how it works (Hardin, 2003), people tend to construct 'mental models' and theories about its workings as a way of navigating and interacting with the world (see, for example, Orlikowski & Gash, 1994). Despite explicitly pointing out that they did *not* know the algorithm, most participants had more or less elaborate theories about what the Facebook algorithm is and ought to be. Kayla, for example, says she has 'no idea what the algorithm is' but suspects it works in response to all the data tracked by Facebook. Similarly, Michael has 'no clue what the actual algorithm is' but still had a clear idea how best to construct a status update in order to increase the likelihood of getting his posts widely distributed.

Far from naming an illusory relation, the algorithmic imaginary is a powerful identification that needs to be understood as productive. The sites and situations through which people encounter and experience algorithms arguably shape ways of thinking, talking and feeling about them. While seeing an ad for wrinkle cream may not be surprising when you are 45, or an ad for a dating site when you have declared yourself as 'single' on Facebook, these connections may not *feel* incidental. Algorithms create a 'cybernetic relationship to identification' by constructing 'categories of identity' (Cheney-Lippold, 2011, pp. 168, 172). These statistically derived patterns of cybernetic categorisation, however, may be in conflict with how users feel about and see themselves. Some participants, such as Shannon and Kayla, feel uncomfortable with the ways in which they are apparently being categorised, while others, such as Lena and Larry, feel distanced and even angry at the algorithm for 'thinking' they would be the kinds of persons who would actually be interested in the content they get served. While it might be difficult to escape the digitally constructed categories of identity, affect, as Papacharissi (2014) suggests, may extend beyond 'just emotions and feelings to describe driving forces that are suggestive of tendencies to act in a variety of ways' (p. 12). Whether or not the algorithm makes a correct inference does not necessarily matter. For example, a child who gets wrongfully addressed as an adult may like the fact it is being taken 'seriously' and start to behave in a more adult-like manner (De Vries, 2010, p. 78). Similarly, it seemed that Lena's anger at being 'wrongfully' identified and associated with her former class mates provoked her to update even more on the Democrats to counter the algorithm's insistence of showing 'Republican' updates.

The algorithmic imaginary does not merely describe the mental models that people construct about algorithms but also the productive and affective power that these imaginings have. Some participants attempt to make themselves more readily 'recognizable' to the algorithm (Gillespie, 2014) by acting in a way that would serve their individual purposes, for example, as Larry does, hiding posts in order to train the algorithm to show more interesting content on their news feed. Others try to make themselves more unrecognisable. Louis, a respondent from the Philippines, says he is deeply fascinated by the Facebook algorithm; yet, he thinks of it as a trap. As Louis contends:

> The Facebook algorithm is like a Lotus flower. It makes you want for more; yet, it traps you from really getting what you want. You like the sensation of being on it, but you have no idea what it actually does to you.

Unlike participants who have 'learned to live with' the algorithm, Louis thinks a better option would be to develop strategies to counteract the algorithm in different ways. Indeed, as Hill (2012) argues, 'resistance cannot merely be about opting out, but about participating in unpredictable ways' (p. 121). As Louis sees it, 'privacy online does not really exist. So why not just confuse those who are actually looking at your intimate information? That way it misleads them'. Some respondents reported engaging in activities of data obfuscation, both explicitly and implicitly. Lena has been trying to 'manipulate content' she interacts with in order to 'control the suggestions' Facebook gives her, while Jessa attempted to confuse the algorithm by liking contradictory things.

As we have seen, the ways in which algorithms are experienced and encountered as part of everyday life become part of 'force relations' that give people a 'reason to react'. Affective encounters between people and the Facebook algorithm are not just productive of different moods and sensations, but also play a generative role in moulding the algorithm itself. Driven by machine learning, the Facebook algorithm evolves and changes as a result of being exposed to an ever-increasing set of data (Introna, 2016). As Rader and Gray (2015) point out, the feedback-loop characteristics of these systems make user beliefs an important component in shaping the overall system behaviour. When users 'click consciously', disrupt their 'liking' practices, comment more frequently on some of their friends posts to support their visibility, only post on weekday nights, or emphasise positively charged words, these movements or reactions are not just affected by the algorithm (or, rather, by people's perceptions of the algorithm), these practices also have the ability to affect the very algorithms that helped generate these responses in the first place. If we want to understand the social power of algorithms, then, critiquing their workings is not enough. While algorithms certainly do things to people, people also do things to algorithms. The social power of algorithms – particularly, in the context of machine learning – stems from the recursive 'force-relations' between people and algorithms.

Concluding remarks

People experience algorithms in all kinds of situations. As this article has shown, the lived reality of the Facebook algorithm generates a plethora of ordinary affects from the frustration of not getting any 'likes' to the strange sensation of thinking 'who are these people who suddenly show up'? To understand the spaces where people and algorithms meet, this article proposed the notion of the algorithmic imaginary. As algorithms are becoming a ubiquitous part of contemporary life, understanding the affective dimensions – of how it makes people feel – seems crucial. If we are to consider the future of the algorithmic intensification, questions arise as to what possibilities for living with and alongside algorithms do these forces of encounter inspire? How does the algorithm perceive its subjects, and to what extent does it influence their sense of self? How, in turn, does the way in which people perceive algorithms affect the logic of the system? Contrary to the notion that 'the individual user is incapable of really experiencing the effect that algorithms have in determining one's life as algorithms rarely, if ever, speak to the individual' (Cheney-Lippold, 2011, p. 176), this article suggests that people do experience algorithms; and, while algorithms might not speak to individuals, they might speak through them. Despite the difficulty in accessing or discovering people's personal encounters with algorithms, it might just be a matter of *where* we as researchers go to look for these meetings. Sometimes, it is not a matter of peeking inside the black box of code but getting behind the tweets.

Disclosure statement

No potential conflict of interest was reported by the author.

References

Agger, B. (2012). *Oversharing: Presentations of self in the internet age*. New York, NY: Routledge.
Amoore, L. (2009). Lines of sight: On the visualization of unknown futures. *Citizenship Studies, 13*
(1), 17–30. doi:10.1080/13621020802586628

Beer, D. (2013). *Popular culture and new media: The politics of circulation*. New York, NY: Palgrave Macmillan.

Berlant, L. G. (2011). *Cruel optimism*. Durham, NC: Duke University Press.

Bucher, T. (2012). Want to be on the top? Algorithmic power and the threat of invisibility on Facebook. *New Media & Society, 14*(7), 1164–1180. doi:10.1177/1461444812440159

Cheney-Lippold, J. (2011). A new algorithmic identity soft biopolitics and the modulation of control. *Theory, Culture & Society, 28*(6), 164–181. doi:10.1177/0263276411424420

Chun, W. (in press). *Habitual new media*. Cambridge, MA: MIT Press.

Deleuze, G., & Guattari, F. (1987). *A thousand plateaus*. Minneapolis: University of Minnesota Press.

Deuze, M. (2012). *Media life*. Cambridge, UK: Polity.

De Vries, K. (2010). Identity, profiling algorithms and a world of ambient intelligence. *Ethics and information technology, 12*(1), 71–85. doi:10.1007/s10676-009-9215-9

Diakopoulos, N. (2015). Algorithmic accountability: Journalistic investigation of computational power structures. *Digital Journalism, 3*(3), 398–415. doi:10.1080/21670811.2014.976411

Elmer, G. (2004). *Profiling machines: Mapping the personal information economy*. Cambridge, MA: MIT Press.

Eslami, M., Rickman, A., Vaccaro, K., Aleyasen, A., Vuong, A., Karahalios, K., Hamilton, K., & Sandvig, C. (2015). "I always assumed that I wasn't really that close to [her]": Reasoning about invisible algorithms in the news feed. In *Proceedings of the 33rd Annual SIGCHI Conference on Human Factors in Computing Systems* (pp. 153–162). New York, NY: ACM. doi:10.1145/2702123.2702556

Fuchs, C., Boersma, K., Albrechtslund, A., & Sandoval, M. (2012). *Internet and surveillance: The challenges of Web 2.0 and social media*. New York: Routledge.

Gillespie, T. (2014). The relevance of algorithms. In T. Gillespie, P. Boczkowski, & K. Foot (Eds.), *Media technologies: Essays on communication, materiality, and society* (pp. 167–194). Cambridge, MA: MIT Press.

Gregg, M., & Seigworth, G. J. (2010). *The affect theory reader*. Durham, NC: Duke University Press.

Hardin, R. (2003). If it rained knowledge. *Philosophy of the Social Sciences, 33*(1), 3–24.

Hill, D. W. (2012). Jean-François Lyotard and the inhumanity of internet surveillance. In C. Fuchs, K. Boersma, A. Albrechtslund, & M. Sandoval (Eds.), *Internet and surveillance: The challenges of Web* (pp. 106–123). New York, NY: Routledge.

Introna, L. D. (2016). Algorithms, governance, and governmentality on governing academic writing. *Science, Technology & Human Values, 41*(1), 17–49.

Kitchin, R., & Dodge, M. (2011). *Code/space: Software and everyday life*. Cambridge, MA: MIT Press.

Knuth, D. E. (1998). *The art of computer programming: Sorting and searching* (Vol. 3). Boston: Addison-Wesley.

Marwick, A. & Boyd, D. (2011). I tweet honestly, I tweet passionately: Twitter users, context collapse, and the imagined audience. *New Media & Society, 13*(1), 114–133. doi:10.1177/1461444810365313

Merleau-Ponty, M. (1962). *The phenomenology of perception*. London: RKP.

Orlikowski, W. J., & Gash, D. C. (1994). Technological frames: Making sense of information technology in organizations. *ACM Transactions on Information Systems (TOIS), 12*(2), 174–207. doi:10.1145/196734.196745

Papacharissi, Z. (2014). *Affective publics: Sentiment, technology, and politics*. New York, NY: Oxford University Press.

Rader, E., & Gray, R. (2015). Understanding user beliefs about algorithmic curation in the Facebook news feed. In *CHI'15 proceedings of the 33rd annual ACM conference on human factors in computing systems* (pp. 173–182). New York: ACM. Retrieved from http://dl.acm.org/citation.cfm?id=2702174

Stewart, K. (2007). *Ordinary affects*. Durham, NC: Duke University Press.

Trottier, D., & Lyon, D. (2012). Key features of social media surveillance. In C. Fuchs, K. Boersma, A. Albrechtslund, & M. Sandoval (Eds.), *Internet and surveillance: The challenges of Web 2.0 and social media* (pp. 89–105). New York, NY: Routledge.

Van Dijck, J. (2013). *The culture of connectivity: A critical history of social media*. Oxford: Oxford University Press.

Appendix 1. List of participants

Australia: Steven (24, graphic designer).

Canada: Jolene (22, fashion blogger), Nora (20, student), Larry (23, works in television), Anthony (64, art professor), Richard (41, manual labourer), Alex (age unknown, occupation unknown).

Norway: Sarah (33, biologist).

Philippines: Louis (20s, former student, current occupation unknown).

United Kingdom: Jacob (38, on leave from a university degree).

United States: Amber (25, student), Kayla (23, student), Michael (21, Musician), Rachel (24, journalist), Jessa (20s, journalist), Lucas (25, Quality Assurance Engineer), Shannon (45, career counsellor), Lena (20s, graduate student), Chris (20, student), Albert (42, works in advertising), Kate (36, former school teacher), Nancy (age unknown, public policy associate), Caitlyn (30s, teacher).

Unknown location, age and occupation: Tom, John.

Algorithmic IF … THEN rules and the conditions and consequences of power

Daniel Neyland and Norma Möllers

ABSTRACT

The introduction to this special issue suggests we need to develop 'a greater understanding of what might be thought of as the social power of algorithms'. In this paper, 'social power' will be critically scrutinised through a study of the entanglement of algorithmic rules with contemporary video-based surveillance technologies. The paper will begin with an analysis of algorithmic 'IF … THEN' rules and the conditions (IF) and consequences (THEN) that need to be accomplished for an algorithm to be said to succeed. The work of achieving conditions and consequences demonstrates that the form of 'power' in focus is not solely attributable to the algorithm as such, but operates through distributed agency and can be noted as a network effect. That is, the conditions and consequences of algorithmic rules only come into being through the careful plaiting of relatively unstable associations of people, things, processes, documents and resources. From this we can say that power is not primarily social in the sense that algorithms alone create an impact on society, but social in the sense of power being derived through algorithmic associations. The paper argues that this kind of power is most clearly visible in moments of breakdown, failure or other forms of trouble, whereby algorithmic conditions and consequences are not met and the careful plaiting of associations has to be brought to the fore and examined. It is through such examinations that the associational dependencies more than the social power of algorithms are made apparent.

Introduction

Power is a major theme in the recent literature on algorithms. Concerns refer, for example, to the roles of algorithms in processes of discrimination (Barocas & Selbst, in press), the sorting and ordering of populations (Lyon, 2003) or the (e)valuation and governance (Aneesh, 2009; Rouvroy, 2013) of social life. Furthermore, work on algorithms points to their relative inaccessibility, which renders both analysis and political intervention notoriously difficult. Although we share these concerns, we also find that scholarship on algorithms is often based on implicit, underlying assumptions that there is 'something special' about algorithms which makes them powerful. Lumped together in these assumptions are questions of the ontology, agency and ability of algorithms. In this paper we seek to focus on how we can understand algorithms' agency and power.

What makes algorithms powerful entities? The way we pose this question already points to the argument we set out in this paper: by asking 'what makes algorithms powerful?' we question who and what need to be drawn together to yield effects that are recognisable as powerful. We argue that the 'social power' of algorithms, just like that of any other artefact, is an effect and not a cause of events, and which is not given but needs to be achieved (cf. Latour, 1986, 2005). Rather than understanding algorithms as having power, an agency through which they create an effect, we argue that power derives from algorithmic association. By 'algorithmic association' we mean the assemblage of people, things, resources and other entities held together by practice and process. From this perspective, what algorithms do and how algorithms accomplish effects are inextricably tied to the situations in which they operate and which they help to reproduce.

We set out our argument drawing on two ethnographies of the development of algorithmic surveillance systems. These systems were designed to alert security personnel in transportation hubs (i.e., airports and train stations) in case of an undesirable event. Central to these systems were algorithmic IF ... THEN rules which established the conditions (IF) and consequences (THEN) required to produce an effect (such as alert security personnel). However, in our field sites neither conditions, nor consequences were inherent to the system; both needed to be achieved through the careful plaiting of relatively unstable associations of people, things, processes, documents and resources. The continuous work needed to achieve conditions and consequences suggests that we cannot attribute 'power' solely to the algorithm as a single entity. Rather, the algorithms in our study operated through distributed agency among an array of people and things. This perspective shifts attention from purported impacts of algorithms on society to the variety of algorithmic associations that need to be established, as well as the conditions which render them more or less stable.

The structure of this paper is as follows. We begin by discussing how algorithms might be implicated in power relationships, drawing on the idea of 'associations' as a concept. We then introduce a study of two algorithmic surveillance systems in order to consider algorithmic rules, their design, development and possible effects. By analysing the conditions and consequences of these rules, we show the associations needed to achieve conditions and consequences. We conclude by suggesting that 'looking for trouble' – moments of breakdown, failure or other problems – is productive for emphasising the centrality of associations, rather than social power, to achieving algorithmic effects.

Algorithms and power

A number of authors have recently considered algorithmic power. For example, Lash (2007, p. 71) argues: 'power is increasingly in the algorithm'. Beer (2009, p. 994) further suggests: 'algorithms have the capacity to shape social and cultural formations and impact directly on individual lives'. Spring (2011) argues that algorithms trap individuals and control their lives, while Slavin (2011, n.p.) is clear that algorithms 'acquire the status of truth ... They become real'. Within these accounts of algorithmic activity, it is the algorithms which are the entities of concern; the algorithms are noted as powerful, agential and central to the distribution of consequences. These concerns lead to various calls

(Diakopoulos, 2013; Kitchin, 2014; Seaver, 2013) for algorithms to be held to account, governed and regulated. However, the challenge in accomplishing such a task is made complicated by proprietary interest in keeping algorithms enclosed, the technical difficulties involved in making an algorithm transparent (Slavin, 2011) or the problems involved in removing algorithms from their black boxes (Bucher, 2012).

This suggests two problematic issues: first, algorithms are agential, powerful and consequential; second, algorithms are almost impossible to know. However, several recent studies point towards the possibilities for engaging up close with algorithms in order to explore their technicalities and consequences (as this paper will also do) and recent studies have begun to question some of the power attributed to algorithms. Hence, Drucker (2013, n.p.) argues that although algorithms are instructions for processes 'whose outcomes may usually be predictable', algorithms can also be 'as open to error and random uncertainties in their execution as they are to uncertain outcomes in their use'. Diakopoulos (2013, p. 2) also suggests that algorithms can not only be beneficial, but also involved in mistakes. This focus on algorithmic mistakes might not diminish the concerns we have with algorithms (their mistakes may be just as consequential and difficult to account for), but it does seem to modify somewhat the ways we might engage with algorithmic power. Instead of treating the algorithm as agential and consequential, we might also have to explore its limitations and the problems it causes for those people, organisations and activities which have become arrayed through algorithms.

Other work pushes these points further. For example, Kushner (2013, p. 1242) suggests that in the case of translation, algorithms need human 'help' in order to become a 'freelance translation machine, an assemblage of circuits and flesh that transforms text from one language to another with a computer's efficiency and the sensitivity of the human mind'. Furthermore, Hallinan and Striphas (2014) argue, in their study of an online recommendation system, that the algorithm cannot work with various oddities in customer preference and instead of being resolved, these oddities need to be worked around. In these accounts, not only is the algorithm made accessible to research, but it is also decentred in its agential consequences. The algorithm needs assistance.

Taken together with recent studies of algorithms in Science and Technology Studies (STS) (Gillespie, 2011, 2014; Neyland, 2015) and geography (Kitchin, 2014), this suggests we need to understand the algorithm-in-action as situated (Suchman, Randall, & Blomberg, 2002) among a variety of people, things, processes, documents, resources and technologies. It suggests we could use this situatedness to explore a distinct approach to power which shifts attention away from the algorithm as *the* agential and consequential entity. Treating the algorithm as the agential entity requires an approach to power predicated on an asymmetrical distribution of the ability to create consequences for others. In this way algorithms would hold power over those subject to algorithmic decision-making through this asymmetry. If we instead treat asymmetry as an achieved effect, we can explore how asymmetries are composed.

One means to do so would be to extend Latour's (2005) work on association into algorithms. Latour (2005) suggests that associations are forms of interaction through which things take a social shape. However, according to Latour, one should not jump from recognising the presence of an interaction, to considering that interaction is characterised by a social force (2005, p. 65). In this way, power (as social force) does not precede interaction, neither is it a property of ossified societal structures, nor is it a context 'which makes the many participants in the action move' (2005, p. 83). Instead, 'Power and domination have to be produced, made up, composed' (Latour, 2005, p. 64). Rather than treating power as resulting from an asymmetrical distribution of the ability to create a consequence for others, this line of argument suggests making sense of asymmetries through close study of the ongoing associations through which an asymmetrical effect is achieved. This approach does not then deny that algorithms might participate in producing asymmetrical consequences, but instead explores how asymmetrical effects are achieved. To understand the ways in which algorithms are tied up with forms of power, we might thus explore their associations. If we follow Latour (2005), we would not look to explain power as an agential characteristic of algorithms, but instead seek to make sense of asymmetries composed through the associational life of algorithms. However, in recognising the situated character of algorithms, we need to provide precise detail on the nature of such algorithmic associations. In order to further explore the ways in which situated algorithms produce asymmetrical effects through their associations, we will turn attention to our empirical study of the development of two algorithmic surveillance systems.

Algorithmic surveillance

This paper engages with two 3-year-long projects which experimented with video analytic algorithms. Video analytics is a developing field in which algorithms and associated software/code sift through streams of digital video data, selecting out data that fit within prescribed patterns of relevance. Such patterns are often referred to as moments of 'event detection' in which algorithms and associated software/code demarcate relevant from irrelevant data and draw the relevant data to others' attention. In our pursuit of algorithmic association and the means by which asymmetrical effects are achieved, this initial distinction of relevance and irrelevance is key – to be deemed 'relevant' rather than 'irrelevant' can often mean to be noted or not within a video analytic surveillance system. Yet to produce such an asymmetry and maintain the relevance–irrelevance demarcation requires continuing effort, as we will go on to explore.

Briefly stated, the two projects that we will consider were designed to work in the following way. Daniel's project involved a management consultancy firm as coordinators, a large technology firm, two teams of academic computer scientists and a team of social scientists given ethnographic access to the project. The project also involved a national European rail operator and a large city airport where the system would be developed and tested. An experimental aim of the research was to work through the possibilities of using algorithms to detect events such as people moving in the wrong direction (counterflow) through airport security or through entry and exit points of train stations, moving into inappropriate areas (intrusion) such as train tracks or closed airport offices, and abandoned luggage.

Norma's project involved behaviour analysis software for video surveillance systems. The project incorporated four teams of academic researchers (computer scientists, geoscientists and legal scholars), two private research institutes (the members of which were mainly computer scientists by training), a consulting agency that carried out cost–benefit analyses, an IT company which was supposed to integrate the system for technology transfer as well as officers from regional police crime units who were expected to share their expertise in detecting criminal behaviour. The group's goal outlined in the grant proposal was to mechanise surveillance processes in order for the system to identify 'dangerous' situations and behaviour automatically and in real time and send alerts to operators who would no longer have to watch screens at all times. The idea was to facilitate intervention before the fact, and would also reduce personnel cost through automation. The project was funded by the German government.

In the following sections we consider three areas of activity that provide insight into the situated character of algorithmic systems and enable us to explore more precisely the forms of association involved and how these go towards building asymmetries. We will begin by looking at the algorithms themselves and the means by which they establish conditions and consequences. We will then explore the further work required to achieve these conditions (through classifications and maps) and consequences (through bricolage and demonstrations).

Algorithmic IF ... THEN rules

The algorithms for event detection used in video analytic systems are a designed product. They take effort and work and thought and often an amount of reworking. The algorithms establish a set of rules which are designed to contribute to demarcating relevant from irrelevant video data. In this way, such rules could be noted as central to the kinds of algorithmic power that generate asymmetries between people and things that can be ignored and people and things that might need further scrutiny. If such a focus could hold together, the rules would be central to the 'power' of algorithms. The algorithmic rules as set out in Figure 1 were developed for detecting abandoned luggage in Daniel's project:

What seems most apparent in these rules is the IF ... THEN structure. At its simplest, the 'IF' acts as a condition and the 'THEN' acts as a consequence. In this particular algorithm, the IF ... THEN rules were designed to operate in the following way. IF an object was

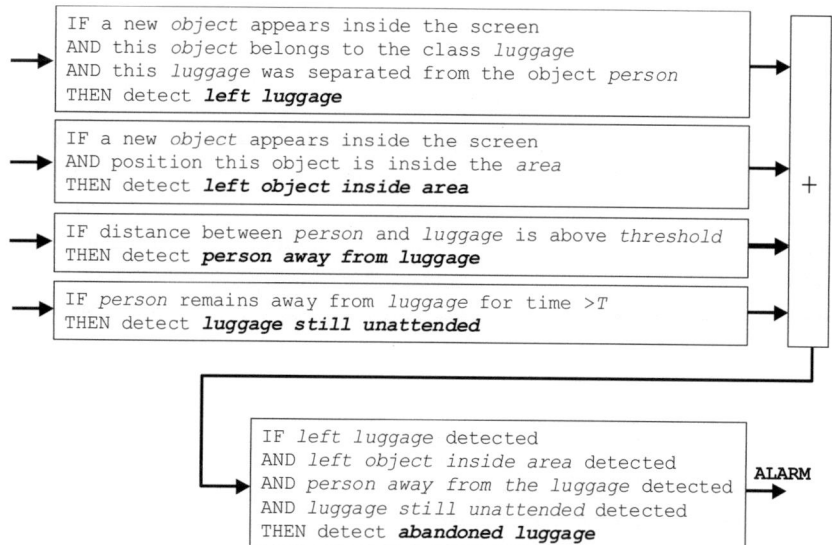

Figure 1. IF ... THEN rules for abandoned luggage.

detected within an area (for example, a train station or airport under surveillance), THEN the object could be tentatively allocated the category of potentially relevant. IF that same object was deemed to be in the class of objects 'luggage', THEN that object could be tentatively allocated the category of potentially relevant item of luggage. IF that same luggage-shaped object was separate from a human-shaped object, THEN it could maintain its position as potentially relevant. IF that same luggage-shaped object and human-shaped object were beyond the distance threshold currently set by the system (say 2 or 10 metres) and the same objects were beyond the temporal threshold currently set by the system (say 30 seconds or 1 minute) – that is, if the luggage and person were sufficiently far apart for sufficiently long, THEN an alarm could be sent to surveillance operators.

If this structuring and division of various entities (humans, luggage, time, space, relevance and irrelevance) occurred straightforwardly and endured, it might be tempting to argue that this is where the social power of algorithms is located or made apparent. A straightforward shortcut would be to argue that the algorithm structures the social world and through this kind of statement, we could then find Lash's (2007) powerful algorithm, and Beer's (2009) algorithm which shapes the social world. As a result of an asymmetrical distribution of the ability to cause an effect, the algorithm would have social power. However, such a shortcut creates a leap from algorithmic rules to their consequences. If instead we pay attention to the situated work required for algorithmic conditions and consequences to be achieved, what we find is not that the algorithm structures the social world. Instead, efforts are made (and fail, are remade, reworked and then sometimes fail again or work to a small extent) to constitute the conditions required for the structure, or the structure gets rewritten to fit new versions of the conditions. This continual rewriting and efforts to achieve conditions and consequences are not only axiomatic to computer science, but are also where associations are made, and are made available for scrutiny. It is also where the asymmetry between relevant and irrelevant data is continuously in the process of being made. In the following analysis of algorithmic conditions and consequences, we will explore the associational effort required to constitute a structure that gives asymmetrical effect to algorithmic rules.

Achieving conditions

In the two projects we consider in this paper, for the IF conditions of an event detection algorithm to be achieved required co-ordinated work to bring together everyday competences (among surveillance operators and computer scientists), the creation of new entities (including lines of code), the further development of components (from algorithmic rules to new forms of classification) and the development of particular theories of the world in which the algorithms would operate (such as a train station or airport), but also subtle changes in that world. These continual associations were the basis for achieving conditions. In order to illustrate the complexity of achieving conditions, we will focus here on a comparison of the two projects' work on classification and maps.

Achieving conditions – classifications

Both projects depended on classification work to bring about a condition necessary for the algorithmic system to asymmetrically divide relevant data from irrelevant data. However, classification systems are necessarily incomplete – there is always something that 'falls through the cracks' (Bowker & Star, 2000). This incompleteness means that ambiguity about the objects and subjects to which algorithms refer is inserted into the development process. To varying degrees, developers then need to create workarounds to compensate for such incompleteness. In extreme cases, the world the algorithms are supposed to refer to has to be remodelled (and simplified) according to the availability of data.

In Daniel's project for an event detection algorithm to pick out, for example, an item of suspicious luggage and issue an alarm to operators, various classifications had to be made. Objects had to be classified, for example, as luggage shaped or human shaped and the states of those objects also required classification, for example, as moving or not moving. Object classification involved algorithmically sifting through the stream of digital data produced by the video surveillance system in the airport and train stations. Classification depended upon models that were built to parameterise potential objects. This involved establishing edges around what a human-shaped object was likely to be (in terms of height, width and so on). Other models then had to be built to parameterise other objects, such as luggage, cleaners' trolleys, sign posts and other non-permanent attributes of the settings under surveillance. The models relied on a 200-point vector analysis to set in place what made up the edges of the object under consideration and then to which model those edges suggested the object belonged. This was designed to produce rapid, real-time classifications within the airport and train stations.

Parameterisation was presented by the computer scientists as a form of classification that the developing algorithmic system could manage without using too much processing power (as it also had to take on other tasks) and without having to take too much time. In this way, parameterisation would act as an initial but indefinite basis for object classification that could be confirmed by surveillance operators when shown images of, for example, an apparently suspicious item of luggage.

In Daniel's project object classification did not just depend on parameterisation. Object tracking was required to ascertain the state of the objects being classified. To achieve the conditions established in the IF … THEN rules of Figure 1, the system had to identify that a potential item of luggage was no longer moving and its human owner had moved at least a certain distance from the luggage and for a certain time. In order to track objects that had been given an initial and hesitant classification, human-shaped objects and luggage-shaped objects would be given a bounding box. This was a digitally imposed stream of metadata that would create a box around the object according to its already established edges. The box would then be given a metadata identity according to its dimensions, location within the airport or train station (for example, which camera it appeared on) and its direction and velocity. IF a human-shaped object split from a luggage-shaped object, IF the human-shaped object continued to move, IF the luggage-shaped object remained stationary, IF the luggage-shaped object and human-shaped object were over a certain distance apart and IF the human-shaped object and luggage-shaped object stayed apart for a certain amount of time, THEN this would achieve the conditions under which the algorithmic system could issue an alert. In place of the algorithm (in the form of IF … THEN rules) having power, it seems instead that a series of people, things, actions and relations have to come about to provide a set of conditions through which an asymmetry can be composed, relevant data divided from irrelevant data and an event detected. In this sense, the algorithmic system comes to be what it is through a carefully maintained series of associations (Latour, 2005); it is the associations through which any sense of power might be said to operate and any asymmetry between relevant and irrelevant data achieved.

The importance of these associations can be made clear by comparing the forgoing analysis with classification in Norma's project. Here, the focus was not specifically on objects and people, but rather the actions of people in relation to other people. The main event detection algorithm in Norma's project detected patterns of aggregated movements across the monitored space through what the computer scientists termed 'unsupervised learning', analysing 'what most people do'. The underlying idea was the following: if a single individual behaves significantly differently from the majority of people in a given space, then there is an increased chance that this person is exhibiting the kind of behaviour the system is supposed to detect. In this theory, 'conformity' means 'what most people do', and deviance is then designated as everything else. Classification would thus operate in the following manner: if a moving object was detected within the monitored area, and it could be assigned the class of person, and this person's movement trajectory diverged significantly from the movements of most people in this space, then the camera would zoom in on this person, sending an alarm and the live video feed to the surveillance operators' screens. In this second project, then, the algorithmic system is nothing without the associational effort to asymmetrically divide normality from abnormality.

Before one jumps too swiftly to assume that algorithms 'have' associational power and that this creates effects, it should be noted that this particular arrangement (using unsupervised learning to distinguish normal and abnormal behaviour) itself emerged from failure. Initial project aims involved classifying actions into 'dangerous' and 'safe' behaviour. Here the researchers had struggled with three interrelated problems: First, they recognised that social behaviour is indexical and can only be meaningfully understood in its context. For them, this meant that they were not able to teach the algorithm how to meaningfully interpret behaviour in order to make definitive decisions. The behaviour was situated. One example they frequently raised was how they would be able to tell whether converging movement trajectories (two people moving towards each other) meant that these people were engaging in, for example, illegal substance trade or simply having a friendly conversation. Second, the police officers in the project were not able to turn their implicit police knowledge (they had learned in years of training) into knowledge explicit enough to satisfy the software requirements for well-defined categories and rules (cf. Goodwin, 1994; Sacks, 1972). Third, because the researchers consequently had more discretion over the definition of 'dangerous' behaviour than they wished for, they did not want to assume responsibility for potentially making wrong decisions. In this sense, to assume that the algorithms 'have' power is to overlook the entangled associations of people, things, decisions, processes and resources within which the algorithm is situated and from which effects are noted (or not), and, from which moment, changes are made (or not). As one researcher noted:

> You know, the rules don't fall from the sky, someone has to specify them. Ideally, the person who runs the transportation hub puts in his knowledge. But really, the core of the problem is this: What is aberrant behaviour, and what is the concrete situation? ... There is definitely a knowledge gap between theory and practice, the police and us. Experts are capable of certain classifications that you simply cannot imitate with technical means. (Norma's field notes, September 2011)

What we can note here is that the associations are not a straightforward condition to be achieved – there are various ways in which algorithmic rules and software/code might be written, various aims put forward and changed, various early test results that require changes, different claims to expertise that require consideration and expectations of expertise that require revision. How different associations are made (between different people and objects, between assumptions about what a stream of video data does tell us or can tell us about suspicion or normalcy), operate in conjunction with a continual reconsideration of the conditions to be achieved. The conditions to be achieved will change with the associations. In this sense it is too simplistic to suggest that algorithms 'have' power; any accomplishment of effect emerges from continual reconfigurations of the entities involved. It is an occasional accomplishment of effect (in other words, the system manages to do something) that can lead to either a conformation or a rewriting of the conditions to be achieved. Asymmetries, such as demarcations of relevant from irrelevant data, can then also change as an upshot of transformations in the conditions achieved through the work of the project participants.

Achieving conditions – mapping

The contrast between achieving a condition and maintaining it as part of the algorithmic system and not achieving a condition and so rewriting the basis for what ought to count as an effect can be seen in comparisons between the two projects' efforts to map space. In Daniel's project, in order for an object to be classified (as in the preceding analysis), first the very notion of a moving object had to be identified and to do this, the computer scientists looked to use a standard technique in video analytics: background subtraction. This method for identifying moving objects was somewhat time-consuming and processor-intensive, but these efforts could be 'front-loaded' prior to any active work completed by the system. 'Front-loading' in this instance meant that a great deal of work would be done to produce an extensive map of the fixed attributes of the setting (airport or train station) prior to attempts at classification work. Mapping the fixed attributes would not then need to be repeated unless changes were made to the setting (such changes included in this project a change to a shop front and a change to the layout of the airport security entry point). Producing the map provided a basis to inform the algorithmic system what to ignore. Fixed attributes were thus nominally collated as non-suspicious in ways that people and luggage, for example, could not be, as these latter objects could not become part of the map of attributes (the maps were produced based on empty airports and train stations). Having a fixed map then formed the background from which other entities could be subtracted. Anything that the system detected that was not part of the map would be given an initial pixel mask which could then feed into the aforementioned processes of object classification and tracking.

In contrast to this approach to mapping, in Norma's project, the teams of researchers were not able to implement their software in the fixed environment needed to make maps. This was because the group worked out of different organisations distributed all over Germany, and only met every three months to integrate their work; and because they did not cooperate with a transportation hub which would put the infrastructure of a monitored space at their disposal. This meant that all of the technical equipment had to be moved and reconfigured from lab to lab, and to the spaces in which it was to be tested and presented. The many 'moving parts' in this project highlight the efforts of communication and collaboration and the careful combination of people, things, processes and resources, which needed to be aligned to achieve the conditions for the algorithms to 'do' anything.

The basis for demarcating relevance from irrelevance in both projects was thus distributed between various different entities (computer scientists and their understanding of spaces such as airports, maps that might be programmed to ignore for a time certain classes of objects, and classification systems that might then also – if successful – provide a hesitant basis for selecting out potentially relevant objects). Here again it becomes clear that anything that algorithms were able to 'do' was situated in continual reconfigurations of the entities involved, and that the agency of algorithms thus needs to be understood as distributed. The 'power' of the algorithmic system to asymmetrically divide relevant data from irrelevant data was an upshot of these associations and not a precondition for achieving effects.

What we suggest is that an understanding is required of the achievement of conditions in order to make sense of algorithms. This approach is important for emphasising the situated efforts required to design a set of algorithmic rules and achieve conditions for their operation (through, for example, classification and mapping). We have also tried to show the ways in which algorithms are part of quite precarious arrangements at times, with the very conditions to be achieved subject to rewriting according to the effects a system manages to show or not show. By considering the effects of an algorithmic system as an upshot of its associations and by emphasising the work required to make and maintain and also change those associations, we have attempted to move away from any assumption that it is the algorithm itself that is in some way powerful. Our suggestion is that asymmetrical effects – such as demarcations between relevance and irrelevance – are achieved (if at all) through associations, rather than through a precondition characteristic of algorithms which gives them the power to act independently on people and things. In the next section, we will explore this further through the second part of algorithmic IF … THEN rules, moving from conditions to consequences.

Achieving consequences

Although we have somewhat separated algorithmic conditions and consequences in this paper, we would like to stress that in practice achieving conditions is inseparable from achieving consequences. Even a cursory look at Figure 1 will reveal that various IF-conditions and THEN-consequences are nested within the single set of algorithmic rules. Moreover, the consequences of the algorithmic system (for example, issuing an alarm to operators of the system) cannot be achieved without the conditions (making the maps, classifying objects), but the conditions are also meaningless without the consequences (the maps are made to aid in the issue of alarms and problems with the conditions may lead to a rewriting of anticipated consequences). What is clear in the two projects is that achieving consequences through algorithmic systems involved distinct types of activity in comparison to achieving conditions. We will compare two examples of trouble in achieving consequences across the two algorithm projects to highlight two different forms of activity that occur in response. Assessing moments where the projects ran into trouble is particularly useful as these are where detailed considerations of associations, their strengths and failures are made apparent to everyone in the project. Running into trouble provides a basis for considering the fragility of such associations. Trouble was also, as we will show, a continual matter of concern for the participants in these two algorithm projects.

In Daniel's project, the main consequence to be achieved was to produce alerts for system operators of such matters as abandoned luggage. The computer scientists sought to test out if the new algorithmic system could produce such alerts more effectively, or at least as effectively, as the conventional video surveillance system in the end-user sites (train stations and an airport). Taking the example of abandoned luggage at the airport, operators would conventionally scan the monitors in their control room in the airport and seek out items which appeared out of place. Items would then be given some scrutiny and if they appeared to be luggage which had been abandoned, operators would radio through to security on the terminal floor who would move to inspect the item. Operators suggested, on average, they would detect one such object per hour. This set a benchmark for the new algorithmic system. The computer scientists set up the system to run for 6 hours taking a live feed from the airport cameras and expected to discover around 6 objects. The system was left to run for 6 hours in the airport as a redundant system (conventional surveillance would continue to operate and provide the basis for any necessary interventions). The computer scientists were present in the airport to collect and analyse results. They were interested not only in the number of correct alerts issued, but also in the number of false positives (seeing things that were not there) and false negatives (not seeing things that were there). In the 6 hours that the system ran, in place of detecting approximately 6 items of potentially lost or abandoned luggage, the algorithmic system detected 2654 potentially suspicious items.

The working assumption of the computer scientists was that there were likely to be around 2648 false positives. In later checking of a random sample of alerts, it turned out the system was detecting as abandoned luggage such things as reflective surfaces, sections of wall, a couple embracing and a person studying a departure board. The computer scientists worked through the results and identified 'confounding' variables such as camera angles not favoured by the system (for example, being too low and hence unable to see through crowds), changing lighting conditions (which cast shadows in different directions, changing not only the system's view of the edges of objects, their initial classification but also their tracking between frames and cameras) and different flooring materials in different parts of the airport (which meant that certain objects stood out against the background in different ways in different spaces). Running into trouble in this way was particularly significant for the project team, as at the time of this test they were only weeks away from giving a final demonstration of the technology 'live' to the project funders. The carefully plaited associations between various entities, which each made demands on the system to asymmetrically divide relevant from irrelevant footage, were now to be made available for reconsideration.

This kind of trouble was not unusual in algorithm projects. Norma's project ran into a number of issues. For example, having no single fixed location in which to demonstrate the technology (such as a transport hub) and having to transport technology to the relevant location on each occasion when it would be demonstrated to the funding institution and industry posed significant difficulties for the project. Every single part of the system had to be reconfigured to each other and to the physical space in which they wanted to demonstrate the technology – associations were thus made and remade frequently and at pace, as this note from Norma's field work shows:

Dennis approaches me and asks me what I'm up to. 'I just wanted to see the work on the cameras, and Marco just explained to me that they're configuring the cameras.' Dennis nods and explains: 'Yeah, their problem is that the cameras vibrate. I think they always work with fixed cameras and you don't have that problem with those.' I don't understand. 'Well, we only were allowed to attach the cameras with strings, and in order not to damage the columns we put foam in between; but that's not helping the problem, either. And they're not able to calculate the errors out'. (Norma's field notes, November 2011)

In the above case, vibrating cameras meant that the tracking algorithms mistook their own movement for movement in the monitored space, and this in turn meant that it would track every single pixel in the image. In a quite literal sense, no asymmetry could be drawn between relevant and irrelevant data as every pixel was constituted as potentially in need of further scrutiny. Further trouble emerged when construction workers changed the pattern of the floor tiles in the days preceding a project demonstration (see below), which was a serious problem for synchronising the cameras with the other system components. Finally, other events in the hall during the preceding weeks repeatedly changed the appearance of the monitored space, which meant that producing the maps needed to reduce processing resources was continuously interrupted. In other words, the architecture, construction workers, other events in the hall and a variety of other factors intervened with the functioning of the algorithmic system. Associations were made radically contingent by the continual uncertainties posed by moving components from one location to another; as the vibrating cameras showed, components and thus their ability to associate were transformed by changing locations. Encountering these kinds of trouble caused problems for the project's attempt to demonstrate the utility of the technology to the funders and a wider audience:

Everyone is gathered around the big touch screen in the hall. Other than the researchers, there are industry representatives, police officers, security services companies, and the funding institution representatives present. Dennis introduces the 'use case': he explains that someone will steal the painting they put in the middle of the hall, and that the system will send an alarm to the screen when that happens. This would be based on the analysis of the video material. 'So who wants to steal the painting? Jakob?' Before Jakob can answer, a very excited looking Professor Bode jumps up, raises her hand, and walks towards the painting. Everyone's heads turn back and forth between her and the screen, looks of anticipation on their faces. The professor finally reaches out to the painting and takes it from its easel. Everyone's attention shifts to the screen. Anticipation turns into extreme awkwardness when nothing happens. The researchers look at the screen with horror. Dennis tries to salvage the situation with some self-deprecating humour: 'I forgot to say that this is also an opportunity to see work in progress'. (Norma's field notes, November 2011)

In a similar manner to the computer scientists in Daniel's project who had to post-rationalise failure in their abandoned luggage test, here the computer scientists had to work to come up with a means to narrate the collapse of associations. They suggested that tiny errors in the messaging formats – such as a missing hyphen – could cause malfunction as the analysis algorithm would send a message to the graphical user interface which could not be read. Both projects, then, faced problems in achieving the kinds of consequences they had initially anticipated – both primarily focused on issuing alerts to operators.

We can note across both projects two common types of response to trouble. A first type of response can be most clearly illustrated through Norma's project. This response to trouble occurred both in computer scientists' everyday work and on occasions of demonstrations, and involved continual tinkering with code. A kind of ongoing bricolage (MacKenzie & Pardo-Guerra, 2014) took place through which ideas of what the surveillance system was supposed to achieve were translated into rules and commands that could be read and executed by a computer. And when trouble emerged in achieving consequences, computer scientists would search for bits of code in open-source libraries, piece these together and modify them, test them and, if they did not work the first time, look for the source of error. This was dull, routine work, often not welcomed by the computer scientists.[1] It was also irritatingly complicated for the computer scientists; as the code ran to hundreds of thousands of lines and was drawn together on occasions from existing non-proprietary sources which were not fully understood by the computer scientists, searching for errors was very time-consuming. Associations within the hundreds of thousands of lines of code had to be dragged to attention by computer scientists, inspected and passed or altered. The following event illustrates a typical situation of what happened when this kind of trouble was encountered:

> I ask Marco if they also thought to include parameters such as age and gender. He declines, but says that he's working on such algorithms in a different project. He gets really excited and offers to demonstrate the algorithm. 'And how does it work?' I ask. I'm interested whether the algorithm is based on machine learning, or classifications made by developers. 'Well the computer learns what features to look for' he replies. He moves his laptop to a different desk and connects to one of the PTZ cameras in the room. He runs the program and a window pops up on the screen, showing the camera footage of Marco and me looking at his laptop screen. Marco adjusts the camera so my face is centred on the screen. He points to numbers and letters which appear next to my face, and to my great amusement the algorithm tells us that I'm a man in my mid-40s [despite being female and in my mid-twenties]. While I'm still laughing, I see that Marco isn't so amused. He opens the window with the code and starts looking through the lines of code, mumbling 'hmmm … but this looks pretty good … why doesn't it work … I can comment this line out, although it's nice, but … '. He crouches behind his laptop, starts typing and mumbling to himself and the screen, and stops paying attention to me. (Norma's field notes, May 2011)

This kind of routine response to trouble involved continual iterations of translating consequences into code, by piecing together bits of software the computer scientists took from open-source libraries, fitting them together, modifying them to their needs, testing the software, looking for bugs, troubleshooting and then doing it all over again. Rather than understanding coding as a straightforward, planned and throughout intentional activity, we need to understand it as importantly including tinkering, troubleshooting, debugging and finding workarounds – a kind of bricolage (MacKenzie & Pardo-Guerra, 2014) through which associations between entities are continually reconfigured and the nature of entities also called to consideration, prior to any consequences at some point being accomplished.

A second type of response to trouble can be illustrated through Daniel's project. The project team looked to respond to the problems met in attempting to identify abandoned luggage 'live' in the airport. The disappointing results of these tests might appear to undermine assertions regarding the 'power' of the algorithm to achieve much at all. However, within a few weeks of the abandoned luggage tests being carried out, the algorithmic system was successfully demonstrated 'live' in the airport to research funders. The response to trouble in this project did not focus so much on bricolage as what we might term the production of a contained effect (drawing inspiration from the work of Muniesa & Callon, 2007). A laboratory, according to Muniesa and Callon (2007), creates a set of controlled and contained conditions idealised for the demonstration of a specific effect. Any attempt to achieve this same effect in moving out into the world beyond the laboratory would require extending the controlled conditions of the laboratory out into the world. Within the controlled and contained conditions of the laboratory, the associations would be at their purest, with no confounding variables. To transform a busy airport into such a controlled environment in order to demonstrate an algorithmic contained effect would also require that the airport in a small, contained way would become the algorithmic system's purified laboratory.

Making the system work, creating a contained effect, required careful management of the different components and their associations. The 'confounding variables' of crowds, distinct flooring materials and inconsistent lighting that had been held responsible for the previous poor results would have to be managed away from the system in transforming the airport into the laboratory. The airport was monitored by the project coordinators with advice from the airport's security manager to ascertain when there were fewest crowds. If fewer people moved through the airport, there was a reduced chance that objects the system needed to parameterise, classify and track (such as luggage-shaped objects) would be occluded (for example, by multiple legs walking between the camera and object). Also, if the abandoned luggage object were to be initially tracked in the moments prior to abandonment between certain locations and cameras where the lighting conditions and flooring conditions were consistent (for example, in those areas towards the rear of the terminal away from natural light where the floors were covered with non-reflective grey tiles), this might 'idealise' conditions for a test. If the person-shaped object 'abandoning' the luggage-shaped object could also leave the luggage in a location where it was not occluded from cameras (by, for example, a pillar) and then the person-shaped object were to also leave via a route with consistent lighting conditions and flooring materials, this would further 'idealise' the airport in order that it might become the algorithmic system's laboratory. Finally, if the luggage-shaped object being abandoned fitted a particular set of parameters, this might aid the system in accomplishing object classification as it would 'know' what it was looking for.

The response to trouble was thus to produce a contained effect by contriving a set of laboratory conditions for showing research funders that the system 'worked' – at least within a narrowly bounded set of associations that could endure within one part of the airport and for one moment. The research funders were made aware that an item of luggage was unlikely to be abandoned in the airport at precisely the time they were present for a demonstration and elements of the 'abandonment' would be staged. However, this abandonment might still appear somewhat genuine – or less contained – if the algorithmic system itself did not 'know' of the artifice of laboratory conditions. If the system was sifting through the streams of digital video data, using maps to perform background subtraction, object classification through parameterisation and tracking to issue an alarm for abandoned luggage – in other words, if the system was operating within the set of associations initially marked out by the computer scientists – and while operating within these associations, the system could pick up the item of abandoned luggage, this might still demonstrate the system's effectiveness in demarcating relevance from irrelevance. But knowledge of the abandonment was not so unevenly distributed between funders, human project participants and the algorithmic system.

Producing an 'idealised' contained space by filtering out confounding variables as far as possible provided a prior basis for background subtraction, parameterisation and then subsequent classification and tracking. In this way, the associations of the algorithmic system could endure as the system 'knew' what it was looking for, where and when and what it ought to do next. As a result, the 'abandoned' luggage was identified by the system during the demonstration; this success was the result of the contained effect. The project team did not need to reproduce the contained effect in the world beyond the 'idealised' conditions of this particular space and time of the airport. Instead, the possibilities of achieving the same effect in the world outside the laboratory-airport only needed to be pointed towards.[2] Much of this pointing involved critiquing existing airport terminals for their inadequate architecture (such as low ceilings), poor lighting and flooring, and outdated cameras systems. In other words, any future failure of the algorithmic system's associations to endure beyond the contained effect achieved in this particular airport could be explained through the absence of conditions which favoured the algorithmic system. For the algorithm to demonstrate and consistently produce an asymmetrical effect by distinguishing relevant and irrelevant video data required the rest of the world (or at least those locations where the system would be used) to match those conditions of the contained effect that would enable its associations to endure.

Conclusion

We have argued in this paper for the importance of moving away from considering algorithms as having social power in the sense that the algorithm itself would be noted as the agential character in the drama, able to cause an effect on society. Instead, we have suggested it is necessary to recognise the situated character of algorithmic systems. That is, algorithmic systems come to make sense through their situatedness, wherein distinct components are designed and reworked and come together with rules, people, processes and specific kinds of relationships. We have sought to extend existing work on algorithmic systems (Gillespie, 2011; Neyland, 2015) by drawing on the work of Latour (2005), to explore a particular approach to power. This has enabled us to move from a treatment of algorithms as having power derived from an asymmetrical distribution of the ability to act independently on others, to exploring asymmetries as an achievement and 'power' as constituted through associations. Such an approach does not entail abandoning the idea that consequences follow from the introduction of algorithmic systems. But it does mean, that, if we want to understand how algorithms are implicated in power relationships, we need to cast a wider net and explore the heterogeneous practices and materials, going everywhere from labs, companies and control rooms to transportation hubs.

We were particularly interested in the ways in which algorithmic systems became involved in the production of an asymmetric effect, distinguishing relevant from irrelevant data. Our purpose in turning to associations is to direct attention to the ways in which such effects as the production of asymmetries are made and endure (or collapse) through the composition (and decomposition) of associations.

The algorithmic IF … THEN rules of the projects analysed in this paper provided a basis for considering particular types of associations and the effects that emerged. In particular we explored the IF-conditions of classification and mapping and the THEN-consequences and trouble that ensued. We suggested that both classification and mapping were ongoing, quite precarious achievements that resulted from the associating of a number of different kinds of entities and distributions of roles and responsibilities which followed from the articulation of conditions that also either confirmed or led to a rewriting of those conditions. The trouble that occurred for both projects in trying to achieve consequences – namely, the issue of an alert to surveillance system operators as a product of successfully producing an asymmetrical distribution between relevant and irrelevant data – was instructive for shedding further light on the nature of algorithmic associations. Both projects were characterised by an ongoing failure of association which led to similar responses.

First, project members responded to trouble through a kind of ongoing bricolage. In Norma's project, failure to recognise expected features of the world (the theft of a painting and Norma's age and gender) led to bricolage in the form of searches in software libraries for pre-existing solutions, efforts to stop cameras vibrating and dredging up lines of code from within the system, and everything from external confounding variables to hyphens in lines of code was made available for reinspection. Similar tinkering took place in Daniel's project in trying to repair classifications. Second, project members also responded to trouble – for example, a failure to detect abandoned luggage or dangerous behaviour – by producing a contained effect. In Daniel's project, a small section of the airport where the demonstration would take place was transformed into a controlled, laboratory-like space in which confounding variables could be manipulated away from the algorithmic system as a basis for demonstrating that effects could be achieved (albeit under very purified conditions). In Norma's project, the same was true for the university hall in which they demonstrated the technology a second time (Möllers, in press).

What we would like to suggest is that this focus on association, while decentring the algorithm as *the* cause of effects, also points up what we might term the associational dependencies required for the algorithmic system to operate. The need to continually rework the bases for doing classification and mapping, the purification of conditions required to demonstrate the contained effect and the bricolage necessary for reworking failed lines of code all suggest particular kinds of associational dependence. Classification could not happen without maps or stable cameras or predefined parameters; maps could not happen without a stable location or coordinated effort to continually work out the permanent attributes of a setting; contained effects could not be demonstrated without purification and the exclusion of confounding variables and bricolage could not take place without computer scientists, their training and open-source libraries. Our suggestion is that future studies of algorithms pay further attention to these associational dependencies – it is through making and holding together these dependencies that algorithmic effects are achieved.

Notes

1. In Norma's project not every computer scientist understood coding as part of their work, and troubleshooting, debugging and tinkering often were seen as nuisances. Such differential

valuation of tasks in developing algorithmic systems is a topic which deserves investigation in its own right.

2. Future research could explore the questions raised by the ongoing operation of algorithmic systems beyond these moments of demonstration. For example, what form does trouble take in systems that are accepted as 'working'?

Acknowledgements

Daniel would like to acknowledge the contributions of Patrick Murphy, Inga Kroener, Sveta Milyaeva and Vera Ehrenstein.

Disclosure statement

No potential conflict of interest was reported by the authors.

Funding

The research leading to these results has received funding from the European Union Seventh Framework Programme (FP7/2007-2013) [grant agreement numbers 261653 and 313173]. Parts of Norma's research have been funded by the German Federal Ministry of Education and Research (BMBF) [project no. 19N10959].

References

Aneesh, A. (2009). Global labor: Algocratic modes of organization. *Sociological Theory, 27*(4), 347–370.

Beer, D. (2009). Power through the algorithm? Participatory web cultures and the technological unconscious. *New Media & Society, 11*(6), 985–1002.

Bowker, G., & Star, S. L. (2000). *Sorting things out.* Cambridge, MA: MIT Press.

Bucher, M. (2012). Want to be on top? Algorithmic power and the threat of invisibility on Facebook. *New Media and Society, 14*(7), 1164–80.

Barocas, S., & Selbst, A. D. (in press). Big data's disparate impact. *California Law Review.* Retrieved July 18, 2015, from http://papers.ssrn.com/sol3/Delivery.cfm/SSRN_ID2615343_code1328346. pdf?abstractid=2477899&mirid=1

Diakopoulos, N. (2013). *Algorithmic accountability reporting: On the investigation of black boxes.* Retrieved October 21, 2014, from http://towcenter.org/wp-content/uploads/2014/02/78524_Tow-Center-Report-WEB-1.pdf

Drucker, J. (2013). Performative materiality and theoretical approaches to interface. *Digital Humanities Quarterly, 7*(1), n.p.

Gillespie, T. (2011). Can an algorithm be wrong? Twitter trends, the specter of censorship, and our faith in the algorithms around us. *Culture Digitally.* Retrieved December 17, 2015, from http://culturedigitally.org/2011/10/can-an-algorithm-be-wrong/

Gillespie, T. (2014). The relevance of algorithms. In Tarleton Gillespie, Pablo J. Boczkowski, & Kirsten A. Foot (Eds.), *Media technologies. Essays on communication, materiality, and society* (pp. 167–193). Cambridge, MA: The MIT Press.

Goodwin, C. (1994). Professional vision. *American Anthropologist, 96*(3), 606–633.

Hallinan, B., & Striphas, T. (2014). Recommended for you: The Netflix prize and the production of algorithmic culture. *New Media and Society, 18*, 1–21.

Kitchin, R. (2014). Thinking critically about and researching algorithms (The Programmable City Working Paper 5). Retrieved from http://papers.ssrn.com/sol3/papers.cfm?abstract_id=2515786.

Kushner, S. (2013). The freelance translation machine: Algorithmic culture and the invisible industry. *New Media and Society, 15*(8), 1241–1258.

Lash, S. (2007). Power after hegemony. *Theory, Culture and Society, 24*(3), 55–78.

Latour, B. (1986). The powers of association. In John Law (Ed.), *Power, action and belief. A new sociology of knowledge?* (pp. 264–280). London: Routledge.

Latour, B. (2005). *Reassembling the social.* Oxford: Oxford University Press.

Lyon, D. (2003). Surveillance as social sorting: Computer codes and mobile bodies. In David Lyon (Ed.), *Surveillance as social sorting: Privacy, risk, and digital discrimination* (pp. 13–30). New York, NY: Routledge.

MacKenzie, D., & Pardo-Guerra, J. P. (2014). Insurgent capitalism: Island, Bricolage and the re-making of finance. *Economy and Society, 43*(2), 153–182.

Möllers, N. (in press). Shifting in and out of context: Technoscientific drama as technology of the self. *Social Studies of Science.*

Muniesa, F., & Callon, M. (2007). Economic experiments and the construction of markets. In D. MacKenzie, F. Muniesa, & L. Siu (Eds.), *Do economists make markets?* (pp. 163–88). Oxford: Princeton University Press.

Neyland, D. (2015). Bearing account-able witness to the ethical algorithmic system. *Science, Technology and Human Values, 41*(1), 50–76.

Rouvroy, A. (2013). The end(s) of critique: Data-behaviourism vs. due-process. In Mireille Hildebrandt & Katja de Vries (Eds.), *Privacy, due process and the computational turn: The philosophy of law meets the philosophy of technology* (pp. 143–167). Abingdon: Routledge.

Sacks, H. (1972). Notes on police assessment of moral character. In D. Sudnow (Ed.), *Studies in social interaction* (pp. 280–93). New York, NY: Free Press.

Seaver, N. (2013, April). *Knowing algorithms.* Paper presented at the Media in Translation 8, Cambridge, MA, USA.

Slavin, K. (2011). *How algorithms shape our world.* Retrieved February 14, 2014, from http://www.ted.com/talks/kevin_slavin_how_algorithms_shape_our_world.html

Spring, T. (2011). *How Google, Facebook and Amazon run the internet.* Retrieved February 14, 2014, from http://www.pcadvisor.co.uk/features/internet/3304956/how-google-facebook-andamazonrun-the-internet/

Suchman, L., Randall, T., & Blomberg, J. (2002). Working artefacts: Ethnomethods of the prototype. *British Journal of Sociology, 53*(2), 164–79.

Algorithmically recognizable: Santorum's Google problem, and Google's Santorum problem

Tarleton Gillespie

ABSTRACT
Because information algorithms make judgments that can have powerful consequences, those interested in having their information selected will orient themselves toward these algorithmic systems, making themselves *algorithmically recognizable*, in the hopes that they will be amplified by them. Examining this interplay, between information intermediaries and those trying to be seen by them, connects the study of algorithmic systems to long-standing concerns about the power of intermediaries – not an algorithmic power, uniquely, but the power to grant visibility and certify meaning, and the challenge of discerning who to grant it to and why. Here, I consider Dan Savage's attempt to redefine the name of U.S. Senator Rick Santorum, a tactical intervention that topped Google's search results for nearly a decade, and then mysteriously dropped during the 2012 Republican nominations. Changes made to Google's algorithm at the time may explain the drop; here, they help to reveal the kind of implicitly political distinctions search engines must invariably make, between genuine patterns of participation and tactical efforts to approximate them.

Recent scholarship about algorithms and their social effects asks what it means when algorithmic information systems are inserted into social processes where (human) judgment matters (Barocas, Hood, & Ziewitz, 2013; Beer, 2009; Gillespie, 2014; Kitchin, 2014; Seaver, 2013; Ziewitz, 2015. For a growing list, see Gillespie & Seaver, 2015). Whether those judgments are about what is most relevant amid a web of information, what symptoms indicate a particular disease, or which market palpitations warrant investment or panic, the kinds of associations, categorizations, and distinctions that algorithms are designed to make threaten to join, even supplant, those made by human decision-makers. Concerns about algorithmic bias and discrimination (boyd, Levy, & Marwick, 2014; Diakopoulos, 2015; Granka, 2010; Grimmelmann, 2008; Introna & Nissenbaum, 2000; Noble, 2012; Pasquale, 2015; Tufekci, 2015) represent the applied edge of this conceptual concern. If our participation in public life (Crawford, 2015; Grosser, 2014; Pariser, 2012; van Dijck, 2013), our ability to seek educational advantages or work opportunities (Pasquale, 2015), or our position in the market (Citron & Pasquale, 2014; Poon, 2007) is being determined, or at the very least adjudicated, by algorithmic systems, then we must know more about the assumptions upon which they are based, the information about us upon which they act, the priorities they serve, and the ways in which they shape, distort, or tip the process (Ananny, 2015; Bucher, 2012; Cheney-Lippold, 2011; Graham, 2005; Hallinan & Striphas, 2014; Mager, 2012; Rieder, 2012).

However, this tendency to treat algorithmic systems as new, hidden, and powerful mechanisms with built-in values can pull our work toward some predictable potholes: treating the technology as a singular object, distinct from human operators and institutional arrangements; treating the algorithm as a secret, tightly guarded and therefore protected from critique; and treating the world in which the algorithmic system operates as otherwise simple, untouched, and vulnerable to manipulation.

Grimmelmann (2014) recognizes this problem best in his analysis of the legal implications of search results. He notes that opinions about search engine liability fall into two camps, one treating the search engine as a neutral conduit delivering results to users, the other treating it as having a kind of editorial power to pick and choose. He suggests that both views are incomplete, because both overlook the user as the third point in this triangular relationship. Search engines act more like advisors to the user, responsive to the query and suggesting which results are most relevant. It is an important reminder, one that undercuts the objective/subjective binary that seems to constrain discussions of algorithmic systems and their impact.

I want to make a parallel argument to Grimmelman's, that too often we treat the information providers as independent of search engines, as if they are merely standing on the edge of the field waiting to be picked for the team. I believe that this profoundly overlooks the strategic efforts of the content providers. Precisely because information algorithms make judgments that can have powerful consequences, those interested in having their information selected as relevant will tend to orient themselves toward these algorithmic systems, to make themselves *algorithmically recognizable* (Gillespie, 2014), in the hopes of being amplified by them.

As soon as nascent search engines began to mediate users' interaction with the web, so also emerged a range of tactics for trying to be recognized by them. In his discussion of the politics of search, Grimmelmann (2008) noted some of these: Googlebombing, link farms, government intervention. But I think it goes further. Web design handbooks and etiquette guides offered tips for designing web pages to be congruent with how search engines index and judge sites as relevant. Bloggers and video creators asked readers to link back, like, retweet, or otherwise circulate that content, in the hopes of generating the signals that search engines value; search engine optimization (SEO) firms and spammers developed techniques, premised on guesses about how search algorithms worked, to boost their clients ranking and gain additional traffic. To some degree, every contribution to the public web in some way desires to be seen, which generally requires being recognized and amplified by Google.

These strategies of visibility are analogous to efforts to be recognized and amplified by other kinds of intermediaries: sending press releases to news organizations, staging events with the visual impact that television craves, or making spokespeople and soundbites available in ways convenient to journalists. 'Generators of information for the press anticipate the criteria of the gatekeepers in their efforts to get through the gate … How do you get a piece of information to 'pass' as news?' (Schudson, 1989, p. 265). Such tactics belie the myth of a world waiting to be reported upon and journalists independently seeking the most important parts, and trouble the distinction between a genuine desire to be heard and a strategic effort to game the system. These also have much in common with tactics of avoidance and obfuscation in the face of surveillance systems (Brunton & Nissenbaum, 2015; Marx, 2009): in this case, it is the aim not to be seen, but in the same way actors will engage in 'neutralization techniques' (Marx, 2009) that must understand the workings of the surveillance system and fit themselves to the contours of its attention and inattention.

Search algorithms have a set of organizing criteria for the kind of phenomena they seek: particular kinds of websites, particular patterns of incoming links, and particular behaviors of users, all read as signals of a genuinely emergent and non-strategic demonstration of a site's true relevance. Being algorithmically recognizable, then, means simulating this particular (ideal/idealized) type of activity. And it means doing so amidst others also trying to simulate that same activity, for a variety of reasons of their own. As we all jostle for recognition, it falls to search engines not just to determine what is relevant, but to distinguish between genuine signals and 'gaming the system' – a distinction that is arbitrary but conventional.

Rather than thinking in terms of algorithms and their values, we might take a lesson from Brunton's (2013) discussion of spam and spam filters. Brunton notes that all communication is tactical; rather than a coherent genre, spam is whatever is defined away as illegitimate by the mechanisms designed to do so. Not only is Google a spam filter too, but the judgments of relevance Google must make must cope with the fact that all communication is tactical, proclaims its own value, wants to be recognized, turns to face the microphone, performs that value in social terms, and tries to appear legitimate in its eyes. Google must discern the relevant from the irrelevant, amid a shifting sea of bids to appear so. Search algorithms may have political ramifications, but our understanding of them will be richer if we see them not as having built-in values but in terms of the tactical and ad hoc ways in which they make determinations of relevance, even as what they are judging is shifting so as to benefit from that determination.

In this essay, I will look at the decade-long effort by sex columnist Dan Savage to criticize U.S. Senator Rick Santorum by popularizing an alternative definition of his name. Savage's site quickly became the top Google search result for 'Santorum' and retained that position above official biographies, news coverage, and even the Wikipedia entry on Sen. Santorum, until those results abruptly changed in 2012 during Santorum's effort to win the Republican nomination for the U.S. presidential election. This case, on one level, could be understood as a powerful example of the political values built into search algorithms. But by focusing on the tactical moves made by Savage, Santorum, and Google, I hope to instead highlight (1) the way public actors attempt to make themselves recognizable to information intermediaries, and (2) the way information intermediaries, algorithmic or otherwise, are forced to discern between acceptable and unacceptable efforts to be seen, when being seen has political currency.

Spreading it around

In 2003, then U.S. Senator Rick Santorum shocked even the AP reporter interviewing him when, in a comment defending laws that curtail private sexual acts,[1] he equated homosexuality with adultery, polygamy, and incest, and then with 'man on child, man on dog, or whatever,' all behaviors he felt 'undermine the basic tenets of our society and the family.' Like many others, sex columnist Dan Savage took umbrage with Santorum's remarks; unlike many others, he wrote an angry op-ed in the *New York Times* in response.[2] That could have been the end of it, except that one of his readers proposed that Savage and his audience should respond by naming a sex act after the Senator.[3] Savage turned this idea back to his readers, and after receiving over 3000 suggestions, Savage invited readers to vote on the best,[4] then announced[5] that 'santorum' should now and forever be defined as – brace yourself – 'the frothy mixture of fecal matter and lube that is sometimes the byproduct of anal sex' (Figure 1).

At first, the act of selecting the winning definition seemed to be the entirety of Savage's political gesture. But soon after, he purchased the web domains santorum.com and spreadingsantorum.com, and posted his new definition at both. On the splash page, both the definition itself and the words 'santorum, senator, rick santorum' were included in the <meta> tags, an (old) technique for drawing the attention of search engine indexing bots. As readers, bloggers, and the press began linking to and commenting on the site, the site quickly became the top search result returned in Google to the query 'Santorum.' At least within Google's index, and for unsuspecting Google users, the Senator's name had been successfully redefined. Many surmised, though it is hard to know, that Savage's site and its prominence in Google's results were influential in Santorum's re-election loss in 2006.

Others had already proven that Google's algorithm could be manipulated. Early tricks to boost a page's ranking included loading it with popular but irrelevant meta tags, filling the bottom of the page with invisible text, and including links out to popular sites. Other tactics, that were perhaps less about 'gaming' the algorithm and more about being recognized by it, included 'web rings' and 'blog rings' where sites with shared interests would agree to link to each other, and search registration services that would alert search engines to a new site and invite them to index it. Eventually, an entire industry offering 'SEO' emerged, offering consultation on how to design websites to boost their ranking on major search engines, based on some divination of Google's evaluative criteria. And

Figure 1. Splash page, Spreadingsantorum.com. Used with permission from Dan Savage.

then there was a practice known as 'Google bombing' (Grimmelmann, 2008): get enough people to link the phrase 'miserable failure' to President George Bush's biography, and watch as the search for 'miserable failure' delivers up Bush's site as the top result.[6] (The trick, though, requires telling people to search for 'miserable failure'; it does not affect what results return to a query about Bush himself. This makes it fundamentally an inside joke.) 'Squatters' registered domain names that represented well-known names or brands, hoping to draw users searching for their favorite store or celebrity. The white supremacist group Stormfront extended this technique further, quite effectively and reprehensibly. In 1999, the group secured the domain martinlutherking.org, posting there what appeared on first glance to be an encyclopedia entry on the civil rights leader; examined more closely, it was in fact a skewed and slanderous profile of the man that betrayed the site's extremist beliefs. For years, their site was the top result in Google to the query 'Martin Luther King Jr' – the site remains in the first page of results.

What Savage and his readers did, as one critic put it, was 'calculated character assassination'[7] – calculated both as in deliberate, and as in mathematical. But it was not Googlebombing. He and his readers deliberately and successfully unseated other sites, including Santorum's official website, securing theirs as the 'legitimate' top result to the query 'santorum.' It is one thing to knowingly look up a specifically worded criticism, to see it turn up a public figure's name; it is another to have all searches for the public figure's name point, first, to a critical parody that figure. (In this sense, it is closer tactically, if not politically, to the Stormfront site.)

The campaign to algorithmically redefine Santorum's name required, first, a not insignificant number of users to link to Savage's site, and in a way that Google's algorithm would recognize as akin to linking to the 'correct' or 'most relevant' site: for instance, by making the word 'Santorum' the text anchor for their link back to spreadingsantorum.com. Google's indexing tools noted these links, and included them in their calculations as indicators of value, boosting the PageRank of Savage's site.

This also required a great deal of coordination. Google designed its search algorithms to recognize patterns that represent the separate and aggregate the links and clicks of millions of users. To trump the algorithm, Savage's coordinated effort would have to be on the scale of other kinds of less coordinated behavior, like supporters of Santorum who might often link to his campaign site. But Savage is no ordinary user. He is a public figure with a great deal of credibility, from his syndicated newspaper column and podcast, his public appearances, and his activism in the gay rights movement. He has a devoted readership, many of whom were already in on the campaign from the start. And his readership overlapped with a broader community of gay activists who already had experience in the tactics of political visibility, including online.

There is a distinction often made, between coordinated efforts to 'game' a search engine (like Googlebombing and SEO tactics) and the 'genuine' output of independent web producers and users, demonstrating the value of a site from their linking and clicking behaviors. The distinction is a false one. Most contributions to the web are somewhere in the middle, where people in some way coordinate their efforts in order to help make their content visible to a search engine, out of a 'genuine' desire for it to be seen. Activist organizations publicize their efforts and gather supporters online; companies urge their customers to post about their product, sometimes in exchange for rewards; writers send their posts to their friends or tweet them to their followers. It is not easy to distinguish, ethically or even practically, between link spam, paying for links, encouraging readers to link, enjoying links generated by people already invested in your project, sharing the content through public networks in the hopes that it will circulate further, or achieving links organically when people stumble onto your site. In more cases than we might care to admit, search rank is a product of a combination of these; the last one, so often held up as the ideal, may be increasingly rare. Not only is there a gray area between 'genuine' linking behaviors and coordinated efforts to game the search engine, it is not even clear that the two are all that different.

Making it stick

The spreadingsantourm.com site remained the top result on Google to the query 'santorum' through the remainder of Santorum's Senate term, his failed re-election bid in 2005–2006, and on through to 2011, when Santorum announced his run for the Republican presidential nomination. After having allowed the spreadingsantorum.com site to stagnate, Savage added a blog that tracked criticism of Santorum and any coverage of the 'frothy' definition, and share buttons allowing users to 'like' the site on Facebook and Google+.

Some wondered whether Santorum's reappearance in national news coverage would help more official, legitimate content supplant Savage's site in the Google index; timely headlines in major news outlets might very well supersede a nearly decade-old site with very little new content. But the press and political humorists also helped to revive the association between Santorum and Savage's definition, and in doing so, likely strengthened it in Google's ranking. News coverage of the lengthy nomination process needed to fill countless broadcast hours and regularly refresh their sites. Reporters desperate for any topic related to the race often found the 'santorum' neologism, and then wrote about whether Savage's campaign might affect Santorum's chances. Even news coverage decrying Savage's site could become fodder for Google's calculations: even if an article did not link to Savage's site, it may spur readers to conduct a search of their own and click on Savage's site as the result. Every mention by John Stewart, Stephen Colbert, or Bill Maher on their late night programs, and there were many, provoked queries for 'santorum.' And Savage noted these on his blog, which both added new content to the site (Google factors a site's 'freshness' into its calculations[8]) and refracted those mentions back to his fans, potentially generating even more queries and links. Since the crux of Savage's critique is not the site itself, but the fact that it tops Google's results, part of the political theater for users who support Savage, or are just curious, involves enacting that theater themselves: searching for the term, seeing it appear, and (perhaps) clicking through to the site. All of this provides Google further data confirming the site's relevance.

It is easy, but misleading, to think of the web as a pile of undifferentiated sites, all independently generated and vying for attention, to which the algorithm discerns and selects the most relevant. Even the interface of Google's search engine suggests this, the way search results are lined up in marching order, ranked only by Google's judgment of their relevance to the query. This notion radically masks the fact that, while sites may be independently authored, they are coordinated by professional routines, world events, the rhythms of other media and information sources, and the quirks of circumstance. Google's search engine cannot return a result as first simply because it has the greatest number of hits that day or the greatest number of incoming links; those may be artifacts of the rhythms of information production and public attention that surge through the web like tides pushed by the moon. The moon, in this metaphor, could be many things: election cycles that generate news stories at particular moments and with particular velocities; media events that provoke bursts of writing about the same thing at the same time; the daily and weekly cycles of information professionals like journalists; the unexpected velocity of a cultural phenomenon or viral bit of content; the deliberate efforts of industries dedicated to shaping the public information landscape, from advertisers to promoters to spin doctors to activists to search engine optimizers to spammers. The success of Savage's campaign depended not only on Savage, his readers, amused bloggers, and gay rights activists. It also benefitted from the dynamics of media cycles and election cycles, which together helped to generate recurring attention and links to Savage's site. This is not exactly coordinated activity designed to game the search engines, the way the initial tactics of Savage and his readers arguably were. But the user activity Google pays attention to is coordinated, by powerful forces.

This posed an additional distinction for Google to make: should incoming links, some from high-status news and commentary sites, further legitimate Savage's page and boost its ranking? Does a surge in attention provoked by the media represent the kind of interest search engines should reward, or counterbalance? Google designers probably have a unique understanding of the complicated and overlapping rhythms of information production online. In every case, Google must decide what to make of these rhythms, how to value them in relation to each other, and how to incorporate them into the calculations that produce search results.

Keeping it clean

As Santorum's fortunes in the 2012 Republican nomination improved, the political press paid more and more attention to him, and paid more and more attention to Savage's site and its prominence in Google's search results. Or to say it another way, Santorum's public visibility, driven by his own strategic campaign efforts and the efforts of his political supporters, and amplified by the media cycles attendant to the U.S. presidential race, challenged the visibility of Savage's campaign as well.

Reporters began to ask Santorum if he would request that Google remove the site from its index. Santorum gave three different answers over the course of 2011, demonstrating a range of available positions one might regarding the nature of Google's algorithm. First, he said he would not ask Google to remove the site, a position that either sees Google's algorithm as beyond intervention, or sees intervention as an ineffective or politically risky move. Drawing attention to Savage's site might even strengthen its ranking by leading even more people to it. Later, he lambasted both Savage and Google in a fundraising letter – leaving Google's algorithm intact, but finding a different kind of (financial) value in it. Finally, in September 2011, he asked Google to remove Savage's site from their index. As he put it, 'If you're a responsible business, you don't let things like that happen in your business that have an impact on the country.'[9] This suggestion, that Google shares some responsibility for how their search results might have political impact, was paired with a dig at Google's possible bias as a company – 'I suspect if something was up there like that about Joe Biden, they'd get rid of it'[10] – akin to the charge of 'liberal bias' so often leveled at broadcast media.

Google was then faced with a choice: remove Savage's site, or let it stand in the rankings. Either decision would be a political one, and would be perceived as such. Over its history, Google has been nearly unwavering in its stance that its search results should not be altered or censored. Famously, in 2004, Google refused to alter the index when the hateful, anti-Semitic site JewWatch ranked at the top of the search results for the term 'Jew' (Grimmelmann, 2008).But this stance is not without exceptions. Google removes spam sites, sites charged with being defamatory, and sites challenged as copyright infringement under the Digital Millennium Copyright Act (DMCA).[11] On several occasions, they have temporarily demoted commercial sites, including J.C. Penney[12] and Overstock[13] for optimizing their sites in ways Google deemed unacceptable. And they have, on occasion, removed content for being offensive. In 2009, a racist image of Michelle Obama turned up as the top result for her name on Google's image search. In response to criticism, Google first refused to remove it. But after continued criticism, Google delisted the image from the index, indicating on the results page that it had done so. (They later were able to remove the image from the source, as it happened to be on a blog hosted on Blogger, a Google-owned site.) Recently, Google began to voluntarily remove links to revenge porn. And the new European 'right to be forgotten' rule, Google and all search engines must remove specifically requested links pointing to 'inaccurate, inadequate or no longer relevant' pages from the search results for a given person's name.

In a public response to Santorum's request, Google refused to alter the index. 'Google's search results are a reflection of the content and information that is available on the Web. Users who want content removed from the Internet should contact the webmaster of the page directly.'[14] A Google spokesperson did note that Google does not 'remove content from our search results, except in very limited cases such as illegal content and violations of our webmaster guidelines.' Or, 'Search engines pride themselves on being automated, except when they aren't' (Grimmelmann, 2008, p. 950). Google's statement carefully figures the algorithm as unmanaged, while also leaving room for the fact that Google does alter the index, not just under legal obligation, but under specific guidelines – guidelines that they crafted, which means of course that they could alter the index in this case if they so chose. They also noted that Savage's 'spreadingsantorum' site *was* already blocked, at least for some users: Google's SafeSearch function already prevented Savage's site from turning up for users in 'restricted' mode. Google noted that it uses algorithmic methods to identify sites that should be restricted by SafeSearch.[15] This will be important in a moment.

Perhaps the most intriguing aspect of Google's response was a separate comment made by their head of global communications, who noted that, 'There definitely are people who are finding this to be the best answer to their question, and they are indicating this by either clicking on this result or linking to this result as the best answer to that question.'[16] We could take this comment two ways. Either he means that Google does not really care about meaning, it cares about user satisfaction: if more users querying 'santorum' click Savage's link, then in Google's estimation, it is the more relevant link, because it is what users chose. The site's rank in the results is confirmed by users selecting it, which justifies its rank. Or, more radically, he is reminding us that some users entering the query 'santorum' *are* in fact looking for Savage's definition; for those users, the meaning of 'santorum' *is* 'a frothy mixture ... ' and Savage's site *is* the correct response to the query. For some users, the term has already been redefined and, coming full circle, Google's results confirm it. In this loop, Google is responding to the popular sense of meaning, indicative of it, constitutive of it, and proof of it, all at once.

Something different in the back end

However, not long after Google asserted that their algorithm is impartial, sacrosanct, and maybe even correct, something did change. In late February 2012, search engine watchers noticed that Savage's site had dropped in Google's rankings for the search 'santorum,' so much so that it no longer made the first page of results. This precipitous drop did not happen on competitors Bing or Yahoo (at least at first). It was a small victory for Santorum, perhaps, though a largely pyrrhic one: curiously, the Urban Dictionary definition that explains (and repeats verbatim) Savage's neologism had claimed the first place on Google, above Santorum's own campaign site and Wikipedia's entry; and the blog run by Savage within spreadingdsantorum.com appeared in the fourth position.

Google has not been particularly forthcoming about the change. Some surmised that Google had caved to political pressure – a reminder that, no matter why the change occurred, it is extremely difficult for intermediaries to avoid the charge of censorship (Gillespie, 2012). Few expert commentators, however, believed that Google had directly manipulated Savage's ranking. As Danny Sullivan of Searchengineland.com noted,

> To date, Google has refused to make any change specifically to the listing, which is pretty much in keeping with how it approaches these types of issues. Instead, Google prefers to resolve tricky issues like these by looking for solutions that may impact a wide range (of) listings.

Sullivan found it telling the splash page was not gone from the index altogether, which might suggest a complete removal. He also noted that, just the day before, Google had announced a bundle of changes to its algorithm.

Google has made hundreds of updates to its search algorithm over the years, a fact that should (but for some reason does not) undermine the veneer of impartiality it continues to enjoy. SEOmoz counted 92 major updates between 2000 and October 5, 2012,[17] and claims that Google makes 500–600 smaller changes every year. These adjustments represent Google engineers' effort to deliver ever more 'relevant' results, and to stay ahead of spammers, content farms, and SEO tactics. Such updates are in fact many changes bundled together, each of which has been tested in-house and, in some cases, in 'A/B' tests[18] where thousands of users unwittingly use a version of Google's search algorithm with the proposed changes, and their usage is compared to those still using the previous version. (Between ongoing A/B testing and the personalization and localization of results, not only do 'we' not get the same results from Google's search engine, but it is hard to say that there even *is* a single search engine. Google is making available many, overlapping algorithms that only appear to be a single tool.)

When Google changes the criteria by which their algorithm determines relevance in one of these major upgrades, almost by definition, some sites rise in the ranking and others drop, sometimes precipitously. These are hard to pinpoint, however, because changes to the algorithm are not always announced publicly, and because shifts in results can occur for other, exogenous reasons. Nevertheless, businesses can go bankrupt when Google changes their algorithm (Battelle, 2005) Google is keenly aware of this, though they are adamant that these effects are not a reason not to make these changes – they are precisely proof that changes should be made. Anticipating criticism from affected sites, Google commented on a significant update in 2011:

> We can't make a major improvement without affecting rankings for many sites. It has to be that some sites will go up and some will go down. Google depends on the high-quality content created by wonderful websites around the world, and we do have a responsibility to encourage a healthy web ecosystem. Therefore, it is important for high-quality sites to be rewarded, and that's exactly what this change does.[19]

Changes to the algorithm are always positioned as new progress toward an unchanging goal.

Could the update explain the sudden and precipitous drop in Savage's site? The timing certainly suggests it, but pinpointing the change responsible is less simple. The February 2012 update included 40 distinct changes to the algorithm, the most Google had ever rolled into a single upgrade.[20] Sullivan identified two changes that might have inadvertently demoted Savage's site. First, Google claimed to have improved their techniques for identifying 'official' pages and ranking them more highly than others. Second, Google had adjusted the Safesearch algorithm, hoping to improve the identification of 'adult' content and more effectively exclude it from searches that are not adult in nature. (In other words, when you search for the term 'toys,' the algorithm should not return links to sex toys, even if they otherwise rank highly for the term.) After some hypothesizing, Sullivan was contacted by a Google representative, who confirmed that it was the changes to Safe-Search that had demoted Savage's 'spreadingsantorum' site.[21]

Still, this is not an entirely satisfying explanation. Urban Dictionary's entry for 'santorum,' which includes Savage's definition, still ranked at or near the top after the change. With the identical words, this page is presumably just as 'adult' as Savage's, and should also have been tagged by Google's algorithms – even more so, as Urban Dictionary is an entire site dedicated to unsavory definitions, many much more 'adult' than Savage's. Urban Dictionary's entry soon also dropped in the rankings for a search on 'santorum' as well, suggesting that it had eventually also been flagged as 'adult'. But it seems odd that it would not have already been identified as such.

Others disagreed with Sullivan's theory, even after it was confirmed by Google. Rishi Lakhani, interviewed at Searchenginewatch.com, suggested that

> in general, it looks like a result of poor SEO … Google muddied the water by blaming safe search, but that appears totally untrue. They don't want people to have a potentially strong example of their new 'official page detection' (OPD) algorithm shift.[22]

According to his theory, Savage's splash page may have long been incorrectly identified as an 'official' page for Rick Santorum, an error corrected by the new upgrade. This would explain why Savage's site had ranked so highly for so long even with so little new content. But it does not fit neatly with the fact that Savage's site ranked so highly at the start, before a page's 'official' standing was even a part of Google's calculations.

A third possibility is that Savage's site was snared in Google's ongoing efforts to fight spam. In February 2011, Google introduced a major update called Panda, designed to identify 'shallow and low-quality' sites that were enjoying higher ranking in their results than sites with more informative content. The impact of Panda, according to Google's own statement, was significant, affecting nearly 12% of results. This was way before Savage's site dropped – but Panda was not a one-time intervention: on a monthly basis, Google updated Panda, each time blocking more sites. So, it is also possible that, with the latest update to Panda, Savage's front page and the incoming links that pointed to it were interpreted as spam, and de-listed as such. This does not fit neatly, however, with the fact that the Savage splash page only dropped, but did not disappear entirely.

Other commentators had still different ideas. It is, of course, possible that Google used the update as political cover, a chance to specifically demote Savage's site without having to admit to doing so. It is even possible that Google engineers do not even know why it changed. Because changes to the algorithm are opaque to both users and critics, debating what caused Savage's site to drop requires a kind of mental reverse engineering, and cannot offer a clear, convincing, or even stable answer.

It is unlikely that Google directly manipulated this particular search result. But the implications are actually far more significant if they did not. Let us assume that Google did not demote Savage's site specifically, and did not purposefully conjure up the update just to cause it to drop. Let us assume that Google made a policy decision in 2011 to leave the index alone, despite Santorum's request; that they made the February 2012 upgrades to the algorithm in order to serve up more relevant results, in their best assessment of relevance; and that the drop in Savage's rankings is the result of either the changes to how Safesearch handles adult content for non-adult queries, or the recognition and elevation of sites deemed official, or its classification as spam. Google may not engage in manipulation, but it must make categorical and *a priori* distinctions about what kinds of results to prioritize, when, and for whom. And it must do so with an eye toward how information providers will then try to emulate these distinctions.

While the Google team responsible for improving the algorithm may have been unaware of the effect it would have on Savage's site, the changes it made were nevertheless animated by specific political presumptions: about the proper contours of quality public discourse, about the difference between rich content and shallow, about where adult content should appear, about the importance of official sources of information, about the difference between activism and spam. For each, Google must algorithmically distinguish between highly valued and 'genuine' signals of relevance, and the specious simulation of those very same signals.

Adult/non-adult: From one perspective, the quiet exclusion of adult content from searches deemed to be 'not adult' makes a certain sense. It is clear why Google would not want users to be regularly confronted by unexpected pornographic results to their innocent queries – imagine the child searching for 'barbie doll' or the cancer patient searching for 'breast exam,' startled to encounter X-rated alternatives amid their results. There are, of course, challenges in making such distinctions: what makes a site adult, and what makes a search not adult. On the other hand, search engines can count on the fact that it is far worse (publicly, ethically, and economically) to deliver 'sex toys' links to the user who asked simply for 'toys,' than it is to make the user searching for sex toys have to clarify their initial query. However, deciding that adult content should not be returned to a non-adult query also disables precisely the kind of political speech Savage was engaged in, a kind that has played an important part of Western political discourse (Naron, 1991). One might argue that this tactic is more damaging to the public discourse than whatever valid political point it might make; many critics have said as much. But this was (likely) not Google attempting to clean up political discourse; it was a decision based on protecting users from accidental offense that, as an unintended consequence, may have also demoted one form of political rhetoric.

Official/unofficial: That Google attempts to identify 'official' pages and elevate them in the ranking also makes sense. While Google's algorithm began by calculating the relevance of a site based on incoming links, rejecting the editorial approach of Yahoo for a kind of 'wisdom of the crowd' quantified populism, a lot has changed since then. The web has grown from a collection of home pages and special interest sites to a massive information archive that millions of users count on for reliable information, trustworthy commercial transactions, and accurate news. But to algorithmically identify 'official' pages and weigh them more heavily than others is a specific intervention, one infused with a particular theory of democracy in it. To privilege official sites over unofficial ones is to amplify those official voices in the public square. To put it another way, the algorithm could be designed to do the exact opposite: it could grant 'unofficial' pages (like Savage's) higher standing, precisely because they do not have the benefits of amplification that official information sources usually do (other outlets of speech, financial resources, built-in credibility). This is not to argue that this would be the 'right' design, only that every design has a theory about quality public discourse embedded within it.

Coordinated political action/spam: Search engines must seek out and block ever more sophisticated forms of spam. This now includes what Brunton (2013) calls 'spam created by machines for machines' (p. 115), including planting links that point back to a target site in the comment spaces on blogs, entire 'link farm' websites with links back to thousands of target sites, and simulating user traffic in ways that the search engine will treat as true signals. Search engines are now in the business of discerning 'genuine' online activity (commenting, linking, and user traffic) from the spam simulation of it; and spammers are in the business of emulating the way people use the web, so as to be mistaken for genuine by search engines. Spam works by veering as close as possible to other kinds of legitimate public activity: people using the medium of communication available, to draw attention to a particular resource, by gathering up support from others to demonstrate its importance. Sounds like spam, but also savvy political organizing. As Brunton (2013) notes, 'there is always friction not around the most egregious case … but at the blurry places where spam threatens to blend into acceptable use, and fighting one might have a deleterious effect on the other' (p. 163). When Google must discern link spam from other forms of strategic and coordinated meaning making, they have an important and precarious job on their hands.

We all do it

Rather than seeing search engines as interveners in a waiting field of content, we must recognize that information producers vie for attention, and are aware that search engines can give it. Authors aim their contributions toward the available mechanisms that could amplify and certify them. Remembering that information is not raw and information producers are not passive sets up a more sophisticated story about the workings and implications of the (algorithmic) mechanisms that may act upon them. And while Google's algorithm may be premised on the links and clicks of individuals, as if those links are unaware of Google's attention to them as signals, public expression is in fact collective and collaborative. Political actors like Savage and his readers will turn together to face these information intermediaries as one and make themselves recognizable as relevant.

These efforts to face the algorithm, which require anticipating its workings and designing contributions so as to be recognized by it, can help shed light on the algorithmic systems themselves. What they do in anticipation of algorithms tells us a great deal about what algorithms do in return. While not all stakeholders have a sophisticated and accurate understanding of how an algorithmic system actually works, often depending on ad hoc, inaccurate, and outdated lay theories (Sandvig, Hamilton, Karahalios, & Langbort, 2014), their tactics can nonetheless be revealing of how an algorithmic system works, how it is imagined to work, and how users believe it *should* work.

So, we cannot simply study algorithms and their effects; rather, we must study the interaction between providers of information and algorithmic assessors of information, sometimes a confluence of interests and sometimes a contest, and the results that these interacting forces generate. And the jostling of interested voices that search engines encounter are themselves bound up in complex cycles of production motivated by other intermediaries: the cycles of traditional media, the rhythms of political campaigns, the disruptions of external events. These cycles are themselves sometimes fueled by highly motivated and organized efforts to gain public visibility by particular stakeholders.

This offers a strong reminder that, while algorithms may introduce some unique dynamics into how information is evaluated, specific to their particular computational, automated, and data-centric affordances, these are in another sense just media. They are socio-technical institutions that generate, select, and circulate public information – they mediate – and so are analogous in many ways to all the media that predate algorithms and even computation: publishers, libraries, broadcasters. By and large, questions of the power of algorithms to discern and amplify some information over others are (and should be) the same questions we have asked for decades, about the power of intermediaries.

One might argue, in fact, that Santorum's 'man-on-dog' statement about homosexuality, the one that angered Savage and his listeners and started this whole business, was much the same tactic. It was a deliberately constructed effort to express a political opinion in such a way that it would be amplified by the medium to which it was addressed – in this case, television and newspapers – so that, with the prominence and legitimacy afforded to it, it would thereby shape the debate. So while Savage may have been trying to game Google's algorithm so that an outrageous statement could enjoy more visibility than it deserved, Santorum's sound bite might have been similarly gaming the AP and cable news: a 'broadcast meme', or 'broadcast spam,' similarly designed to take advantage of a system that circulates such things.

When we are concerned about the power of information intermediaries, algorithmic or otherwise, we are fundamentally concerned about questions of visibility and meaning. This is nowhere more apparent than for search engines, which grant order web pages not just from first to last but, in doing so, from most visible to least. And in doing so, search engines stabilize meanings by offering up certain results in response to particular queries. As Thompson (2005) notes, 'Mediated visibility is not just a vehicle through which aspects of social and political life are brought to the attention of others: it has become a principal means by which social and political struggles are articulated and carried out' (p. 49). This was a question for traditional media long before it was one for search engines. But again, visibility is not simply granted by the search engine: visibility is a prize that is actively sought and sometimes vigorously fought over. The results of that tussle, both between competing information providers and between those information providers and the search engine, results in the results.

Politics too is often a struggle for visibility. Any community trying to enact political change must struggle in some sense to be visible on the public stage. For those wishing for their political perspectives to be heard, those mechanisms that grant or withhold public visibility are of signal importance (Gitlin, 1980). Visibility generates audiences, and the anointing of a particular perspective as relevant grants it public legitimacy. Politics is also often a struggle over meaning. While Savage's site may be an extreme case, where what is being contested is the meaning of a man's own name, it is easy to point to more reasonable examples: much of the political debate over climate change, or universal health care, or gay marriage, or corporate speech, involves contested definitions of the terms themselves. To some degree, political campaigning is in part a semiotic undertaking, designed to confer and stabilize a set of meanings attached to a candidate's name: on his 2016 campaign website, Santorum's 'about' page begins 'Rick Santorum is a conservative committed to restoring the American Dream for hardworking Americans.'[23] This is just as much of a semiotic assertion as 'Santorum: the frothy mixture … ' is. But we see this one as more legitimate because Santorum is defining himself – or, in fact, a network of campaign advisors and staffers with his guidance, supported by thousands of volunteers who help his campaign in part by restating that definition in their own public contributions. Santorum's Republican rivals also tried to 'define' Santorum, as too conservative or unprepared for office or not as likely to win a general election; these too were efforts to associate a meaning with a name, and they too depended on information intermediaries to amplify and certify those meanings. It is left to Google and other information intermediaries to decide whether each of these semantic, collaborative, and tactical affirmations are genuine, or just designed to assert one interpretation over the rest, and whether to pick up on and certify those signals as legitimate or to downplay those meanings as mere political gamesmanship.

Savage wanted public visibility for his message, a message in which he challenged the meaning of a term. He had the resources and the expertise to mobilize people to help him make this contested political claim, and found a clever strategy for amplifying that collective political expression by making it 'algorithmically recognizable' to Google's search engine. This required flirting with the obscene, giving an unofficial site the trappings of an official one (or a carnivalesque version of it), and getting dangerously close to being spam. Google and other search engines are in a position of power, not because they are algorithmic, but because they sit in a uniquely powerful position where they get to grant visibility and certify meanings.

Those who distribute public discourse must draw distinctions between that which we want to avoid, even when it tries to look like what we want to protect, and what we want to protect, even when it looks a lot like what we want to avoid. The greater the demand for making that distinction, either from users or critics or whoever pays the bills, the greater the risk that will befall those who end up on the wrong side of that distinction. How the distinction is made, both technically and institutionally is an important cultural and political question. And it is a question we have grappled with around information intermediaries long before the introduction of computers and algorithms. These are well-worn political dilemmas, about the role of intermediaries doing their business among competing cultural and political interests, leaning on and reifying categories of distinction, with consequences for what is visible and what is not, and for stabilizing contested political meanings.

Notes

1. Associated Press. (2003, April 2003). Except from Santorum interview. Retrieved from http://usatoday30.usatoday.com/news/washington/2003-04-23-santorum-excerpt_x.htm.
2. Dan Savage. (2003, April 25). G.O.P. Hypocrisy. *New York Times*. Retrieved from http://www.nytimes.com/2003/04/25/opinion/25SAVA.html.
3. Dan Savage. (2003, May 15). *Savage Love*: Bill, Ashton, Rick. *The Strangler*. Retrieved from http:::/www.thestranger.com/seattle/SavageLove?oid=14267.
4. Dan Savage. (2003, May 29). *Savage Love*: Do the Santorum. *The Strangler*. Retrieved from http://www.thestranger.com/seattle/SavageLove?oid=14422.
5. Dan Savage. (2003, June 12). *Savage Love*: Gas Huffer. *The Strangler*. Retrieved from http://www.thestranger.com/seattle/SavageLove?oid=14566.
6. Marissa Mayer. (2005, September 16). Googlebombing "failure". *Google Official Blog*. Retrieved from https://googleblog.blogspot.com/2005/09/googlebombing-failure.html.
7. "Pro-Family" activist calls on Dan Savage to fix Rick Santorum's "Google problem". (2012, January 5). *Huffington Post*. Retrieved from http://www.huffingtonpost.com/2012/01/05/dan-savage-rick-santorum-google_n_1186784.html.
8. Amit Singhal. (2011, November 3). Giving you fresher, more recent search results. *Google Inside Search*. Retrieved from https://search.googleblog.com/2011/11/giving-you-fresher-more-recent-search.html.
9. John Sutter. (2011, September 21). Santorum asks Google to clean up search results for his name. *CNN.com*. Retrieved from http://www.cnn.com/2011/09/21/tech/web/santorum-google-ranking/.
10. Alexander Burns. (2011, September 20). Santourm: Google spreads "filth". *Politico*. Retrieved from http://www.politico.com/story/2011/09/santorum-google-spreads-filth-063952#ixzz1YZ3jT247.
11. Google, 'Removal Policies'. Retrieved from https://support.google.com/websearch/answer/2744324?vid=1-635805400558656442-723298935.
12. David Segal. (2011, February 12). The dirty little secrets of search. *New York Times*. Retrieved from http://www.nytimes.com/2011/02/13/business/13search.html.
13. Matt Rosoff. (2011, February 23). Google busts Overstock.com for search spam. *Business Insider*. Retrieved from http://www.businessinsider.com/google-busts-overstock-for-search-spam-tactics-2011-2.
14. John Sutter. (2011, September 2011). Santorum asks Google to clean up search results for his name. *CNN.com*. Retrieved from http://www.cnn.com/2011/09/21/tech/web/santorum-google-ranking/.
15. Matthew Panzarino. (2012, December 12). Google tweaks image search algorithm and SafeSearch option to show less explicit content. *The Next Web*. Retrieved from http://thenextweb.com/google/2012/12/12/google-changes-search-image-safesearch-explicit/.
16. Laura Sydell. (2012, January 2012). How Rick Santorum's 'Google problem' endured. *NPR*. Retrieved from http://www.npr.org/2012/01/06/144801671/why-santorums-google-problem-remains.
17. Moz, 'Google algorithm change history'. Retrieved from http://www.seomoz.org/google-algorithm-change.
18. Brian Christian. (2012, April 25). The A/B test: Inside the technology that's changing the rules of business. *Wired*. Retrieved from http://www.wired.com/2012/04/ff_abtesting/.

19. Finding more high-quality sites in search. (2011, February 24). *Google Official Blog*. Retrieved from http://googleblog.blogspot.com/2011/02/finding-more-high-quality-sites-in.html.

20. Search quality highlights: 40 Changes for February. (2012, February 27). *Google Inside Search*. Retrieved from http://insidesearch.blogspot.com/2012/02/search-quality-highlights-40-changes.html.

21. Though Sullivan received this confirmation directly, Google did not issue this explanation publicly, nor did the company publicly discuss the change in Savage's site ranking. Settling questions about the specific implications of an algorithm tend to remain frustratingly murky and open to dispute, and not just because the algorithm itself is kept secret.

22. Miranda Miller. (2012, March 1). Spreading Santorum loses its frothy spot atop Google. Retrieved from http://searchenginewatch.com/article/2156606/Spreading-Santorum-Loses-Its-Frothy-Spot-Atop-Google.

23. Learn about Former Senator Rick Santorum. Retrieved from http://www.ricksantorum.com/about_rick.

Disclosure statement

I am currently employed by Microsoft, a competitor to Google in the area of search. My research for this essay was conducted before that employment began. Nevertheless, it could be perceived to be a conflict of interest. I hope it is clear that the aim of the essay is not to criticize Google's specific role in this incident, but to use the case to raise broader questions about algorithmic intermediaries and public discourse.

References

Ananny, M. (2015). Toward an ethics of algorithms: Convening, observation, probability, and timeliness. *Science, Technology & Human Values*, *41*(1), 93–117.

Barocas, S., Hood, S., & Ziewitz, M. (2013). Governing algorithms: A provocation piece. Retrieved from http://papers.ssrn.com/sol3/papers.cfm?abstract_id=2245322

Battelle, J. (2005). *The search: How Google and its rivals rewrote the rules of business and transformed our culture*. New York, NY: Portfolio.

Beer, D. (2009). Power through the algorithm? Participatory web cultures and the technological unconscious. *New Media & Society*, *11*(6), 985–1002.

boyd, d., Levy, K., & Marwick, A. (2014). The networked nature of algorithmic discrimination. Open Technology Institute. Retrieved from http://www.danah.org/papers/2014/Data Discrimination.pdf

Brunton, F. (2013). *Spam: A shadow history of the Internet*. Cambridge, MA: The MIT Press.

Brunton, F., & Nissenbaum, H. (2015). *Obfuscation: A user's guide for privacy and protest*. Cambridge, MA: The MIT Press.

Bucher, T. (2012). Want to be on the top? Algorithmic power and the threat of invisibility on Facebook. *New Media & Society*, *14*(7), 1164–1180.

Cheney-Lippold, J. (2011). A new algorithmic identity: Soft biopolitics and the modulation of control. *Theory, Culture & Society*, *28*(6), 164–181.

Citron, D., & Pasquale, F. (2014). The scored society: Due process for automated predictions. *Washington Law Review*, 89. Retrieved from http://papers.ssrn.com/sol3/papers.cfm?abstract_id=2376209

Crawford, K. (2015). Can an algorithm be agonistic? Ten scenes from life in calculated publics. *Science, Technology & Human Values*, *41*(1), 77–92.

Diakopoulos, N. (2015). Algorithmic accountability: Journalistic investigation of computational power structures. *Digital Journalism*, *3*(3), 398–415.

van Dijck, J. (2013). *The culture of connectivity: A critical history of social media*. Oxford: Oxford University Press.

Gillespie, T. (2012). Can an algorithm be wrong? *Limn*, *1*(2). Retrieved from http://escholarship.org/uc/item/0jk9k4hj

Gillespie, T. (2014). The relevance of algorithms. In T. Gillespie, P. Boczkowski, & K. Foot (Eds.), *Media technologies: Essays on communication, materiality, and society* (pp. 167–194). Cambridge, MA: MIT Press.

Gillespie, T., & Seaver, N. (2015). Critical algorithm studies: A reading list. *Social Media Collective*. Retrieved from http://socialmediacollective.org/reading-lists/critical-algorithm-studies/

Gitlin, T. (1980). *The whole World is watching: Mass media in the making & unmaking of the new left*. Berkeley, CA: University of California Press.

Graham, S. D. N. (2005). Software-sorted geographies. *Progress in Human Geography*, *29*(5), 562–580.

Granka, L. A. (2010). The politics of search: A decade retrospective. *The Information Society*, *26*(5), 364–374.

Grimmelmann, J. (2008). The Google dilemma. *New York Law School Law Review*, *53*, 939–950.

Grimmelmann, J. (2014). Speech engines. *Minnesota Law Review*, *98*(3), 868–952.

Grosser, B. (2014). What do metrics want? How quantification prescribes social interaction on Facebook. *Computational Culture*, *4*. Retrieved from http://computationalculture.net/article/what-do-metrics-want

Hallinan, B., & Striphas, T. (2014). Recommended for you: The Netflix prize and the production of algorithmic culture. *New Media & Society*, *18*(1), 117–137.

Introna, L. D., & Nissenbaum, H. (2000). Shaping the Web: Why the politics of search engines matters. *The Information Society*, *16*(3), 169–185.

Kitchin, R. (2014). Thinking critically about and researching algorithms. Retrieved from http://papers.ssrn.com/sol3/Papers.cfm?abstract_id=2515786

Mager, A. (2012). Algorithmic ideology: How capitalist society shapes search engines. *Information, Communication & Society*, *15*(5), 769–787.

Marx, G. T. (2009). A tack in the shoe and taking off the shoe: Neutralization and counter-neutralization dynamics. *Surveillance & Society*, *6*(3), 294–306.

Naron, G. R. (1991). With Malice toward all: The political cartoon and the law of libel. *Columbia-VLA Journal of Law & the Arts*, *15*, 93–116.

Noble, S. U. (2012). Missed connections: What search engines say about women. *Bitch Magazine*, *54*, 36–41.

Pariser, E. (2012). *The filter bubble: How the new personalized web is changing what we read and how we think* (Reprint ed.). New York, NY: Penguin Books.

Pasquale, F. (2015). *The Black box society: The secret algorithms that control money and information*. Cambridge, MA: Harvard University Press.

Poon, M. (2007). Scorecards as devices for consumer credit: The case of Fair, Isaac & Company Incorporated. *The Sociological Review*, *55*(s2), 284–306.

Rieder, B. (2012). What is in pageRank? A historical and conceptual investigation of a recursive status index. *Computational Culture*, *2*. Retrieved from http://computationalculture.net/article/what_is_in_pagerank

Sandvig, C., Hamilton, K., Karahalios, K., & Langbort, C. (2014). Auditing algorithms: Research methods for detecting discrimination on internet platforms. Paper presented to "Data and Discrimination," a pre-conference of the 64th annual meeting of the International Communication Association, Seattle, WA, USA.

Schudson, M. (1989). The sociology of news production. *Media, Culture & Society*, *11*(3), 263–282.

Seaver, N. (2013). Knowing algorithms. *Media in Transition 8*. Cambridge, MA. Retrieved from http://pubsonline.informs.org/doi/abs/10.1287/opre.42.2.201

Thompson, J. B. (2005). The new visibility. *Theory, Culture & Society*, *22*(6), 31–51.

Tufekci, Z. (2015). Algorithmic harms beyond Facebook and Google: Emergent challenges of computational agency *Colorado Technology Law Journal*. v13 n2. Retrieved from http://ctlj.colorado.edu/wp-content/uploads/2015/08/Tufekci-final.pdf

Ziewitz, M. (2015). Governing algorithms: Myth, mess, and methods. *Science, Technology & Human Values*, *41* (1), 3–16.

Computing brains: learning algorithms and neurocomputation in the smart city

Ben Williamson

ABSTRACT

This article examines IBM's 'Smarter Education' program, part of its wider 'Smarter Cities' agenda, focusing specifically on its learning analytics applications (based on machine learning algorithms) and cognitive computing developments for education (which take inspiration from neuroscience for the design of brain-like neural networks algorithms and neurocomputational devices). The article conceptualizes the relationship between learning algorithms, neuroscience, and the new learning spaces of the city by combining the notion of programmable 'code/space' with ideas about the 'social life of the brain' to suggest that new kinds of 'brain/code/spaces' are being developed where the environment itself is imagined to possess brain-like functions of learning and 'human qualities' of cognition performed by algorithmic processes. IBM's ambitions for education constitute a sociotechnical imaginary of a 'cognitive classroom' where the practices associated with data analytics and cognitive computing in the smart city are being translated into the neuropedagogic brain/code/spaces of the school, with significant consequences for how learners are to be addressed and acted upon. The IBM imaginary of Smarter Education is one significant instantiation of emerging smart cities that are to be governed by neurocomputational processes modelled on neuroscientific insights into the brain's plasticity for learning, and part of a 'neurofuture' in-the-making where nonconscious algorithmic 'computing brains' embedded in urban space are intended to interact with human cognition and brain functioning.

In recent years, urban environments have been reimagined as 'smart cities of the future' with the computational capacity to monitor, learn about, and adapt to the people that inhabit them (Batty et al., 2012). As geographers have detailed, the smart city is an urban environment governed by the capacities of coded devices and infrastructures (Kitchin, 2014a), a 'programmable environment' (Gabrys, 2014) structured and supported 'line by line, algorithm by algorithm, program by program,' 'by code using data as fuel' (Thrift, 2014, p. 10). To some degree, smart cities are even 'sentient' spaces that 'think of us' (Crang & Graham, 2007, p. 792), with some form of reflexive awareness as learning environments. This article provides a case study of the 'Smarter Education' initiative of IBM's global 'Smarter Cities' program, focusing on its educational ambitions to create classrooms with in-built capacities for learning as an exemplar of its wider efforts to make cities into programmable learning spaces. Smarter Education itself is premised on technologies of learning analytics and cognitive computing. These are both highly algorithm-driven technologies: learning analytics depends on machine learning algorithms trained on data to analyse students' performance on tasks; cognitive computing relies on neural networks algorithms and associated neurotechnologies based on neuroscientific models of brain functioning, and has led to the creation by IBM of 'cognitive tutors' that can 'personalize' and 'optimize' learning according to each student's predicted progress. IBM's promise of the learning algorithms of educational data analytics and cognitive computing is to transform schools into 'smarter schools' – brainy spaces where the environment itself has been encoded with capacities for learning – which might act as templates for increasingly 'cognitive cities' that are 'configured for advanced mental processing' (Dunn, Cureton, & Pollastri, 2014).

The learning algorithms of learning analytics and cognitive computing applications imagined by IBM contain particular models of learning processes that are themselves becoming active much more widely in how the smart city as a learning environment is enacted. The central contribution of the article is to identify how IBM is promoting processes of algorithmic learning that are integral to its vision of smarter cities. Its glossy imaginary of Smarter Education acts as a seemingly desirable model not just for the future of schools in software-enabled urban environments, but as a diagram for future cities that are to be treated as learning environments and enacted by increasingly cognitive forms of computing technology. Smarter Education is one significant instantiation of emerging smart cities that are to be governed by neurocomputational processes modelled (in part) on the brain's pliability for learning – but with the capacity to compute beyond human perceptibility and consciousness – wherein brain-based devices embedded in urban space are imagined to have the capacity to optimize human neural morphology and cognitive functioning. A reimagining of the human subject is instantiated by such developments. As Rose (2016) asks, why do some dream that new neurotechnologies will make it possible to 'read' the brain, what practical applications might such technologies lead to, and what mutation in our understandings of the human might result from their development? As an exemplar 'neurofuture-in-the-making' (Williams, Katz, & Martin, 2011, p. 143), IBM's own agenda is based on a dream of modelling the brain, is leading to the design of new computational applications (exemplified in its education programs and its aspirations for more cognitive smart cities), and is contributing to a reimagining of the human subject – one understood algorithmically in terms of computable cognition and programmable brain functions.

IBM imaginaries

A number of organizations associated with smart cities have begun to produce materials envisaging education as a smart social institution situated in digitally mediated urban infrastructures. Like the city, the school is treated as a 'code/space' (Kitchin & Dodge, 2011) in these imaginings, where code and algorithms play an integral part in the functioning of the built environment itself. For Kitchin and Dodge (2011) the term 'code/space' articulates how the functioning of spaces is translated into coded processes that then act recursively to alter them. Elsewhere, Kitchin (2014a) refers to the 'programmable city' as a prototypical code/space, where urban functions are delegated to software systems which then transform how they perform. However, the educational dimensions of smart cities remain empirically neglected and critically under-conceptualized. This is significant since the smart city visions of major software vendors such as IBM and Microsoft posit a direct relationship between education and the future city – not just in educating 'smart citizens' to participate in it (Williamson, 2015), but insofar as they treat programmable urban spaces as learning environments that utilize the power of machine learning and cognitive computing algorithms to learn about the people and things that inhabit them.

As a way of opening up this gap into a research agenda around education in smart cities, I analyse the 'sociotechnical imaginary' of IBM's Smarter Education program. Sociotechnical imaginaries are collectively held, institutionally stabilized, and publicly performed visions of desirable futures that are animated by imagined forms of life and made attainable through the design of technological projects (Jasanoff, 2015). The code/spaces of smart cities are in this sense sociotechnical imaginaries materialized and operationalized through specific technological innovations and practices. In particular, I focus on IBM as a key organizational actor that has emphasized learning analytics and cognitive computing in its global Smarter Education program. Smarter Education articulates an imagined future for educational spaces and practices being operationalized by IBM in specific technological projects: it acts as a model for the future of schooling that IBM assumes is both attainable and should be attained through the application of technical products, and that also illustrates how algorithmic forms of learning are imagined by IBM as integral to the functioning of the smart cities to which it is seeking to sell its technical solutions.

Methodologically, researching IBM's imaginary has involved searching its promotional and scientific literatures, websites, infographics, press releases, and news features, and tracing the connective tissues between IBM's scientific claims and knowledges, its human actors, its technical applications, and its production of visions of a future in which its applications are to be operationalized. While cautious that much of this material is largely promotional and serves IBM's marketing aspirations as a global smart cities software solutions vendor, I emphasize how its materials 'frame and represent alternative futures' and 'naturalize ways of thinking about possible worlds' and associated forms of social life and behaviour (Jasanoff, 2015, p. 35). In particular, I explore what models of learning and brain functioning underpin IBM's production of machine learning and cognitive computing applications, critically considering their possible consequences for the shaping of desired behaviours and practices in an imagined neurofuture of education. These are algorithmic processes being mobilized in the present that possess both a past life in the practices of IBM's R&D labs and a future life in the IBM imaginary of Smarter Education. While empirical data on the smarter classrooms imagined by IBM are not currently available, by analysing the sociotechnical imaginary of IBM's Smarter Education initiative I examine how learning algorithms might participate in the smart city itself by advancing the idea of 'brain/code/space.' Brain/code/space articulates how environments are becoming increasingly programmable, but also how such spaces are becoming dependent upon encoded models of human cognitive functioning to become adaptive learning environments, and represents the material and spatial instantiation of imagined computational neurofutures-in-the-making.

Modelling algorithms

Learning analytics and cognitive computing are both fundamentally algorithm-driven. A growing body of research has begun to engage with algorithms both as social products – designed by technical experts in specific social settings – and as socially productive systems that interact with diverse practices. As products, Kitchin (2014b) characterizes algorithms variously as 'black boxes' that are hidden inside intellectual property and proprietorial code; as 'heterogeneous systems' in which hundreds of algorithms are woven together; as 'emergent' systems that are constantly being refined, reworked, and tweaked; and as complex, unpredictable, and fragile systems that are sometimes miscoded, buggy, and 'out of control.' Beyond their properties as products, these vastly complex algorithmic systems can then 'do things,' and exert material effects 'on themselves, on machines and on humans' (Goffey, 2008). As a consequence, algorithms are becoming an integrated part of everyday social processes that can reinforce, maintain, or even reshape visions of the social world, knowledge, and encounters with information (Beer, 2013).

It is important to distinguish such claims from simplistic technological determinism, and to acknowledge algorithms as products of social practices. Gillespie (2014, n.p.) argues that 'sociological analysis must not conceive of algorithms as abstract, technical achievements, but unpack the warm human and institutional choices that lie behind these cold mechanisms.' In particular he highlights the importance of examining how complex human and social activities – and the values and assumptions held about them – are operationalized by being translated into a functional interaction of models, goals, data, variables, indicators, and outcomes. The algorithm itself, in this sense, may not be as important an object of inquiry as the underlying 'models' – including models of human action – on which algorithms are intended to operate within 'the social world of the algorithmic system' (Neyland, 2015, p. 128).

In the below examples, the emphasis is on those models of human learning and cognition that are built into the learning analytics systems and cognitive classroom spaces being developed by IBM. While it is beyond the scope of this article to penetrate the technical complexity of IBM's algorithmic systems, it is possible to analyse the available documentation emerging from IBM to discern what kinds of assumptions, models, and desired outcomes its algorithms are intended to operationalize. IBM's imaginary of Smarter Education is a documentary construction of a desired future world 'out there' that IBM is seeking to build 'in here, in the algorithmic machine' (Neyland, 2015, p. 129).

Learning analytics

Learning analytics software is designed to enable students to be tracked through their digital data traces in real time and to provide automated predictions of future progress (Siemens, 2013). Fundamentally interdisciplinary, the emerging field of learning analytics consists of expertise in statistics, computer science, information science, machine learning, psychology, and neuroscience (Piety, Hickey, & Bishop, 2014). Within the field itself, learning analytics is often considered in terms of both its techniques and applications

(Siemens, 2013). Techniques involve the specific algorithms and models for conducting analytics; applications involve the ways in which insights generated from analytics are then codified into software products to improve teaching and learning. As Siemens (2013, p. 1386) details, 'an algorithm that provides recommendations of additional course content for learners can be classified as a technique. A technique, such as prediction of learner risk for dropout, can then lead to an application, such as personalization of learning content.'

A key organizational developer of learning analytics techniques and applications is IBM, which houses its learning analytics R&D within its Smarter Education program, itself a subtheme of its global Smarter Cities agenda. Smarter Education is based on a series of assumptions about the real-time availability of educational data about what students learn and how they progress, and about the beneficial uses of data analytics for institutional and systemic improvement (IBM, 2015a). According to its paper on 'the future of learning':

> Analytics translates volumes of data into insights for policy makers, administrators and educators alike so they can identify which academic practices and programs work best and where investments should be directed. By turning masses of data into useful intelligence, educational institutions can create smarter schools for now and for the future. (IBM, 2014)

In detailing its imaginary of 'smarter schools,' the report particularly emphasizes the use of 'academic analytics' to enable institutions to analyse data for insights into their effectiveness, and 'learning analytics' to facilitate the interpretation of students' actions. These analytics include both 'predictive tools' – which model probable future progress on data from past activities – and prescriptive analytics – which automate appropriate pedagogic responses: 'these two dimensions of smarter analytics enable educational leaders to detect patterns that exist in masses of data, project potential outcomes and make intelligent decisions based on those projections' (IBM, 2014, n.p.). To this end, IBM has established its own high school chain in the US, P-TECH, which exemplifies how schools could generate real-time data on student activities, but also make future-tense predictions of their likely outcomes and prescribe pedagogic interventions. The ambition of P-TECH is 'to build for schools what its operations center is for cities: a single system for collecting, aggregating and analyzing data from students and teachers alike, then writing algorithms to prescribe how to cope' (Linday, 2013, n.p.). As an operationalization of the Smarter Education imaginary, P-TECH makes every aspect of institutional and individual performance into a real-time and future-focused process of data collection, analysis, and feedback.

Given the focus in this paper on the modelling that must take place for algorithms to function, it is important to note that learning analytics is fundamentally underpinned by techniques of user modelling. For example, Siemens (2013, p. 1386) explains how 'new data-based discoveries are made and insight is gained into learner behavior ... through models and algorithms.' Learner modelling, cognitive modelling, behaviour modelling, probability modelling, and 'knowledge domain modelling' (the mapping of the knowledge structure of a discipline) are crucial elements in any learning analytics platform. Once these models are combined, they can be used to produce predictive models of learner progressions. Here machine learning algorithms and predictive analytics are significant. 'Machine learning' consists of software systems that utilize adaptive algorithms, techniques of 'deep learning,' and statistical models to analyse users' data and anticipate or even predict their future actions by 'transforming data on events, actions, behaviours, beliefs and desires' into probabilistic predictions of the future that then can be used to decide on action to be taken in the present (Mackenzie, 2013, p. 399). The practical 'production of prediction,' as Mackenzie (2015a, p. 436) terms it, depends on a range of mathematical, statistical, logistic, and calculative practices that are rooted in particular predictive styles and machine learning settings, and situated in the province of experts such as engineers, mathematicians, and statisticians working in university and industry research. Predictive modelling is thus highly contingent on the situatedness of its production in fields of technical expertise and experimentation.

It is important to reiterate that the object of inquiry here is the interaction of the algorithm with the underlying model that has been constructed from the data. As Gillespie (2014, n.p.) notes, 'the "algorithm" comes after the generation of a "model," i.e. the formalization of the problem and the goal in computational terms.' Moreover, in order for the algorithm to function – particularly the case with machine learning algorithms – it must first be 'trained' with existing data 'so that it may "learn"' (Gillespie, 2014), and need to be constantly re-trained in an iterative process of monitoring, adjusting, revising, and optimizing as the accuracy and generalizability of the predictive models it generates are themselves checked and analysed (Mackenzie, 2015a). The models and the training data are always constructed and operationalized according to the values and assumptions of their designers. Fundamentally, learning analytics such as those being developed and deployed by IBM depend on the construction of models of learner actions, and learning processes, which can then be subjected to algorithmic processes that have themselves been designed to learn. These models are the product of complex sociotechnical practices and are embedded in the methodological commitments, assumptions, values, and styles of thinking of their designers, such as those associated with Smarter Education at IBM.

Although the specific internal practices of IBM are beyond the empirical scope of this study, it is possible to see from its documentary resources how a particular set of assumptions about the use of learning analytics and machine learning algorithms is circulating within the institutional context of the company. There is, in other words, an institutional social life to the algorithmic data practices that IBM is developing as part of Smarter Education. From the documentary traces that constitute its imaginary of smarter schools, it is possible to discern that IBM is seeking to model different aspects of education, including practices of learner modelling and behaviour modelling, as a means towards generating predictions of future actions and outcomes. Further empirical investigation of these practices would seek to examine the institutionalized processes involved in training and re-training the machine learning algorithms that will interact with those models to generate insights into the behaviour of the learner and to make the learning process known and thus amenable to intervention. One significant modelling technique being developed by IBM to this end is cognitive modelling of the neural structure of the 'learning brain.'

Cognitive classrooms

An emerging development in IBM's learning analytics and associated machine learning techniques is 'cognitive-based learning systems' based on neuroscientific methodological innovations, technical developments in brain-inspired computing, and neural networks algorithms. IBM's promotion of cognitive learning systems within education is part of a proliferating discourse of educational neuroscience, or 'the dispersal of neurobiological language, imagery, symbolism and rhetoric within formal and informal learning environments' (Busso & Pollack, 2015, p. 169). The discourse of contemporary education is increasingly infused with references to 'neuroscience in education,' 'neuroeducation,' and 'neuropedagogies.' These terms reflect how neuroscientific understandings of the learning process have been used to inform the design and application of better pedagogies, though many neuroeducational approaches treat the functional architecture of the brain in explicitly determinist terms, and even 'reduce learning to an algorithmic or computational process' (Pykett, 2015, p. 97). In applying its expertise in cognitive computing to education, IBM is taking a particular algorithmic model of brain functioning as the basis for imagining new neurocomputational systems that might intervene in young people's own learning processes – processes taking place in a 'learning brain' that itself has been conceptualized algorithmically through IBM's own laboratory studies.

Cognitive modelling of the kind promoted by IBM has long been an aspiration of learning analytics developers. Cognitive modelling is concerned with developing systems that possess a 'computational model capable of solving the problems that are given to students in the ways students are expected to solve the problems,' and thus since 'cognitive processes can be modeled, software (tutors) can be developed to support learners in the learning process' (Siemens, 2013, pp. 1383–1384). With the current development by IBM of cognitive-based learning technologies built on the idea that the architectures and functions of the brain can now partly be modelled computationally, cognitive modelling is seen within the learning analytics field as more attainable. It is seen as possible to create technologies that function more like human brains than programmed software; technologies that can then be embedded into schools as a cerebral augmentation to the cognitive capacities of the learner. The promise here is of technologies that can learn from the user, through processing data collected during their digital learning activities, and then adapt and respond to that user's individual needs, preferences, and dispositions in ways that are more 'natural' than hard-programmed computing systems. IBM's cognitive systems, its advocates claim, 'learn at scale, reason with purpose and interact with humans naturally,' thanks to their 'human qualities, such as self-directed goals, common sense and ethical values' (Kelly, 2015, p. 5).

Over the last decade, IBM has positioned itself as a dominant research centre in cognitive computing, with huge teams of engineers and computer scientists working on both basic and applied research in this area. The development of cognitive computing with 'human qualities' at IBM – again linked to its Smarter Cities agenda – closely mirrors current scientific R&D around 'neural networks' algorithms and 'neuromorphic' hardware in the analysis of big data. The emerging discourse of cognitive computing is replete with references to the brain as a 'big data processor,' 'brain-like computations,' 'algorithms that learn,' 'neural network learning algorithms,' 'brain-inspired algorithms,' and 'deep learning algorithms.' Building on such developments, IBM has positioned cognitive computers as 'decision support systems' that 'can process natural language and unstructured data and learn by experience, much as humans do,' in contrast to expert systems that are hard coded by programmers (IBM Research, 2015, n.p.). It has even produced its own visionary book, *Smart machines: IBM's Watson and the era of cognitive computing* (Kelly & Hamm, 2014). Perhaps the most well-known IBM cognitive computing development is Watson, a massively advanced cognitive supercomputer promoted by IBM for its capacity to process and learn from natural language and other unstructured data:

> Watson is a cognitive technology that processes information more like a human than a computer – by understanding natural language, generating hypotheses based on evidence, and learning as it goes. And learn it does. Watson 'gets smarter' in three ways: by being taught by its users, by learning from prior interactions, and by being presented with new information. (IBM, 2015b, n.p.)

Watson has become the subject of almost feverish R&D both within IBM and among the vast network of partners and subsidiaries in the 'Watson ecosystem' of application developers, content providers, and 'talent partners.' Watson has already been applied in healthcare, higher education, the culinary sector, banking, and business, as well as in 'citizen services' in cities (Terdiman, 2015). IBM's wider R&D network in cognitive computing is based on many years of neuroscientific research at its 'Brain Lab,' much of it supported by the US Defense Advanced Research Projects Agency (DARPA), as part of its Systems of Neuromorphic Adaptive Plastic Scalable Electronics (SyNAPSE) program to build 'artificial brains,' with hundreds of millions of US dollars funding (Artificial Brains, 2013).

Much of IBM's cognitive computing R&D is based on the neo-cortical principles of the brain as a synaptic memory system determined by computable neuronal patterns, rather than human-engineered architectures. Its Brain Lab has provided the neuroscientific insight for these developments. While IBM itself is not seeking to build an artificial brain but 'a computer inspired by the brain,' it claims that 'cognitive computing aims to emulate the human brain's abilities for perception, action and cognition,' and has dedicated extensive R&D to the production of 'neurosynaptic chips' that can 'emulate the neurons and synapses in the human brain' (IBM Research, 2014, n.p.). In 2014 IBM engineers published a major article in *Science* that was featured in its leader comment and front cover (Merolla et al., 2014; Service, 2014). In a series of related articles in both specialist and non-specialist publications, IBM engineers claimed to have created a 'one million neuron brain-inspired processor,' a 'brain chip' that is 'capable of 46 billion synaptic operations per second, per watt–literally a synaptic supercomputer in your palm' (Modha, 2014, n.p.). These neurosynaptic chips can also be tiled together into 'scalable neuromorphic systems' of several millions of neurons and billions of synapses, referred to in promotional IBM literature as 'computing brains,' 'systems that can perceive, think and act,' or even a 'brain-in-a-box' at a 'roughly human scale' (Modha, 2013, n.p.).

The elision of computation and the brain by IBM is both a marketing strategy and an engineering innovation. As marketing, it positions IBM as a solutions-provider for complex data analysis problems. As an engineering innovation, it proposes a new model for computation that, according to the *Science* article, displaces previous 'programmable' approaches to algorithm design and machine learning. Whereas conventional machine learning algorithms depend on being programmed and trained with example data (sometimes termed 'supervised learning'), cognitive computing systems such as IBM's brain chip are designed with the capacity to process and learn from natural language, interactions with users, and other unstructured data ('unsupervised learning') in ways that emulate the neural networks of the human brain. The development path of IBM's 'brain chip' and 'computing brains,' recorded in a series of published scientific articles, has proceeded from neuroscience and neuroanatomy to supercomputing, to a new computer architecture, to a new programming language, to algorithms, and applications, all underpinned by its understanding of the human brain's synaptic plasticity developed within IBM's own Brain Lab. Plasticity is the understanding that the brain's neuronal architecture is itself pliable, flexible, and constantly adapting to environmental input, and is the basis for much neural networks R&D. IBM's cognitive computers are, therefore:

> designed to learn dynamically through experiences, find correlations, create hypotheses and remember – and learn from – the outcomes, emulating the human brain's synaptic and structural plasticity (or the brain's ability to re-wire itself over time as it learns and responds to experiences and interactions with its environment). (IBM Research, 2011, n.p.)

IBM's engineers are modelling the neural plasticity of the learning brain in silicon.

To apply its cognitive computing applications in education, IBM has developed a specific 'Cognitive Computing for Education Transformation' program, led by its own 'Program Director and Master Inventor,' though care needs to be taken to differentiate the cutting edge of IBM's R&D from the imaginaries of application that have quickly surrounded it. IBM's cognitively 'smarter classroom' initiative is just one such imaginary application of cognitive computing, part of a series of 'visionary' scenarios for the future that also include healthcare, retail, security, and smart cities that are all imagined as being responsive, real-time, predictive, and highly personalized. Like the IBM smart cities into which it is integrated in these scenarios, IBM's imaginary of a 'smarter classroom' is intended to use cognitive computing applications to analyse massive quantities of student data in real time and then wrap personalized learning experiences around each one:

> IBM envisions educational institutions adopting cloud-based cognitive systems to collect and analyse all of this data over a long period of time – creating longitudinal student records that would give teachers the information they need to provide personalized learning experiences for their students. (IBM Research, 2013a, n.p.)

In its imaginary of the classroom in five years, IBM grandly claims that the IBM 'smarter classroom' is a 'classroom that will learn you' through 'cognitive-based learning systems.' As the IBM promotional website for the 'classroom that will learn you' claims:

> The rapid digitization of educational institutions will allow unprecedented instrumentation of the learning process. Cognitive computing, or learning technologies, will help us calculate everything we can about how each student learns and thrives, then create flexibility in the system to continually adapt and fine-tune what we deliver to that student and how this supports teachers and employers. (IBM, 2013, n.p.)

These claims are reinforced and reiterated in a variety of IBM think pieces, glossy interactive multimedia presentations, and infographics available on the company website. The cognitive classroom promises personalization of the learning experience, real-time feedback on learner performance, adaptive learning software that can learn from and adapt to the learner, and intelligent software tutors that can automate remedial intervention or even prescribe appropriate curricular content.

IBM's Cognitive Computing for Education Transformation program director has presented these as intelligent, interactive systems that combine neuroscientific insights into cognitive learning processes with neurotechnologies that:

learn and interact with humans in more natural ways. At the same time, advances in neuro-science, driven in part by progress in using supercomputers to model aspects of the brain … promise to bring us closer to a deeper understanding of some cognitive processes such as learning. At the intersection of cognitive neuroscience and cognitive computing lies an extra-ordinary opportunity … to refine cognitive theories of learning as well as derive new prin-ciples that should guide how learning content should be structured when using cognitive computing based technologies. (Nitta, 2014, n.p.)

The prototype innovations so far developed by this program include automated 'cognitive learning content,' 'cognitive tutors,' and 'cognitive assistants for learning'; these may be integrated into 'personalized adaptive learning systems,' all 'designed with a deep under-standing of underlying cognitive neuroscience as well as cognitive theories of learning' (Nitta, 2014, n.p.), to provide intelligent computational augmentation to the learner's cog-nitive process. As the IBM Global Manager of Education Solutions for Smarter Cities phrases it, the 'cognitive tutor' application is intended

> to supplement face-to-face teaching and ultimately replace it entirely for subjects and areas where a cognitive agent will, quite simply, do a better job of understanding the learner's needs and provide constant, patient, endless support and tuition personalized for the user. (Eassom, 2015, n.p.)

IBM has also developed an application based on Watson, called Codename: Watson Teacher Advisor, which is designed to observe, interpret, and evaluate information to make informed decisions that should provide guidance and mentorship to help teachers improve their teaching.

The imaginary of the cognitive tutor and the teacher advisor clearly resonates with a longer genealogy of thinking about the automation of teaching (Bayne, 2015), but more uniquely superimposes an emergent computational theory of the brain on to the spaces in which education takes place. The promise of the classroom that can learn you is of a smart environment with its own cognitive faculties, designed according to neuroscientific claims about the brain as a sophisticated algorithmic system that is defined by its capacity as a synaptic memory system that 'spikes' as it receives inputs. It treats the cognitive class-room and the human subjects that inhabit it in increasingly analogous terms. The promise of cognitive computing for IBM is not just of more 'natural systems' with 'human qual-ities,' but a fundamental reimagining of the 'next generation of human cognition, in which we think and reason in new and powerful ways,' as claimed in a recent IBM white paper entitled 'Computing, cognition and the future of knowing':

> It's true that cognitive systems are machines that are inspired by the human brain. But it's also true that these machines will inspire the human brain, increase our capacity for reason and rewire the ways in which we learn. (Kelly, 2015)

The key point here is that IBM's imaginary of smart learning environments has distinctive implications for thinking about smart cities as brain-inspired computational spaces in which the human cognitive capacities of the learning brain might be enhanced. The neu-rocomputationally cognitive classroom that can learn is part of IBM's emerging vision of an 'ecosystem of cognitive environments inhabited by a society of specialized software agents called cogs':

> Cogs work in a mutually beneficial partnership with humans to enable better complex data-driven decision-making. We call these partnerships Symbiotic Cognitive Systems. Cognition does not occur solely (or even mostly) within an individual human mind, but rather is distributed across people, artifacts and environments. … Cogs are designed to follow and interact with humans and other cogs across a variety of everyday environments. They engage individually or collectively with humans … [and] learn and leverage sophisticated models of human characteristics, preferences and biases so they can communicate naturally. (IBM Research, 2013b, n.p.)

IBM's imaginary of the cognitive ecosystem, or a 'symbiotic cognitive system,' is underpinned by an 'infrastructure inhabited by the society of cogs and the devices that let them behave as one shared integrated resource, enabling "human-computer collaboration at the speed of thought"' (IBM Research, 2013b, n.p.). Its cognitive environments include cognitive homes, cognitive offices, cognitive cafes, and increasingly cognitive cities within which each of these environments are networked together. The cognitive classroom that can learn you is one example of such a 'symbiotic cognitive system,' in which cognitive software agents are enabled to interact with users, and to participate in a distribution of cognition across the neurobiology of the human brain and the neurosynaptic devices of cognitive computing. As with the smart city itself, the cognitive environment of the classroom constitutes a code/space where coded devices and infrastructures partially determine individual actions and social activities. Crucially, the cognitive code/spaces imagined by IBM put brain-inspired algorithms directly into interaction with human cognition, mobilizing machine models of neuronal network processes to extend and optimize the capacities of the human mind itself.

Mackenzie (2015b, n.p.) has argued that advances in cognitive computing in places like IBM are based around 'the ideal of something like pattern recognition or indeed conscious awareness' and 'abound in references to cognition, meaning, perception, sense data, hearing, speaking, seeing, remembering, deciding, and surprisingly, imagining and fantasy.' As such, Mackenzie (2015b, n.p.) claims, their 'modelling practices are no longer the statistical rendering of number in the hands of government, science or commerce' but 'as challenges set for an often almost Cyclopean cognition to reorganise and optimise.' Mackenzie terms such technologies 'cognitive infrastructures.' IBM's imaginary of the cognitive classroom can be conceived, then, as a cognitive infrastructure in which cognitive tutors, cognitive learning content, and cognitive assistants are powered by neurocomputational learning algorithms that can be applied to optimize learners' cognition. In such fabricated spaces, the brain functioning of human subjects themselves is rendered reductively as algorithmic or computational processes, which are therefore amenable to being optimized by the application of cognitive computing algorithms. The smarter school is imagined as a brainy space which is located in the cognitive infrastructure of a neurocomputationally smart city that is itself animated by neuroscientific models of the plastic brain but networked together into an ecosystem of distributed intelligences that can out-compute the capacities of human perception, consciousness, and cognition.

Modelling, morphing, and modifying the mind

The application of 'brain-inspired thinking' in IBM's neuropedagogic plans for the cognitive classroom reflects the increasingly prominent application and popularization of 'neuro knowledges' (Pykett, 2013) – those disciplines of the brain sciences with their own styles of thinking, explanations, modes of expertise, and application. However, the different branches of the neuro knowledges assume different working models of the brain, mobilize different methods to measure it, and build different theories and empirical accounts of its functioning, all shaped by specific social, political, cultural, and economic contexts (methodological and technical innovations, political and industrial support, etc.) (Rose & Abi-Rached, 2013). Additionally, much contemporary neuroscience attributes capacities to the brain from experimental findings in artificial laboratory contexts, as 'brain facts' abstracted from embodied life and culture (Rose, 2016; Williams et al., 2011). Neuroeducation, in particular, tends to treat brain processes as if they are computational or algorithmic processes, and is part of an emerging field of policy experimentation that treats reductive forms of neuroscientific evidence about the neurobiological processes of young people as the target for strategic intervention (Pykett, 2015). Through the 'biopolitics of the brain sciences,' the 'cerebral knowledges' of neuroscience are coming to play a significant role in contemporary techniques of governance, whereby 'experts of the brain, rather than of "psy" or society,' are understood to be addressing societal challenges, and 'governing the conduct of human beings [has] come to require, presuppose and utilize a knowledge of the human brain' (Rose & Abi-Rached, 2014, pp. 3–5). As a result, neuroscientific developments have become entwined with strategies designed to govern human conduct by drawing upon the growing availability of empirical knowledge of the brain.

In recent critical science and technology studies, neuroscience has been conceptualized in terms of its 'numerous interpretations, translations, and mediations' rather than an assumed 'neuro-realism' (Williams et al., 2011, p. 139). The neuro knowledges emerging from IBM's Brain Lab and applied in its cognitive computing applications therefore need to be seen as socially situated practices providing a particular neurocomputational model and knowledge of brain processes. Its activities position it as a solutions-provider at a time when governments are seeking to intervene in human lives through the brain itself, not least in education and in response to problems of urban living (Fitzgerald & Rose, 2015). If the social power of algorithms now plays a part in organizing everyday life (Beer, 2013), then the algorithmic power of brain-based cognitive computing in particular poses significant issues for the ways individuals and collectives are targeted for intervention through human–computer interaction with learning algorithms. The IBM imaginary of cognitive computing in education is part, therefore, of a much wider emerging debate about the influence of neuroscientific thinking in addressing societal challenges and shaping human subjectivity, though care is required to differentiate simplistic claims about brain manipulation from the strategic uses of neuroscientific concepts by political and commercial actors, including IBM, that are increasingly mobilizing neuro expertise in the computational modelling of brain processes as the basis for intervening in the cognitive lives of human subjects.

As noted earlier, one of the key concepts of the brain sciences is neuroplasticity. The understanding of the brain's malleability has become a dominant neuroscientific claim, not just at IBM's Brain Lab. Methodological inquiries have ascertained that the brain is open to environmental input, with the environment shaping the neural architecture and functional organization of the brain through the formation, strengthening and trimming of synaptic connections. As a result of recent discoveries around neural plasticity, there is emerging consensus that neurobiological mechanisms exist through which 'environments get encoded in brains' and aspects of social life are incorporated into neurobiological structures (Fitzgerald & Rose, 2015). The result of this emerging 'imaginary of plasticity' (Rose & Abi-Rached, 2013) is that new techniques are now being devised to recognize and manage the processes involved in shaping and reshaping the brain which promote the idea that the brain is flexible, mouldable, able to be trained, re-wired, improved, and ultimately optimized. The imaginary of plasticity instantiates the social within the neurobiological, with new understandings of 'the social life of the brain' being used to animate policies and practices in healthcare, education, and other social domains (Pickersgill, 2013, p. 322).

IBM's cognitive classroom, as a cognitive environment inhabited by cognitive tutors, is illustrative of the imaginary of plasticity being materialized in pedagogic form. In this imagined space, cognitive systems that have been built to emulate the plasticity and neural networks of the brain are to be put to pedagogic work as cognitive tutors that might 're-wire' the neural circuits underpinning human learning itself. The expert basis for such systems emanates from IBM's own Brain Lab. Its neuroscientific and computational R&D practices have helped identify the neural networking of the social life of the brain itself, and developed ways of modelling such processes computationally in ways that have allowed its engineers to build new neurocomputational applications. Its neuro knowledges have been translated into neural network algorithms and neurosynaptic devices such as the brain chip that it seeks to apply in a social ecosystem of cognitive devices to extend the networks of the mind.

While IBM's elision of the brain and computation may appear dubious, it reflects recent sociological debate about the social life of the brain, as 'the webs of human social and cultural life that we had come to understand as our particular object of knowledge seem more and more open to being figured neuroscientifically' (Fitzgerald & Callard, 2015, p. 4). Media researchers, too, have begun to examine how ideas about the social life of the brain, and its collapsing of taken-for-granted distinctions regarding 'biology' and 'society,' might imply a shift in understanding of human subjectivity. For example, Hayles (2013, p. 10) argues that recent discoveries around neural plasticity support the idea that humans develop through 'epigenetic changes – changes initiated and transmitted through the environment rather than through the genetic code,' and therefore that humans and technologies can be understood to 'coevolve' together 'technogenetically':

> As digital media ... embedded in the environment, become more pervasive, they push us in the direction of faster communication, more intense and varied information streams, more integration of humans and intelligent machines, and more interactions of language with code. These environmental changes have significant neurological consequences. (Hayles, 2013, p. 11)

Elsewhere, Hayles (2014, p. 202) refers to 'nonconscious cognitive systems' that increasingly permeate information and communication networks and devices, so that cognition in some instances may be located in a technical system rather than in the mental world of an individual participant, 'an important change from a model of cognition centered in the self.' This non-anthropocentric view of 'cognition everywhere' accepts that nonconsciously cognitive computing devices can employ learning processes that are modelled like those of embodied biological organisms, using their experiences to learn, achieve skills and interact with people. When nonconscious cognitive devices penetrate into human systems, they can then potentially change the dynamics of human behaviours through changing brain morphology and functioning technogenetically. Models of neural plasticity emerging from neuroscience have thus provided the imaginary necessary for the development of the nonconscious learning algorithms of cognitive computing, which are then used to activate cognitive environments such as IBM's cognitive classroom; a space in which learners are targeted for cognitive enhancement and neuro-optimization through interacting with other nonconscious cognitive agents and environments.

In IBM's imaginaries of Smarter Education and Cognitive Computing for Education Transformation, the brain is to be translated into computational code to enact nonconscious cognitive computing devices; and it is then to be applied in the code/space of the cognitive classroom to alter the functioning of the brain. This is symmetrical with Kitchin and Dodge's (2011) notion of how urban functions can be delegated to software code and algorithms to produce code/spaces that then fundamentally alter the functioning and experience of the city itself. In IBM's imaginary of the cognitive classroom – like that of the cognitive smart city – the human subject is approached as a plastic brain, but a plastic brain that is understood in terms of algorithmic and computational processes. This is a very specific form of neuro knowledge, or rather a neurocomputational knowledge, and it allows IBM to develop its ideas about symbiotic cognitive systems in which algorithmic forms of nonconscious cognition and learning as well as human cognition and learning can be optimized.

One way of conceptualizing the hybridity of programmable spaces with the neuroscientific figuring of the social life of the brain is the notion of a neurocomputational 'brain/code/space.' This term registers how the learning algorithms of data analytics and cognitive computing are weaving constitutively into the functioning and experience of smart cities, including but not limited to the cognitive classrooms of IBM's imagined smarter school. The brain/code/spaces of IBM's smart cognitive classrooms are built around models of the brain that are encoded in the functioning of learning algorithms, inserted into the pedagogic space of the classroom, and that, located there, might act technogenetically to alter brain morphology and enhance cognitive functioning according to expert knowledges about the algorithmic nature of brain processes. IBM's imaginary of the brain/code/spaces of such cognitive learning environments is one instantiation of a new kind of urban cognitive infrastructure in which neuroscientific claims about brain plasticity are built into the learning algorithms that constitute the functioning and experience of the environment itself. There is some resemblance here with recent accounts of biopolitics in which 'the body is increasingly seen not as an organic substratum but as molecular software that can be read and rewritten' (Lemke, 2011, p. 93). The notion of brain/code/space articulates a novel neurocomputational biopolitics in which brain functions are transcoded into data, and then codified into nonconscious cognitive learning algorithms and applications that are designed to augment human cognition. In sum, IBM's claims about the cognitive classroom represent a nexus of neuro knowledges and imagined neurofutures with technical expertise in learning algorithms, neural networks, cognitive computing, and neurosynaptic modelling. These approaches assume that it is now possible to understand and model the learning brain, one that is computationally understood and mapped in terms of the plasticity of its synaptic connections and neural pathways, and transcode it into learning algorithms that can be embedded in the environment. An imagined form of life based on computational models of the plastic, programmable, and optimizable brain animates the technological projects that are transforming IBM's imaginary of Smarter Education into a neurofuture-in-the-making.

Conclusion

This article has offered an initial exploration of the neurocomputational hybridity of technological code/spaces with new conceptions of the plasticity of the 'social life of the brain.' Through an examination of the IBM imaginary of Smarter Education as an exemplar of its aspiration for Smarter Cities, it suggests that smart cities are increasingly being imagined as cognitive learning environments, functioning through learning algorithms and nonconscious cognitive applications that are themselves modelled on the learning brain and are intended to become technogenetically co-constitutive of human brain processes and cognitive functioning. There are traces here of what Fitzgerald and Rose (2015) have termed the 'neurosocial city,' an urban environment characterized by practices that are animated by neuroscientific understandings of citizens. Retooled as a neurocomputational brain/code/space, the emerging cognitive city is an urban environment designed to be more cognitively capable and to impress itself on the cerebral lives of citizens. In this sense, the brain/code/spaces of the smart city are themselves becoming learning environments where the neuroscientific diagrammatization of the brain has been mapped onto the spatial diagrammatics of the city. Education is one space in which learning algorithms are being deployed, but significantly illustrates the far wider implications of the neuro-turn for smart cities as they are being transformed by actors such as IBM into brain/code/spaces where nonconscious computing brains are embedded in the functioning of the environment and intended to weave into the cognitive experience of citizens. Of course, such processes should not be understood deterministically as if they would occur automatically. If, as Pykett (2013, p. 864) claims, the neuro knowledges are becoming part of a 'concerted attempt to re-imagine the human subject,' one identified in terms of the functioning of the brain, then the neuroscientific inspiration for cognitive classrooms and smart cities itself might be understood as changing how subjects are conceived, constituted, shaped, and managed – as subjects with interior plastic brains that can be optimized and modified through their exteriorization into neurocomputational cognitive systems. The neurotechnological dream of IBM is not simply to diagrammatize the brain, but to build brain-inspired applications that might transform current conceptions of the human subject. In doing so, it treats human cognition and computational cognition analogously, as systems of learning algorithms that can be constantly monitored, checked, re-wired, and optimized.

This initial exploration of IBM opens up a research agenda which would interrogate in more empirical depth the practices that brought these knowledges, techniques, and applications into being. With cognitive computing, the remaining sociological challenge is to trace how IBM and other actors have systemized the human brain as a complex neural network – in ways that align brain processes with computational processes – then proceduralized this knowledge in the design of applications that are intended to influence human neural morphology and cognitive functioning through the algorithmic learning environment itself. The plasticity of the socially learning brain modelled and codified in the learning algorithms of cognitive computing platforms is itself the product of practices performed by scientific and technical experts in concrete social and material circumstances, with a long genealogical provenance. Empirical research is required to detail how learning algorithms are designed to learn, to interrogate the models of the plasticity of the learning brain they operationalize, and to unpack the associated assumptions about managing, re-writing, and optimizing the brain on which they proceed.

In conclusion, the design of IBM's smarter classroom is just one instantiation of a contemporary set of algorithmic practices emerging from the fields of machine learning and cognitive computing and the associated imaginaries that animate their development. As a technological project based on a particular sociotechnical imaginary, IBM's Smarter Education ambitions exemplify its wider aspirations to produce smart cities that are conceived as 'naturally' cognitive environments, and where citizens themselves are conceived computationally in terms of their neurobiological malleability and amenability to algorithmic optimization. Its machine learning algorithms, neural networks algorithms, and other neurocomputational techniques of cognitive modelling are being designed to become part of urban environments in which 'an object need not be alive or conscious to function as a cognitive agent' (Hayles, 2014, p. 216). A novel kind of neurocomputational biopolitics is emerging from such practices, whereby the learning brain is imagined to be interacting with, and activated by, learning algorithms and the computing devices they enact in new kinds of brain/code/spaces. The potential consequences of such neurocomputational spaces extend beyond education to smart cities being designed by IBM to function through unsupervised machine learning processes and brain-inspired algorithms that can learn autonomously about and from the people and things that inhabit them. Such spaces are no longer hard-coded 'programmable cities,' but more 'naturally' cognitive cities with 'human qualities.' These neurotechnological applications also register the emergence of imagined 'neurofutures' based on a 'neuro-realist' set of 'brain facts' which assume that 'mental life can be understood, mapped, visualized, maintained, managed, improved, enhanced or optimized today or in the near future in these neuro-related, brain-based ways' (Williams et al., 2011, p. 136). By hybridizing neuroscientific knowledges about neuroplasticity and neural networks with new computational techniques and practices, IBM's imaginary of Smarter Education is part of a neurofuture for cities currently in-the-making, in which mental life is understood algorithmically in terms of the plasticity of neural networks and the brain's amenability to optimization.

Disclosure statement

No potential conflict of interest was reported by the author.

Funding

This research was supported with a grant from the Economic and Social Research Council [ref: ES/L001160/1]: https://codeactsineducation.wordpress.com/

References

Artificial Brains. (2013). DARPA SyNAPSE Program. Artificial Brains: The quest to build sentient machines. Retrieved January 11, 2013, from http://www.artificialbrains.com/darpa-synapse-program

Batty, M., Axhausen, K. W., Giannotti, F., Pozdnoukhov, A., Bazzani, A., Wachowicz, M., … Portugali, Y. (2012). Smart cities of the future. *The European Physical Journal Special Topics, 214*, 481–518.

Bayne, S. (2015). Teacherbot: Interventions in automated teaching. *Teaching in Higher Education, 20*(4), 455–467.

Beer, D. (2013). *Popular culture and new media: The politics of circulation.* London: Palgrave Macmillan.

Busso, D., & Pollack, C. (2015). No brain left behind: Consequences of neuroscience discourse for education. *Learning, Media and Technology, 40*(2), 168–186.

Crang, M., & Graham, S. (2007). Sentient cities: Ambient intelligence and the politics of urban space. *Information, Communication & Society, 10*(6), 789–817.

Dunn, N., Cureton, P. & Pollastri, S. (2014). *A visual history of the future.* Future of Cities: working paper. London: Foresight, Government Office for Science.

Eassom, S. (2015). IBM Watson for education. *IBM Insights on Business.* Retrieved April 1, 2015, from http://insights-on-business.com/education/ibm-watson-for-education-sector-deakin-university/

Fitzgerald, D., & Callard, F. (2015). Social science and neuroscience beyond interdisciplinarity: Experimental entanglements. *Theory, Culture & Society, 32*(1), 3–32.

Fitzgerald, D., & Rose, N. (2015). The neurosocial city. *Urban Transformations.* Retrieved from http://www.urbantransformations.ox.ac.uk/debate/the-neurosocial-city/

Gabrys, J. (2014). Programming environments: environmentality and citizen sensing in the smart city. *Environment & Planning D: Society & Space, 32*, 30–48.

Gillespie, T. (2014). Algorithm. *Culture Digitally.* Retrieved from http://culturedigitally.org/2014/06/algorithm-draft-digitalkeyword/

Goffey, A. (2008). Algorithm. In M. Fuller (Ed.), *Software studies: A lexicon* (pp. 15–20). London: MIT Press.

Hayles, N. K. (2013). *How we think: Digital media and contemporary technogenesis.* London: University of Chicago Press.

Hayles, N. K. (2014). Cognition everywhere: The rise of the cognitive nonconscious and the costs of consciousness. *New Literary History, 45*(2), 199–220.

IBM. (2013). In the future, everything will learn. Retrieved from http://www.ibm.com/smarterplanet/us/en/ibm_predictions_for_future/ideas/

IBM. (2014). *The future of learning: Enabling economic growth.* Somers, NY: IBM Corporation. Retrieved from http://www-01.ibm.com/common/ssi/cgi-bin/ssialias?subtype=WH&infotype=SA&appname=SNDE_ED_ED_USEN&htmlfid=EDW03005USEN&attachment=EDW03005USEN.PDF.

IBM. (2015a). Education for a smarter planet. Retrieved from http://www.ibm.com/smarterplanet/us/en/education_technology/ideas/

IBM. (2015b). What is IBM Watson? Retrieved from http://www.ibm.com/smarterplanet/us/en/ibmwatson/what-is-watson.html

IBM Research. (2011). IBM's first cognitive computing chips mimic functions of the brain. *IBM Research News.* Retrieved August 18, 2011, from http://ibmresearchnews.blogspot.co.uk/2011/08/this-cognitive-computing-chip-taught.html

IBM Research. (2013a). The classroom will learn you: Cognitive systems will provide decision support for teachers. Retrieved from www.research.ibm.com/cognitive-computing/machine-learning-applications/decision-support-education.shtml.

IBM Research. (2013b). A symbiotic cognitive experience: Human-computer collaboration at the speed of thought. Retrieved from http://researcher.ibm.com/researcher/view_group.php?id=5417

IBM Research. (2014). Brain Power: Scientists at IBM research unveil a brain-inspired computer and ecosystem. Retrieved from http://www.research.ibm.com/cognitive-computing/brainpower/

IBM Research. (2015). Cognitive computing. Retrieved from www.research.ibm.com/cognitive-computing

Jasanoff, S. (2015). Future imperfect: Science, technology, and the imaginations of modernity. In S. Jasanoff & S.-H. Kim (Eds.), *Dreamscapes of modernity: Sociotechnical imaginaries and the fabrication of power* (pp. 1–35). Chicago, IL: University of Chicago Press.

Kelly, J. E. III. (2015). *Computing, cognition and the future of knowing: How humans and machines are forging a new age of understanding.* Somers, NY: IBM Corporation. Retrieved from http://www.research.ibm.com/software/IBMResearch/multimedia/Computing_Cognition_WhitePaper.pdf

Kelly, J. E. III, & Hamm, S. (2014). *Smart machines: IBM's Watson and the era of cognitive computing.* New York, NY: Columbia University Press.

Kitchin, R. (2014a). The real-time city? Big data and smart urbanism. *GeoJournal, 79*, 1–14.

Kitchin, R. (2014b). *Thinking critically about and researching algorithms* (The Programmable City working paper 5). Retrieved from http://papers.ssrn.com/sol3/papers.cfm?abstract_id=2515786

Kitchin, R., & Dodge, M. (2011). *Code/space: Software and everyday life.* London: MIT Press.

Lemke, T. (2011). *Biopolitics: An advanced introduction.* London: New York University Press.

Linday, G. (2013). IBM'S department for education: The company that brought you smarter cities moves into schools. *Next City.* Retrieved from http://nextcity.org/features/view/ibms-department-of-education

Mackenzie, A. (2013). Programming subjects in the regime of anticipation: software studies and subjectivity. *Subjectivity, 6*(4), 391–405.

Mackenzie, A. (2015a). The production of prediction: What does machine learning want? *European Journal of Cultural Studies, 18*(4–5), 429–445.

Mackenzie, A. (2015b). Demis Hassabis: Mindful infrastructures and re-concatenated worlds. Retrieved from http://rian39.github.io/infrastructure/2015/02/06/Demis-Hassabis-Mindful-Infrastructures.html

Merolla, J., Cassidy, A. S., Sawada, J., Akopyan, F., Jackson, B. L., Imam, N., … Modha, D. S. (2014). A million spiking-neuron integrated circuit with a scalable communication network and interface. *Science, 345*(6197), 668–673.

Modha, D. (2013). Systems that perceive, think and act. *The Atlantic.* Retrieved June 2013, from http://www.theatlantic.com/sponsored/ibm-cognitive-computing/archive/2013/06/systems-that-perceive-think-and-act/276708/

Modha, D. (2014). Introducing a brain-inspired computer: TrueNorth's neurons to revolutionize system architecture. *IBM Research.* Retrieved from http://www.research.ibm.com/articles/brain-chip.shtml

Neyland, D. (2015). On organizing algorithms. *Theory, Culture & Society, 32*(1), 119–132.

Nitta, S. (2014). Cognitive learning content: A vision for how to make learning deeply engaging as well as intuitive. *IBM Insights on Business.* Retrieved May 14, 2014, from http://insights-on-business.com/education/cognitive-learning-content-a-vision-for-how-to-make-learning-deeply-engaging-as-well-as-intuitive/).

Pickersgill, M. (2013). The social life of the brain: Neuroscience in society. *Current Sociology, 61*(3), 322–340.

Piety, P. J., Hickey, D. T., & Bishop, M. J. (2014, March 24–28). Educational data sciences – Framing emergent practices for analytics of learning, organizations and systems. *LAK '14,* Indianapolis, IN, USA. Retrieved from http://edinfoconnections.com/wp-content/uploads/2014/01/Educational-Data-Sciences-Feb-9.pdf

Pykett, J. (2013). Neurocapitalism and the new neuros: using neuroeconomics, behavioural economics and picoeconomics for public policy. *Journal of Economic Geography, 13*, 845–869.

Pykett, J. (2015). *Brain culture: Shaping policy through neuroscience.* Bristol: Policy Press.

Rose, N. (2016). Reading the human brain: How the mind became legible. *Body and Society.* doi:10.1177/1357034X15623363

Rose, N., & Abi-Rached, J. (2013). *Neuro: The new brain sciences and the management of the mind.* Oxford: Princeton University Press.

Rose, N., & Abi-Rached, J. (2014). Governing through the brain: Neuropolitics, neuroscience and subjectivity. *The Cambridge Journal of Anthropology, 32*(1), 3–23.

Service, R. (2014). The brain chip. *Science, 345*(6197), 614–616.

Siemens, G. (2013). Learning analytics: The emergence of a discipline. *American Behavioral Scientist, 57*(10), 1380–1400.

Terdiman, D. (2015). IBM using Watson to build a "Siri For Cities." *Fast company*. Retrieved July 22, 2015, from http://www.fastcompany.com/3048905/app-built-with-ibms-watson-is-like-a-specialized-siri-for-cities

Thrift, N. (2014). The sentient city and what it may portend. *Big Data & Society, 1*(1). doi:10.1177/2053951714532241

Williams, S., Katz, S., & Martin, P. (2011). The neuro-complex: Some comments and convergences. *Media Tropes, 3*(1), 135–146.

Williamson, B. (2015). Educating the smart city: Schooling smart citizens through computational urbanism. *Big Data & Society, 2*(2), 1–13. doi:10.1177/2053951715617783

Scrutinizing an algorithmic technique: the Bayes classifier as interested reading of reality

Bernhard Rieder

ABSTRACT
This paper outlines the notion of 'algorithmic technique' as a middle ground between concrete, implemented algorithms and the broader study and theorization of software. Algorithmic techniques specify principles and methods for doing things in the medium of software and they thus constitute units of knowledge and expertise in the domain of software making. I suggest that algorithmic techniques are a suitable object of study for the humanities and social science since they capture the central technical principles behind actual software, but can generally be described in accessible language. To make my case, I focus on the field of information ordering and, first, discuss the wider historical trajectory of formal or 'mechanical' reasoning applied to matters of commerce and government before, second, moving to the investigation of a particular algorithmic technique, the *Bayes classifier*. This technique is explicated through a reading of the original work of M. E. Maron in the early 1960 and presented as a means to subject empirical, 'datafied' reality to an *interested reading* that confers meaning to each variable in relation to an operational goal. After a discussion of the Bayes classifier in relation to the question of power, the paper concludes by coming back to its initial motive and argues for increased attention to algorithmic techniques in the study of software.

Introduction

Since the popularization of the Internet, algorithmic procedures for information retrieval, ordering, and filtering have increasingly come into the focus of scholars in the humanities and social sciences. Search engines have been the most noticeable example. Their immense popularity has made the discussion of ranking procedures relevant to wider audiences, and the established field of web search studies (Zimmer, 2010) indicates continuing academic interest. The web also provides many other instances where algorithms select, hierarchize, suggest, and so forth: online sellers make automated product 'recommendations', dating sites calculate 'compatibility' coefficients between members and arrange them accordingly, news aggregators generate front pages according to measures of 'noteworthiness', social networking services filter friends' status updates based on 'closeness' metrics, and micro-blogging services give prominence to 'trending' topics based on sudden spikes in activity.

The terms between quotation marks highlight that we are dealing with cultural and thus highly ambiguous tasks being expressed as and delegated to mechanical procedures. A popular book by Eli Pariser (2011) lists many more cases of 'algorithmic sorting' (p. 72) and argues that the tendency to personalize information runs the risk of enclosing us in 'filter bubbles' that restrict us to 'information that conforms to our ideas of the world' (p. 52). While Pariser's take on the phenomenon is limited in terms of evidence, the book has the merit of having introduced a broad audience to a phenomenon that is undeniably real and arguably significant: algorithmic procedures – and the larger configurations they are embedded in – have indeed started to '[transform] the world we experience by controlling what we see and don't see' (p. 48).

There remains a stark contrast, however, between the increasingly accepted diagnosis that '[s]oftware structures and makes possible much of the contemporary world' (Fuller, 2008, p. 1) and the attention given to specific instances and precise methods. If software has indeed become a technique of power or, more accurately, a medium for designing and deploying complex techniques for 'conducting conduct' (Foucault, 2004a, p. 192), it is disconcerting that the critical analysis of concrete technical objects, procedures, and practices is exceedingly rare. Much like Pariser, scholars in the humanities and social sciences often prefer theorizing the social and political effects of software to the examination of the technical logics and arrangements that produce algorithmic enunciations in the first place. While software studies and related fields have begun to take up this work, there has been a focus on algorithmic *language*, code, rather than algorithmic *literature*, the programs designed and written in concrete settings with concrete goals in mind. While understanding the former is crucial, the actual landscape of existing software does not follow teleologically from the mere existence of computing machinery and programming languages. Software, like language, allow for the expression and mechanization of a wide range of ideas and objectives, even if basic principles and historically accumulated knowledge and convention structure possibilities and actual outcomes.

Some of the most promising efforts to 'study the algorithm' (Lazer, Kennedy, King, & Vespignani, 2014, p. 1205) have come from journalists adapting their 'traditional watchdogging [to] algorithmic accountability reporting' (Diakopoulos, 2015, p. 398), using reverse engineering techniques to reconstruct decision procedures. Emerging research methods for auditing algorithms point in a similar direction (cf. Custers, Calders, Schermer, & Zarsky, 2013; Sandvig, Hamilton, Karahalios, & Langbort, 2014; Sweeney, 2013). But there are limits to what one is able to infer from the outside, since information systems are often both complex and adaptive by design. These systems, however, do not sprout from an intellectual vacuum. Starting from the observation that the design of algorithmic procedures draws on rich reservoirs of knowledge made available by disciplines such as computer science and software engineering, this paper formulates an approach to the analysis of software that sits between broad theorizing and the empirical investigation of concrete applications of information ordering algorithms. This middle ground revolves around the finite set of well-known approaches to information filtering and classification that underpin most running systems. These standardized yet plastic methods, which I propose to call *algorithmic techniques*, are at the core of both software development practice and computer science education. In fact, learning how to program, in the sense of mastering a programming language, makes for only a small part of computer science education at the university level. A much larger portion is concerned with the many different and often math-heavy techniques that can be expressed in code and with how to apply them to the notorious 'real-world problems' students are set to encounter in concrete work settings. Algorithmic techniques are, in that sense, units of knowledge and expertise in the domain of software making. What Wing (2006) and others have called 'computational thinking' is precisely this: the capacity to abstract from a concrete situation to a level where familiar algorithmic techniques can be applied. This brings software specialists[1] in line with other methods experts, such as statisticians, operational researchers, or consultants, who master a set of methods and procedures they readily apply to diverse situations.

While algorithmic techniques are ultimately destined for implementation in software, they often begin with ideas that have little to do with computation. For example, there is nothing intrinsically computational about the inkling that spam messages can be identified by inspecting their textual content. But Graham's (2002) proposal to use a statistical classifier that treats every single word in a message as an indicator for 'spamminess' moves the initial intuition firmly into computational territory, even if actual programs may enact the idea in a variety of ways. The term 'statistical classifier', however, points not only to the larger space of probability theory, but also to a list of well-documented algorithmic techniques for performing statistical classification. Each technique revolves around a central idea, a conceptual core that is normally laid out in a combination of natural language and mathematical notation. The technique provides a general rationale and formal calculative specifications, but implementing these elements in a working system still requires many decisions to be made concerning the units to take into account, the parameters to specify, the tweaks to apply, the outputs to produce, and so forth. I would argue that the most concrete manifestation of cumulative *knowledge* in computer science and related disciplines is an ever-growing archive of techniques, ready to hand for those skilled to apply them. Code, then, is the medium to express these techniques in terms a computer can understand, and concrete algorithms are the outcome of situated encounters between computing environments, algorithmic techniques, and local requirements. I believe that the critical investigation of software and the various social roles it plays could greatly benefit from a deeper understanding of algorithmic techniques. To develop this argument in more detail, I propose to investigate a particular example from the field of information ordering.

The mention of spam filtering already points to the technique I will examine more closely in this paper since *Bayes classifiers* are commonly used for this task. Bayes classifiers are also often referred to as *Bayesian filters*, pointing to the observation that tasks like search, classification, and filtering are closely related from a technical perspective (cf., Belkin & Croft, 1992). I therefore use the term 'information ordering' to address these practices on the whole. Bayes classifiers provide a specific method for making use of statistical inference to sort a new element, for example, an incoming email, on the basis of a decision model derived from previously categorized elements, for example, messages already marked as spam. There are three main reasons for choosing this particular technique. *First*, Bayes classifiers are an instructive *pars pro toto* for contemporary information ordering. Since they are probabilistic (their classifications are not binary but with degrees of certainty), adaptive (they 'learn' from experience), and well suited for personalization, they allow for a discussion of aspects central to the wider field of machine learning. *Second*, the principles Bayes classifiers rely on are sufficiently simple to be laid out in ways that do not require familiarity with probability mathematics. *Third*, Bayes filters are caught up in a historical nexus – early information retrieval and text mining – that is both closely related to politically relevant applications in the present and instructive for the larger theoretical argument I want to make. While Bayes classifiers are only one of many techniques applicable to the tasks that prompt us to question the social power of algorithms in the first place, such as content filtering or recommendation and automated assessment of creditworthiness or job qualification, they represent instances of the *interested reading* of empirical, 'datafied'[2] reality that runs through these examples.

Tackling the question of the social power of algorithms through the critical examination of a particular technique implies a significant deviation from more common approaches that either discuss 'algorithms' as such, generalizing over the vast diversity of existing techniques, or examine a specific application domain (e.g., content filtering or credit scoring) or platform (e.g., Facebook) where algorithms perform crucial roles. The approach developed in this paper, however, aligns with the specific way algorithmic techniques are diverse and general at the same time: while every technique implies a particular way of doing things, they can often be applied to a wide array of domains if some basic requirements are met. As I will lay out in more detail below, these requirements can be quite general: for the application of a Bayes classifier, for example, one merely needs to squeeze the entities to classify into the form of objects that have some quantified properties and decide on a feedback or 'supervision' mechanism to train the statistical model. Besides emails, this can mean almost anything, including people, situations, and ideas.

When it comes to assessing the political significance of what was long called 'computerization', a beautifully unadorned term to capture the digital overhaul so many practices have become subjected to, there are basically three ideal-typical positions to take. The *first* considers that computers, software, and the experts accompanying them follow a singular logic, for example, that of instrumental reason. If that logic is found lacking, the political struggle revolves around the containment or reversal of computerization. This attitude manifests in the work of thinkers like Heidegger and Illich, or, more recently, in Golumbia's (2009) study of 'computationalism'. The *second* position sees technology merely as an epiphenomenon of social or economic forces, which means that studying these forces themselves would tell us all we need to know. Neither social constructivism at the micro level nor Marxist criticism at the macro level would see a particular need to study algorithmic techniques in any detail since they are consequences and not causes. While technology can become relevant through reification or productivity enhancement, the real sites of struggle are elsewhere. A *third* position, however, holds that computing technology can have considerable political significance without necessarily encapsulating a singular logic. This means that different forms of computerization are conceivable. Computers and software, here, are certainly considered to entail their own 'substance', even if their specificity lies not in a singular ideological imprint, but in the particular ways they represent and intervene in the world. This stance can be found in fields such as the 'values in design' movement (Nissenbaum, 2005) or in Philip Agre's work (Agre, 1997), and it implies reform and critical participation. If one espouses one of the first two positions, there is little reason to examine particular techniques in any detail since all they can ever be is the mere expression of broad logics or ideologies. For the third position, however, examining techniques matters, because it leads to an understanding of not only what they actually do and how they do it, but also what they *could* do or could do *differently*. If software is seen as a genuine form of cultural expression and intervention, the conceptual horizon mobilized in technical artifacts is a relevant object of study for the humanities and social sciences as well as a site for political assertion and struggle. This paper emphatically embraces the third position, but strives to remain sensitive to the arguments put forward by the other two. Despite my short and reductive presentation, we should discount neither the homogenizing effects of computational principles, ideas, and conventions, nor their deep entanglement with larger social and economic configurations. The margins of choice the third position emphasizes are not simply there, but need to be created, identified, articulated, and defended. In this spirit, I use the Bayes classifier example both as my case and to make my case.

Discussing a technique that produces a decision model based on the encounter between data and feedback, however, requires a broader introduction. When editors Joseph Becker and Robert M. Hayes (1963) inaugurated the *Information Sciences Series*, an influential book series published by Wiley & Sons from 1963 on, with the statement that '[i]nformation is the essential ingredient in decision making' (p. V), they explicitly tied the nascent discipline to the goal-driven pragmatism of management and operations research rather than to the scientific ideal of disinterested analysis and description. This points to a tradition of applying formal or 'mechanical' reasoning to matters of commerce and government that shares little with Leibniz' famed algebra of thought and the pure universalism of mathematical logic that is often emphasized in histories of computing. But the application of calculation to practical matters and, in particular, to the management of increasing organizational size and complexity (Beniger, 1986) has a long history that culminates in the emergence of statistics as the predominant way to look at and act in a world seen as dynamic and opaque.

Statistics and accounting realism

While the interface between calculation and reasoning has been amply studied through the history of the 'noble' field of logic, it was in the murky arenas of commerce and government that computation became an applied technique for practical decision-making. The advent of double-entry bookkeeping in the fifteenth century and the circulation of *algorismi* – manuals for learning applied arithmetic – both responded to and enabled growth in long-distance trade, where bigger ships and longer routes demanded larger organizational entities that, in turn, required means to manage complex logistics and the sharing of risk and profit. This 'elevated computation to the status of an empirical science' (Swetz, 1987, p. 295) that provided robust tools to control and decide, thereby stabilizing, standardizing, and systematizing how merchants managed their businesses and interacted with their peers. Uncertainty was not eliminated, but quantified as *risk*, calling for insurance rather than avoidance. William Petty's *Political Arithmetik* (1655) is notable for applying these commercial techniques to matters of government, leading to concrete recommendations concerning public investment and economic organization based on what we would today call cost–benefit analysis. Statistics, as the name indicates, is deeply intertwined with such attempts to develop a 'science of the state', a rational means to govern, manage, and decide.

Up to this day, the term statistics has kept a double meaning. On the one side, it refers to the collection of facts or *data*, which, in the nineteenth century, turned into an 'avalanche' (Hacking, 1990, p. 2) or 'deluge' (Cohen, 2005, p. 113) of tabulated numbers concerning many different subjects. This type of 'description by numbers' is what we mean when we talk about accident or employment statistics. On the other side, '[b]y 1889, users of statistics […] had become discontent with the mere presentation of numerical facts, and were looking for more refined methods of analysis' (Gigerenzer et al., 1989, p. 58), which led to the emergence of a series of mathematical techniques used to analyze and find patterns in collected data, for example, dependencies between variables. Both meanings refer to *epistemic* practices, that is, practices caught up in the production and definition of knowledge, but the latter indeed mobilizes mechanical reasoning in its fullest sense, as a purely formal transformation of one set of symbols into another that produces nonetheless an epistemic surplus in the process. The detection of a significant level of correlation between two variables is not simply a 'presentation of numerical fact'; it is a cognitive operation that generates an *interpretation* of the relationship between numbers and, by extension, the world they purport to describe.

At the same time, statistics is tied to a particular class of problems or, rather, of 'problematizations', the specific ways things are brought forward and framed as problems (Foucault, 1984, p. 17f). As a subfield of mathematics, statistics provides techniques for reasoning in situations where large numbers of entities behave in ways that can no longer be accounted for by modeling a single unit. Statistical mechanics, for example, materialized when it became clear that a description of the empirical behavior of gases based on the measurement of individual molecules would be utterly impossible. Similarly, as Foucault (2004b, p. 107f) points out, the study of epidemics and economic dynamics in the nineteenth century undermined the dominance of the family as a model for understanding and governing society. Instead, the *population* emerged as a proper conceptual entity, seen as giving rise to phenomena and dynamics that could not be reduced to its constituent parts. Both molecules and people could no longer be described in deterministic terms when encountered as 'living multiples' (Mackenzie & McNally, 2013). In both cases, statistics would resolve the supposed contradiction between uncertainty and control (Hacking, 1990) by providing the concepts and techniques to reason with and about multiples. The structure and dynamics of sets of similar but shifting entities or cases become, at the same time, *explanandum* and *explanans*. Statistics recognizes the problem of multiples as a defining characteristic of the world and develops notions such as regularity and variation, distribution and tendency, or dependence and correlation to examine, describe, and act on it.

Whether we fully accept the validity and utility of statistics' concepts and tools is secondary here; what counts is that 'in the operations of government, the conduct of business and finance, the activities of science and engineering, and even in some aspects of daily life' (Cohen, 2005, p. 17), statistical reasoning has become, long before the advent of computers, an accepted and 'trusted' (Porter, 1995) form of relating to the world, in terms of both understanding (interpretation) and intervention (decision-making). But as Desrosières (2001) notes, statistics permit different 'attitudes' towards the 'reality' they are meant to describe, different 'orchestrations of reality' (p. 346). 'Metrological realism' (p. 340), the correspondence or equivalence theory of truth, is but one of them. What we find in commerce and government, where statistics have come to play an even larger role than in science, is 'accounting realism', where the '"equivalence space" is composed not of physical quantities (space and time), but of a general equivalent: money' (p. 342). Here, the benchmark for the validity of a technique is no longer disinterested correspondence, but its usefulness for attaining specific goals.

Unsurprisingly, early Information Science turns mainly to statistics to solve its own problem of multiples and largely subscribes to the pragmatism of accounting realism. Not only Bush's (1945) famous paper laments the 'growing mountain of research' (p. 112) bogging down scientists; in the 1950s and 1960s, when many of the techniques and algorithms used to order information today were first laid out, there were few publications that did *not* invoke the growing mass and increased the speed of production of written information. In the process of developing mechanical approaches to *solve* this *problem*, knowledge, long understood as a coherent and consistent whole that needed to be mapped by enlightened individuals, came to be redefined as a complex, dynamic, and sprawling mass of documents that needed to be processed and 'mined' in relation to a specific, situated requirement. This meant a far-reaching investment in knowledge's computable substitute, *information*, and the development of 'information retrieval' (Mooers, 1950) as a set of methods for making decisions about documents.

A statistical approach to computing meaning

Interestingly, information retrieval employs the deeply ambiguous term 'information' first in its everyday meaning as akin to 'stored knowledge'. Unlike Shannon's *Theory of Communication*, which was concerned with the technical aspects of signal transmission, the nascent information sciences targeted what Weaver called the 'level B' of communication, that is, 'the semantic problem' (Shannon & Weaver, 1949, p. 4), that is, *meaning*. Often referred to in less intimidating terms such as 'aboutness' or 'relevance', handling meaning through information ordering became the central focus, even if this initially meant little more than selecting and ranking documents in relation to a query or 'question'. But the field evolved at a rapid pace. If we divide contemporary methods for information filtering into two rough groups, *content-based filtering* using properties of documents to decide what to do with them and *collaborative filtering* relying on social 'recommendation', a considerable part of the first group was essentially in place by 1975[3] and one could argue that the second group is at least partially anticipated by work in citation analysis dating back to the 1960s.

Content-based filtering, the field where Bayes classifiers where first developed, uses text – words, sentences, paragraphs, etc. – as a stand-in for meaning, as a raw material from which to infer 'aboutness' by means of computation. This effort relied on the realization, attributed to Alonzo Church and Alan Turing, 'that numbers were an inessential aspect of computation – they were just one way of interpreting the internal states of the machine' (Barr & Feigenbaum, 1981, p. 4), which meant that the 'digital handling of non-numerical information' (Mooers, 1950) became a plausible endeavor. Like its more illustrious cousin, artificial intelligence, information retrieval set out to extend the scope of mechanical reasoning to a domain previously considered a human privilege: the handling of knowledge. Rather than reconstruct the overall history of information retrieval any further, this section sets out to investigate a particular way this was envisioned concretely.

The Bayes classifier indeed epitomizes the application of statistics to Information Science's mission to process meaning and knowledge. The story begins in the late 1950s when M. E. Maron,[4] an analytical philosopher and cybernetician working at the

Ramo-Wooldridge Corporation and the (infamous) Rand Corporation before becoming a full professor at Berkeley's School of Information in 1966, 'was thinking hard about the problem of information retrieval' (Maron, 2008, p. 971). He was particularly unsatisfied with the practice of indexing documents, where assigning a tag to an item in order to describe its subject was 'a two-valued affair' (p. 971): a term was either attributed or not, nothing in between. The first improvement Maron, in collaboration with colleague J. L. Kuhns, proposed was for indexers to specify a value, somewhere between 0 and 1, to indicate a tag's *relevance* for a document. This method, named *probabilistic indexing*, made it possible, through inverse statistical inference via Bayes' theorem, to provide an automatically ranked result list for a subject query instead of merely an unordered set of documents (Maron & Kuhns, 1960).

Leaving aside its complicated history and various interpretations, Bayes' theorem basically provides a simple method to calculate the probability of a hypothesis based on existing knowledge. For example, if we know the percentage of women in a population and the a priori percentages of women and men with long hair, we can calculate the probability of the hypothesis that a person with long hair we see only from behind is a woman. In our case, the hypothesis concerns the probability that a document (tagged with a number of weighted terms) is relevant for a query (represented by a number of search terms that could also be weighted). Interestingly, Maron proposed from the outset to replace the a priori probability of a document (the equivalent of the 'percentage of women in a population'), which would normally be one divided by the number of documents in the collection, with statistics on document use. This choice introduces the much discussed principle of cumulative advantage or 'Matthew effect' (Merton, 1968) into the process, since documents with greater use will end up higher on the result list, in turn leading to even higher use. In the end, Maron's formula for relevance looked like this, using a dot product[5] to calculate the 'closeness' between query terms ('WordsQuery') and the document terms ('WordsDoc'):

$$P(\text{DocumentIsRelevant}) = (\text{WordsQuery} \cdot \text{WordsDoc}) * P(\text{DocumentUse}). \quad (1)$$

When searching for [hydraulics], a document tagged with 0.7 for that term would thus have a higher 'relevance number' than a document tagged with a value of 0.5. Documents accessed more often also received a higher value. Results were then ranked according to their relevance number. Term combinations and weighted search terms were possible as well. The method was still based on manual indexing, but represented nonetheless 'a theoretical attack which replaced traditional two-valued indexing and matching with a statistical approach [...] to make predictions about the relevance of documents in the collection' (Thompson, 2008, p. 964).

The indexing and ranking technique I just outlined is not a Bayes classifier, however. It introduced Bayes' theorem into information retrieval, but it was a second experiment that went further and attempted to do away with the human indexer – who was regarded by early information scientists as slow, unreliable, and biased – by using the full text of the document itself. Based on the assertion that 'statistics on kind, frequency, location, order, etc., of selected words are adequate to make reasonably good predictions about the subject matter of documents containing those words' (Maron, 1961, p. 405), Maron devised a technique for the automatic classification of documents: the Bayes classifier.

Classification, in terms of the probabilistic approach proposed by Maron, meant that text documents were to be sorted into user-specified subject categories: '[b]ased on some more or less clear notion of the category, we must decide whether or not an arbitrary document should be assigned to it' (Maron, 1961, p. 404). A simple contemporary example is indeed spam filtering: emails are documents and categories are *spam* and *not-spam*. Maron's technique conceived text documents as *objects* having certain *properties* (or features), which simply means that each text was represented by the finite list of words it contained as well as their frequency. These properties were considered to say at least *something* about the subject matter the document discusses – good enough for the pragmatic task of information retrieval. Today, such lists of quantified properties are generally referred to as *vectors* or *feature vectors*.

The first step was then to select a number of characteristic 'training' documents for each one of the subject categories – human intervention was thus rearranged, not eliminated – and to generate a combined word list for each category from the selected documents. Not all words were considered. Very frequent words and very rare words were discarded. The resulting selection was submitted to a technique similar in spirit to the now very common *term frequency – inverse document frequency* (tf*idf) metric introduced by Karen Spärck Jones (1972) in the early 1970s: words that are evenly distributed over all categories are considered inadequate 'clues' and thus rejected. For the words having sufficient 'specificity', an index was generated, where each word was attributed a relevance value for each category, determining 'certain probability relationships between individual content-bearing words and subject categories' (Maron, 1961, p. 405). In a nutshell: if a word appears very often in the training documents assigned to a certain category, but is rare for others, it becomes a strong *clue* or *indicator* for that category.

Once the training phase was complete, human intervention was no longer required: based on the general idea that a document should be attributed to a category if it contains many good indicators for it, new documents could be automatically classified. The calculative procedure was very similar to the ranking procedure outlined above, but instead of calculating the fit between query terms and document terms, the fit between the word list for a category and the word list for each incoming document was calculated. Since many words were taken into account, every document was likely to receive a relevance value for several categories, for example, document n is 0.8 relevant for category i, 0.5 for category j, and so forth, resulting in probabilistic rather than binary classification. The system was *adaptive* in the sense that it could allow for learning beyond the initial training: if a user decides to reclassify a document, the word lists for categories would be recalculated, adding the new 'knowledge' to the statistical model.

This is the basic outline of a Bayes classifier and a surprisingly representative illustration of the larger field of contemporary machine learning techniques. Since the approach assumes statistical independence between words, it is more specifically called a 'naive' Bayes classifier, but almost all modern techniques such as maximum entropy classifiers or support vector machines use the same feature vectors as starting point, even if the mathematical procedures applied differ. There are a number of important aspects to consider.

First, the procedure I have just described is precisely what the term 'algorithmic technique' attempts to thematize. What I have just laid out in plain English is not *yet* an algorithm in a more restrictive understanding of the term, but it outlines a method for classification that entails a way of both looking at and acting in and on the world. It frames and formalizes text documents as word frequency lists, formulates a sequence of stages from training to classification to adjustment, and specifies a number of proto-mathematical functions for weighing and calculating. Any software developer would be able to create a working program from my description, but every implementation would be different since many details remain unspecified and require decisions. Should words be reduced to their stems? Where to cut off frequent and infrequent words? How to calculate word specificity? These and other questions need to be answered when an algorithmic technique is brought to bear on a specific task in a specific operating environment. A concrete algorithm is the outcome of that process. This means that the study of algorithmic techniques is not enough to make sense of actual systems, their behavior, and the many specific commitments they imply. But a robust understanding of common techniques can both ground more general forms of theorizing in the actual rationales underpinning software making and inform more concrete forms of empirical analysis. It can lay the ground work for comparison between different implementations by proving analytical categories – for example, selected units and features, training and feedback setup, and decision modalities – that span these cases.

Second, the given example of text classification is but one application of a more general technique. Maron's work relies on a specific framing of texts as quantified lists of words, completely ignoring aspects such as order, syntax, or style. Meaning is thus conceived in a highly reductive manner and although systems using broader and deeper understandings of language both can and do exist, any running system requires and relies in some way on selection, formalization, and reduction. Datafication thereby translates fundamental assumptions about the application domain into data structures and reifies them. This more often than not implies not only reduction, but also *reduction to a common form*, a movement that underpins generalization and explains how techniques can be applied to a wide variety of domains. Bayes classifiers are applicable to all entities that can be represented as feature vectors, that is, lists of valued properties. Songs can be grouped based on which users listened to them[6]; locations and situations can be classified based on the characteristics and behavior of associated populations; applicants for credit can be approved or denied based on their Facebook profiles. But in all of these cases, *someone* has to make decisions on what and how to formalize and then to specify classes and attribute a minimum number of elements to these classes for the filter to begin its work. Other classification techniques will involve a different dramaturgy of steps and actors, but their field of application is bound to be comparably wide. If we think of user interfaces, tracking techniques, and – increasingly – sensors as devices that channel aspects of human practice into formal data structures, it is no wonder that many of the techniques pioneered in information retrieval from the 1950s on have seen a second spring with the popularization of the Internet. The more things we do with digital appliances involved, the greater the number of entities and phenomena that can be formalized as objects and properties in the way just described. The ensuing proliferation of problems involving large sets of entities in already computerized settings makes algorithmic solutions almost inevitable.

Third, a Bayes classifier arranges decision-making in a way that is profoundly different from the common framing of algorithms as *formulas*. Even in academic publications, the prevalent conception seems to imagine a group of developers enumerating variables to take into account and specifying how to couple and weigh them. The makers of Facebook, for example, would brood over the criteria for Newsfeed filtering, meticulously arranging metrics such as affinity between users, post engagement, and some function of time to produce a clear decision recipe that is guarded like a precious secret. But this conception is increasingly incomplete and outdated; techniques such as Bayes classifiers propose the means to derive decision models from the encounter between some *data*, a *purpose*, and a mechanism for *feedback*. In the case of Bayesian spam filtering, nobody has to manually compile a list of 'spammy' words and weigh them. What happens is that in a first step classes are defined on the basis of what the classification is supposed to achieve, its purpose; in our case the sorting of emails into spam and not-spam. When a user begins to mark messages, the list of weighted words is generated automatically, producing a basis for decision-making that is not a clear-cut formula, but an adaptive statistical model containing potentially hundreds of thousands of variables. When a payday lender uses Facebook data to decide whether an applicant is likely to pay back a loan, there is no need for a Bourdieusian sociologist who tags every possible profile element in terms of class membership. It is enough to have a number of profiles of users who have *already* paid back or defaulted on their loans to generate a model where every single profile item becomes an indicator for 'creditworthiness'. Facebook can develop its Newsfeed filtering engine in a very similar way, using something like 'time on site' or 'ad click probability' as a criterion to determine which visibility parameters are optimal for every user, individually. Instead of selecting and weighing variables manually, the classifier derives – or 'learns' – optimal parameters from the relation between data (posts that have different properties), feedback (a user's engagement with these posts), and a purpose (increasing engagement further). The system is then able to execute the following command: 'show to the user the posts similar to those that previously led to high engagement'. The Bayes classifier is thus neither a static recipe for decision-making nor a theory engaged in ontological attribution; it is a method for making data signify in relation to a particular desire to *distinguish*; it is a device for the automated production of *interested* readings of empirical reality. Maron's goal was not to say anything deep about the relationship between text and meaning, but to design a system that produces 'good' results in the domain of its application. I thus use the term 'interested' to emphasize that the epistemic process is not just tainted by some unavowed bias, but fully designed around an explicit purpose that trumps any epistemological or ontological qualms one may have. Just as Desrosières' (2001) notion of accounting realism suggests, 'the goal is no longer truth, but performativity – that is, the best possible input/output equation' (Lyotard, 1984, p. 46).

Fourth, the technique does not determine the performativity of the resulting algorithm. The Bayes classifier provides the capacity for making interested readings, but specifies neither the purpose nor the way a decision is connected back to the world. Facebook can decide to train its Newsfeed engine based on any criterion the company could come up with. Does this make Bayes classifiers 'neutral' tools? Mackenzie (2015) argues that 'as machine learning is generalized, the forms of value that circulate in the form of commodities alter' (p. 444), emphasizing that the different technical 'styles' of processing 'entail different kinds of value' (p. 436). Seen as interested readings of datafied reality, one could push even further and argue that data mining techniques embody forms of cognition, specific styles of perception that, on the one side, are non-anthropomorphic in the sense that they consist of procedures that can only be enacted by fast computing machinery, and, on the other side, are thoroughly entangled with operational arrangements. On the level of signification, data mining techniques attribute meaning to every variable in relation to a purpose; on the level of performativity, the move to increasingly integrated digital infrastructures means that every classificatory decision can be pushed back into the world instantly, showing a specific ad, hiding a specific post, refusing a loan to a specific applicant, setting the price of a product to a specific level, and so forth. No data point remains innocent. If we consider power to operate as a 'network of relations' (Foucault, 1975, p. 31), we can appreciate how data mining delivers specific ways of establishing, organizing, and modulating relations between datafied entities in service of strategic goals. Even if Bayes classifiers do not determine how their results are used at the interface level and beyond, they stand for a new set of technologies that produce deeply 'interested' knowledge, use it to make decisions with concrete effects, and thereby introduce a 'microphysics'[7] that has the potential to profoundly affect how power operates.

Fifth, as already mentioned, Bayes filters are ideal for personalization and it should come as no surprise that the first attempt (Rich, 1983) to personalize information retrieval for individuals and not just user categories (novice, expert, etc.) relied on a probabilistic method close to the one just described. Although there is, again, no technical imperative to produce a separate statistical model for each user, information retrieval renounced, from the beginning, the universalist notions of order we find in most knowledge classification systems used in libraries or encyclopedias. Even early systems emphasized the query over the database and attempted to transfer as much expressivity as possible to users, generally imagined as scientists who know very well what they are looking for. Systems were not conceptualized as convenient access points to stable trees of knowledge, but as *engines of order*, capable of projecting latent structures present in the data in a myriad of ways. As the filter bubble debate shows, liberal societies in particular are marked by the tension between universalism and perspectivism, and the Internet has further exacerbated the issue by, on the one side, uniting unprecedented numbers of people in front of the very same interfaces and, on the other, making it possible to serve each person something different. Bayes classifiers, as an instance of a larger group of techniques, are at the very center of this conundrum.

Standing in for the wider category of information ordering techniques, Bayes classifiers entangle meaning – and not just the meaning of texts – in complex and often very direct ways with decision-making informed by specific objectives and purposes. In a sense, Bacon's famous distinction between *is* and *ought* disappears in a form of description that is built, from the ground up, on a prescriptive horizon. We no longer (only) decide based on what we know; we know based on the decision we have to make.

To close this paper, then, I want to come back to the beginning of the argument and argue why it is worthwhile to study algorithmic techniques in the first place.

Why study algorithmic techniques?

Our relationship with tools and machines has been – at least since the Industrial Revolution – highly ambiguous. Hailed or derided, technology rarely leaves indifferent, at least until it fades into the fabric of everyday life. Particularly since World War II, humanities scholars have proposed their own assessment, often in rather pessimistic accounts. But in most cases, these accounts have not taken the form of engagement with concrete technical objects and procedures; at the same time, the supposed autonomy of technological development has been regularly lamented. But could it be that this autonomy is a *consequence* of the lack of engagement with technology as technology, that is, as a vast ensemble of objects, techniques, and practices that can only be squeezed into the concept of *techne* at the price of extreme reduction?

For Simondon (2014), the technical object gains its *objectal* dimension, that is, its place in economic, social, and psychosocial relations, on the basis of its *objective* dimension, that is, its technical operation. Technology (*la technique*) is seen as one of the fundamental ways, next to religion, science, or art, in which human beings relate to the world: 'What resides in machines is human reality, human gesture, fixed and crystallized in structures that function' (Simondon, 1958, p. 12, author's translation). It is as 'beings that function' (Simondon, 2014, p. 138) that machines acquire meaning and not merely through cultural embedding. The assessment of the social role a technical object plays must, therefore, start from its 'functional meaning' (p. 28),that is, from what it does and how it does it. Building on this ground, I would like to put forward four arguments in favor of a more extensive engagement with algorithmic techniques.

First, insufficient attention to technical aspects and technical knowledge increases the risk that critique engages a straw man rather than the actual thing. Winner's diagnosis that 'our standard conceptions of technology reveal disorientation that borders on dissociation from reality' (Winner, 1978, p. 8) rings true more than ever. I hope that the Bayes classifier example has made amply clear that contemporary techniques for ordering information, and thus the many entities information can stand for, are not simply transpositions or extensions of older principles of cataloguing and classification into the digital space, even if interfaces employ familiar metaphors. As I have tried to show, there is a certain continuity or resonance with earlier forms and applications of mechanical reasoning. Through statistics, '[p]robability theory has become the arbiter of practical rationality' (Gigerenzer et al., 1989, p. 255), but the computer has greatly enhanced its scope and sheer power. However, when it comes to understanding how software operates, misconceptions abound. We can still read that '[l]ogical rules allow for no substantive ambiguity; either a proposition follows or it does not' (Golumbia, 2009, p. 194), although non-monotonic, many-valued, or probabilistic logics have been central to computer science from its beginning. Bayes classifiers are perfect examples for techniques that will answer the question whether a document belongs to a certain category not with a 'yes' or a 'no', but rather with '0.7'. While the truly continuous, itself cast in doubt by quantum theory, is indeed outside of the domain of (digital) computers, the 'gradable and fuzzy' (Golumbia, 2009, p. 21) has been expressible in computational terms for a long, long time. This is essential to the appreciation of the political dimension of software; when thinking about *control* through algorithms, we should rely less on Leibniz' calculating philosophers as a guiding metaphor, and more on Petty's cost–benefit analyses operating today through concepts such as probability, average, margin, distribution, correlation, order, threshold, variation, tendency, distance, equilibrium, and so forth. Google may be an advertising company first, but it is a statistics company second. In the end, whether politically relevant phenomena such as filter bubbles are an accurate diagnosis, a straw man, or simply a pleasant moral panic needs to be *established*. Technical description is a necessary step toward demystification.

Second, by looking at concrete technical artifacts – whether they are techniques or concrete implementations – the misleading opposition between objectivity and subjectivity and, in particular, the dichotomy between judgment and calculation can be addressed in a different light. The term 'qualculation' (Cochoy, 2002) is useful here, because even purely computational procedures rely on extensive *work* that is not calculative. Maron's decision to formalize texts as word frequencies was designed to enable computation, not a result of computation. Callon and Law's (2005) argument that the notion of calculation should not be contrasted with (human) judgment, but rather extended to include it fully applies. This does not mean that all forms of reasoning are equivalent. One can safely say that Dean Baquet, executive editor of the New York Times, and Krishna Bharat, creator of the automated news aggregator Google News, both hold considerable influence over the news people read every day; but their 'power' is configured quite differently, operating through different techniques and mechanisms. Following Callon and Law, we can describe both configurations as qualculative in the sense that in both cases the decisions leading to actual outcomes combine elements of calculation – even the New York Times does not ignore its sales figures – and judgment. The differences in *how* they qualculate are significant, however. As previously noted, mechanical reasoning does not eliminate power, but reconfigures it and shifts human discretion from the definition of outcomes to the definition of procedures, mechanisms, or techniques that *produce* outcomes. The difference between The New York Times and Google News is important, but it cannot be reduced to the difference between judgment and calculation. Looking at Bayes classifiers, we see that moments of choice abound: the selection of training documents, the elimination of words, the setting of thresholds and cut-off points, the commitment to a rote theory of language that takes word frequencies as indicators of meaning, the various ways of coordinating between the classifier and the interface, and the choice to use *a* probabilistic method and *this* probabilistic method in the first place. Paradoxically, it seems that the more we calculate, the more judgment is required. This change in perspective should prompt us to trade the stale question whether algorithms are 'objective' or not for an investigation into the interpretative commitments, purposes, and benchmarks specific calculative assemblages subscribe to. The study of algorithmic techniques cannot replace the empirical analysis of the concrete sites and implementations where these decisions are ultimately made, but it can go far in informing such an endeavor.

Third, it is becoming increasingly clear that algorithms – often based on probability techniques – are playing a crucial role in deciding how information circulates, how people find and relate to each other, and how conduct is indeed conducted. And while nearly every technique leaves room for many decisions and can be developed into various directions, its conceptual horizon still implies an epistemological orientation and specific forms of intervention. A critique needs to understand the paradoxical relationship between standardization and variation that characterizes software more often than not. Despite my emphasis of the 'purpose' or performance criterion above, the technicity of the Bayes classifier is not dissolved in its finality; rather, it presents a *specific* way to read and act on the world in relation to a specific purpose. A wider theory of Bayes classifiers, and, in extension, of machine learning, is both possible and desirable. Desrosières' (2001, p. 342) argument that accounting realism installs money as general equivalent brings us back to the entanglement with larger social and economic configurations I mentioned above. While I do not believe that there is necessarily a fatal connection between machine learning and advanced capitalism, it is hard to ignore how perfectly the interested readings these techniques perform fit into a system that attempts to extract monetary value from the exploitation of increasingly infinitesimal differences. A general theory of algorithmic techniques will have to accept that the objective and objectal dimensions, to use Simondon's terms again, cannot be held separate indefinitely.

Fourth, a lack of engagement with concrete technological procedures further cements the cultural and epistemological rift between humanists and engineers. There is a vast gap between the well-meant appeals by Pariser (2011), asking companies and engineers to design algorithms that favor 'diversity' and 'serendipity' instead of enclosing us in filter bubbles that narrow our horizon, and the concepts, languages, and techniques that guide actual implementations. This gap needs to be bridged in a more fundamental way than the superficial and increasingly managerial notion of *interdisciplinarity* allows, if we want to make information filtering a political issue in more precise terms. If 'diversity' and 'serendipity' are not to mean randomness, we will have to think about the concrete meaning we want to give to these terms, and this meaning will have to find a way of expressing itself in the medium of computation. This is not simply a translation from one discipline into another, for example, from political science into computer science, but a much more complicated process that requires a painstaking production of a precarious association between fundamentally different forms of expression. While I agree with Mackenzie (2015, p. 436) that it is not essential to have a detailed grasp of how data mining methods work, I believe that an understanding on the more general level of algorithmic techniques is both attainable and necessary. My technical presentation of the Bayes classifier certainly omitted many aspects that any computer or information scientist would consider to be essential. My goal, however, was to find a level of description where an encounter between technical and larger cultural principles becomes possible, a level where neither 'side' is reduced to a caricature. We can certainly envision a broad critique of a particular style of data mining, for example, the probabilistic style. But when we understand that 'probabilistic', here, means that each property of a formalized entity is framed as an indicator for membership in a set of predefined classes, our critique will maybe be able to produce actual suggestions. Could we show users which properties contributed most to a decision? Could we make property or value selection available on the interface? Could we make training principles explicit? Could we make probabilistic associations fade over time? Could we define exceptions? These suggestions are mere stumps, but they can maybe illustrate how a deeper yet still pre-formal understanding of algorithmic techniques in the humanities and social sciences could lead to the emergence of a trading zone where the false opposition between culture and technology (Simondon, 1958, p. 9) no longer applies.

Notes

1. There are considerable differences between types of 'software makers', but all of them employ algorithmic techniques in various ways. The information ordering techniques this paper focuses on result from intensive research activity in academic computer and information science, but they are now readily available to most developers through software libraries and extensive documentation.
2. I use this term in loose reference to Mayer-Schönberger and Cukier's notion of *datafication*: 'data refers to a description of something that allows it to be recorded, analyzed, and

reorganized. [...] To datafy a phenomenon is to put it in a quantified format so it can be tabulated and analyzed' (Mayer-Schönberger & Cukier, 2013, p. 78). I consider datafication not a neutral process, but as always implying purposeful selection, framing, and mediation.

3. This is the year the highly influential 'vector space model' was formally introduced (Salton, Wong, & Yang, 1975). Anecdotally, Salton was the Ph.D. advisor of Amit Singhal, the current head of Google's Search division.

4. This paper focuses on the work by M. E. Maron, although a fuller account would have to include the contributions made by Solomonoff (1957).

5. A dot product is the sum of the products of two sequences of numbers. For example, the dot product between the query {hydraulics: 0.7, car: 0.5} and the document terms {hydraulics: 0.6, car: 0.8} would be 0.7 * 0.6 + 0.5 * 0.8, thus 0.82. The more terms overlap between a query and a document and the higher the weight of the terms, the more 'relevant' the document.

6. In Maron's work, a document was represented as a list of words and their frequency, for example, doc1:{word1:5, word2, 10, ...}. A classification of music according to user listens could represent each song as the list of users that listened to it and how often: song1: {user1:5, user2:10, ...}.

7. Foucault (1975, p. 31) introduces the term to address the many subtle, diffuse, and productive technologies of power that operate on bodies in various ways.

Acknowledgements

The author would like to thank Fernando van der Vlist and the two anonymous reviewers for their valuable feedback.

Disclosure statement

No potential conflict of interest was reported by the author.

References

Agre, P. E. (1997). Toward a critical technical practice. In G. C. Bowker, S. L. Star, W. Turner, & L. Gasser (Eds.), *Social science, technical systems and cooperative work: Beyond the great divide* (pp. 131–156). Mahwah, NJ: Erlbaum.

Barr, A., & Feigenbaum, E. A. (1981). *The handbook of artificial intelligence* (Vol. 1). Los Altos, CA: William Kaufman.

Becker, J., & Hayes, R. M. (1963). *Information storage and retrieval: Tools, elements, theories.* New York, NY: Wiley.

Belkin, N. J., & Croft, W. B. (1992). Information filtering and information retrieval: Two sides of the same coin? *Communications of the ACM, 35,* 29–38.

Beniger, J. R. (1986). *The control revolution. Technological and economic origins of the information society.* Cambridge, MA: Harvard University Press.

Bush, V. (1945, October 9). As we may think. *Life Magazine.*

Callon, M., & Law, J. (2005). On qualculation, agency, and otherness. *Environment and Planning D: Society and Space, 23*(5), 717–733.

Cochoy, F. (2002). *Une sociologie du packaging, ou l'âne de Buridan face au marché*. Paris: Presses Universitaires de France.

Cohen, I. B. (2005). *The triumph of numbers: How counting shaped modern life*. New York, NY: W. W. Norton.

Custers, B., Calders, T., Schermer, B., & Zarsky, T. (Eds.). (2013). *Discrimination and privacy in the information society. Data mining and profiling in large databases*. Berlin, Heidelberg: Springer.

Desrosières, A. (2001). How real are statistics? Four possible attitudes. *Social Research, 68*(2), 339–355.

Diakopoulos, N. (2015). Algorithmic accountability. *Digital Journalism, 3*(3), 398–415.

Foucault, M. (1975). *Surveiller et punir: naissance de la prison*. Paris: Gallimard.

Foucault, M. (1984). *L'usage des plaisirs: histoire de la sexualité II*. Paris: Gallimard.

Foucault, M. (2004a). *Naissance de la biopolitique*. Paris: Gallimard.

Foucault, M. (2004b). *Sécurité, territoire, population*. Paris: Gallimard.

Fuller, M. (2008). *Software studies: A Lexicon*. Cambridge, MA: MIT Press.

Gigerenzer, G., Swijtnik, Z., Porter, T., Daston, L., Beatty, J., & Krüger, L. (1989). *The empire of chance. How probability changed science and everyday life*. Cambridge: Cambridge University Press.

Golumbia, D. (2009). *The cultural logic of computation*. Cambridge, MA: Harvard University Press.

Graham, P. (2002). A plan for spam. Retrieved from http://www.paulgraham.com/spam.html

Hacking, I. (1990). *The taming of chance*. Cambridge: Cambridge University Press.

Lazer, D., Kennedy, R., King, G., & Vespignani, A. (2014). The parable of Google flu: Traps in big data analysis. *Science, 343*, 1203–1205.

Lyotard, J.-F. (1984). *The postmodern condition: A report on knowledge*. Manchester: Manchester University Press.

Mackenzie, A. (2015). The production of prediction: What does machine learning want? *European Journal of Cultural Studies, 18*(4–5), 429–445.

Mackenzie, A., & McNally, R. (2013). Living multiples: How large-scale scientific data-mining pursues identity and differences. *Theory, Culture & Society, 30*(4), 72–91.

Maron, M. E. (1961). Automatic indexing: An experimental inquiry. *Journal of the ACM, 8*, 404–417.

Maron, M. E. (2008). An historical note on the origins of probabilistic indexing. *Information Processing and Management, 44*, 971–972.

Maron, M. E., & Kuhns, J. L. (1960). On relevance, probabilistic indexing and information retrieval. *Journal of the ACM, 7*, 216–244.

Mayer-Schönberger, V., & Cukier, K. (2013). *Big data. A revolution that will transform how we live, work, and think*. Boston, MA; New York, NY: Houghton Mifflin Harcourt.

Merton, R. K. (1968). The Matthew effect in science: The reward and communication systems of science are considered. *Science, 159*(3810), 56–63.

Mooers, C. (1950). *The theory of digital handling of non-numerical information and its implications to machine economics*. Boston, MA: Zator.

Nissenbaum, H. (2005). Values in technical design. In C. Mitcham (Ed.), *Encyclopedia of science, technology, and ethics* (pp. 66–70). New York, NY: Macmillan.

Pariser, E. (2011). *The filter bubble: What the Internet is hiding from you*. New York, NY: Penguin Press.

Petty, W. (1655). *Several essays in political Arithmetik* (4th ed.). London: D. Browne, J. Shuckburgh, J. Wiston, B. White.

Porter, T. (1995). *Trust in numbers. The pursuit of objectivity in science and public life*. Princeton, NJ: Princeton University Press.

Rich, E. (1983). Users are individuals: Individualizing user models. *International Journal of Man-Machine Studies, 18*, 199–214.

Salton, G., Wong, A., & Yang, C. S. (1975). A vector space model for automatic indexing. *Communications of the ACM, 18*, 613–620.

Sandvig, C., Hamilton, K., Karahalios, K., & Langbort, C. (2014, May). Paper presented at the 64th Annual Meeting of the International Communication Association, Seattle, USA.

Shannon, C., & Weaver, W. (1949). *The mathematical theory of communication*. Urbana: University of Illinois Press.

Simondon, G. (1958). *Du mode d'existence des objets techniques*. Paris: Presses Universitaires de France.

Simondon, G. (2014). *Sur la technique (1953–1983)*. Paris: Presses Universitaires de France.

Solomonoff, R. J. (1957). *An inductive inference machine*. IRE Convention Record.

Spärck Jones, K. (1972). A statistical interpretation of term specificity and its application in retrieval. *Journal of Documentation, 28*(1), 11–21.

Sweeney, L. (2013). Discrimination in online Ad delivery. *Communications of the ACM, 56*(5), 44–54.

Swetz, F. J. (1987). *Capitalism and arithmetic. The new math of the 15th century*. La Salle: Open Court.

Thompson, P. (2008). Looking back: On relevance, probabilistic indexing and information retrieval. *Information Processing and Management, 44*, 963–970.

Wing, J. (2006). Computational thinking. *Communications of the ACM, 49*(3), 33–35.

Winner, L. (1978). *Autonomous technology: Technics-out-of-control as a theme in political thought*. Cambridge, MA: MIT Press.

Zimmer, M. (2010). Web search studies: Multidisciplinary perspectives on web search engines. In J. Hunsinger, M. Allen, & L. Klastrup (Eds.), *International handbook of Internet research* (pp. 507–522). Dordrecht: Springer.

'Hypernudge': Big Data as a mode of regulation by design

Karen Yeung

ABSTRACT

This paper draws on regulatory governance scholarship to argue that the analytic phenomenon currently known as 'Big Data' can be understood as a mode of 'design-based' regulation. Although Big Data decision-making technologies can take the form of automated decision-making systems, this paper focuses on algorithmic decision-guidance techniques. By highlighting correlations between data items that would not otherwise be observable, these techniques are being used to shape the informational choice context in which individual decision-making occurs, with the aim of channelling attention and decision-making in directions preferred by the 'choice architect'. By relying upon the use of 'nudge' – a particular form of choice architecture that alters people's behaviour in a predictable way without forbidding any options or significantly changing their economic incentives, these techniques constitute a 'soft' form of design-based control. But, unlike the static Nudges popularised by Thaler and Sunstein [(2008). *Nudge*. London: Penguin Books] such as placing the salad in front of the lasagne to encourage healthy eating, Big Data analytic nudges are extremely powerful and potent due to their networked, continuously updated, dynamic and pervasive nature (hence 'hypernudge'). I adopt a liberal, rights-based critique of these techniques, contrasting liberal theoretical accounts with selective insights from science and technology studies (STS) and surveillance studies on the other. I argue that concerns about the legitimacy of these techniques are not satisfactorily resolved through reliance on individual notice and consent, touching upon the troubling implications for democracy and human flourishing if Big Data analytic techniques driven by commercial self-interest continue their onward march unchecked by effective and legitimate constraints.

1. Introduction

It is claimed that society stands at the beginning of a New Industrial Revolution, powered by the engine of Big Data. This paper focuses on how industry is harnessing Big Data to transform personal digital data into economic value, described by one leading cyberlawyer as the 'latest form of bioprospecting' (Cohen, 2012). Although the term 'Big Data' is widely used, no universal definition has yet emerged. Big Data is essentially shorthand for the combination of a technology and a process (Cohen, 2012, p. 1919). The technology is a configuration of information-processing hardware capable of sifting, sorting and interrogating vast quantities of data very quickly. The process involves mining data for patterns, distilling the patterns into predictive analytics and applying the analytics to new data. Together, the technology and the process comprise a methodological technique that utilises analytical software to identify patterns and correlations through the use of machine-learning algorithms applied to (often unstructured) data items contained in multiple data sets, converting these data flows into a particular, highly data-intensive form of knowledge (Cohen, 2012, p. 1919). A key contribution of Big Data is the ability to find useful correlations within data sets *not capable of analysis by ordinary human assessment* (Shaw, 2014). As boyd and Crawford observe,

> Big Data's value comes from patterns that can be derived from making connections about pieces of data, about an individual, about individuals in relation to others, about groups of people, or simply about the structure of information itself. Big Data is important because it refers to an analytic phenomenon playing out in academia and industry. (2012, p. 662)

It is this understanding of Big Data, as both a methodological approach and an analytic phenomenon, that this paper adopts.

I argue that Big Data's extensive harvesting of personal digital data is troubling, not only due to its implications for privacy, but also due to the *particular way* in which that data are being utilised to shape individual decision-making to serve the interests of commercial Big Data barons. My central claim is that, despite the complexity and sophistication of their underlying algorithmic processes, these applications ultimately rely on a deceptively simple design-based mechanism of influence – 'nudge'. By configuring and thereby personalising the user's informational choice context, typically through algorithmic analysis of data streams from multiple sources claiming to offer predictive insights concerning the habits, preferences and interests of targeted individuals (such as those used by online consumer product recommendation engines), these nudges channel user choices in directions preferred by the choice architect through processes that are subtle, unobtrusive, yet extraordinarily powerful. By characterising Big Data analytic techniques as a form of nudge, this provides an analytical lens for evaluating their persuasive, manipulative qualities and their legal and political dimensions. I draw on insights from regulatory governance scholarship, behavioural economics, liberal political theory, information law scholarship, Science & Technology Studies (STS) and surveillance studies to suggest that, if allowed to continue unchecked, the extensive and accelerating use of commercially driven Big Data analytic techniques may seriously erode our capacity for democratic participation and individual flourishing.

2. Big Data as a form of design-based regulation

My analysis begins by explaining how Big Data algorithmic techniques seek systematically to influence the behaviour of others, drawing on a body of multidisciplinary scholarship concerned with interrogating 'regulatory governance' regimes and various facets of the regulatory governance process.

2.1. Design-based regulatory techniques

Regulation or regulatory governance is, in essence, a form of systematic control intentionally aimed at addressing a collective problem. As Julia Black puts it, '[r]egulation, or regulatory governance, is the organised attempt to manage risks or behaviour in order to achieve a publicly stated objective or set of objectives' (Black, 2014, p. 2).[1] Many scholars analyse regulation as a cybernetic process involving three core components that form the basis of any control system – that is, ways of gathering information ('information gathering and monitoring'); ways of setting standards, goals or targets ('standard-setting') and ways of changing behaviour to meet the standards or targets ('behaviour modification') (Hood, Rothstein, & Baldwin, 2001). Within this literature, the techniques employed by regulators to attain their desired social outcome are well established as an object of study (Morgan & Yeung, 2007). While legal scholars tend to focus on traditional 'command and control' techniques in which the law prohibits specified conduct, backed by coercive sanctions for violation, cyberlawyers and criminologists have explored how 'design' (or 'code') operates as a regulatory instrument (Clarke & Newman, 2005; Lessig, 1999; von Hirsch, Garland, & Wakefield, 2000; Zittrain, 2008). Although design and technology can be employed at the information-gathering phase (e.g., the use of CCTV cameras to monitor behaviour) and behaviour modification phase of the regulatory cycle (e.g., car alarms which trigger if unauthorised interference is detected), design-based regulation embeds standards *into* design at the *standard-setting* stage in order to foster social outcomes deemed desirable (such as ignition locking systems which prevent vehicle engines from starting unless the occupants' seatbelts are fastened), thus distinguishing design-based regulation from the use of technology to facilitate regulatory purposes more generally (Yeung, 2008, 2016).

2.2. Choice architecture and 'nudge' as instruments for influencing behaviour

Since 2008, considerable academic attention has focused on one kind of design-based approach to shaping behaviour – nudge – thanks to Thaler and Sunstein, who claim that a nudge is 'any aspect of choice architecture that alters people's behaviour in a predictable way without forbidding any options or significantly changing their economic incentives' (Thaler & Sunstein, 2008, p. 6). The intellectual heritage of *Nudge* rests in experiments in cognitive psychology which seek to understand human decision-making, finding considerable divergence between the rational actor model of decision-making assumed in microeconomic analysis and how individuals actually make decisions due to their pervasive use of cognitive shortcuts and heuristics (Tversky & Kahneman, 1974, 1981). Critically, much individual decision-making occurs subconsciously, passively and unreflectively rather than through active, conscious deliberation (Kahneman, 2013). Drawing on these findings, Thaler and Sunstein highlight how the surrounding decisional choice context can be *intentionally designed* in ways that systematically influence human decision-making in particular directions. For example, to encourage customers to choose healthier food items, they suggest that cafeteria managers place the healthy options more prominently – such as placing the fruit in front of the chocolate cake (Thaler & Sunstein, 2008, p. 1). Due to the 'availability' heuristic and the influence of 'priming', customers will systematically tend to opt for the more 'available' healthier items.

2.3. Big Data analytics as informational choice architecture

To understand how Big Data analytic techniques utilise nudge, we can distinguish two broad configurations of Big Data-driven digital decision-making analytic processes:

(a) *Automated decision-making processes:* Many common transactions rely upon automated decision-making processes, ranging from ticket dispensing machines to highly sophisticated techniques used by some financial institutions offering consumer credit, such as pay-day loan company Wonga (https://www.wonga.com/loans-online). Although varying widely in complexity and sophistication, not all of which rely on Big Data-driven analytics, these decision-making processes automatically issue some kind of 'decision' without any need for human intervention beyond user input of relevant data (or data tokens) and thus constitute a form of action-forcing (or coercive) design (Brownsword, 2005; Yeung & Dixon-Woods, 2010).

(b) *Digital decision-guidance processes*: In contrast, digital decision-'guidance' processes are designed so that it is not the machine, but the targeted individual, who makes the relevant decision. These technologies seek to *direct or guide* the individual's decision-making processes in ways identified by the underlying software algorithm as 'optimal', by offering 'suggestions' intended to prompt the user to make decisions preferred by the choice architect (Selinger & Seager, 2012).

While automated algorithmic decision-making raises serious concerns (e.g., Citron, 2008; Citron & Pasquale, 2014; Pasquale, 2015), this paper focuses on Big Data-driven decision-guidance techniques. These techniques harness nudges for the purpose of 'selection optimisation'. Consider how Internet search engines operate: in response to a query, Big Data analytic techniques mine millions of web pages with lightning speed, algorithmically evaluating their 'relevance' and displaying the results in rank order. In the Google search engine, for example, the most prominently displayed sites are 'paid for' sponsored listings (thus enabling firms to pay for search engine salience), followed by weblinks ranked in order of Google's algorithmically determined relevance. Although theoretically free to review *all* the potentially relevant pages (from the hundreds of thousands ranked), in practice each individual searcher is likely to visit only those on the first page or two (Pasquale, 2006). Hence the user's click-through behaviour is subject to the 'priming' effect, brought about by the algorithmic configuration of her informational choice architecture seeking to 'nudge' her click-through behaviour in directions favoured by the choice architect. For Google, this entails driving web traffic in directions that promote greater use of Google applications (thereby increasing the value of Google's sponsored advertising space). Other algorithmic selection optimisation techniques operate in a similar fashion, helping the user identify which data items to target from a very large population. For example, so-called 'predictive policing' techniques use Big Data analytics to identify the 'highest risk' individuals or other targets to assist enforcement officials determine their inspection priorities, thereby increasing the efficiency and efficacy of their inspection and enforcement processes (e.g., Mayer-Schonberger & Cukier 2013, pp. 186–189).

Although the concept of nudge is simple, Big Data decision-guidance analytics utilise nudge in a highly sophisticated manner. Compare a simple static nudge in the form of the speed hump, and a highly sophisticated, dynamic Big Data-driven nudge in the form of Google Maps navigation function. In neither case is the driver compelled to act in the manner identified as optimal by the nudge's architect. Hence, a motorist approaching a speed hump willing to endure the discomfort and potential vehicle damage that may result from proceeding over the hump at speed need not slow down. Nor is the driver using Google Maps compelled to follow the 'suggestions' it offers. But if the driver fails to follow a suggested direction, Google Maps simply reconfigures its guidance relative to the vehicle's new location via algorithmic analysis of live data streams that track both the vehicle's location and traffic congestion 'hot spots' that are algorithmically predicted to affect how quickly the vehicle will reach its desired destination.

While the self-executing quality of many static forms of design-based regulatory instruments obviates the need for human intervention, so that the enforcement response is automatically administered once the requisite standard has been reached, this makes them a rather blunt form of control (Latour, 1994, pp. 39–40). Although vehicles should proceed slowly in residential areas to ensure public safety, speed humps invariably slow down emergency vehicles responding to call-outs. In contrast, Big Data-driven nudges avoid the over- and under-inclusiveness of static forms of design-based regulation (Yeung, 2008). Big Data-driven nudges make it possible for automatic enforcement to take place *dynamically* (Degli Esposti, 2014), with both the standard and its execution being continuously updated and refined within a networked environment that enables real-time data feeds which, crucially, can be used to *personalise* algorithmic outputs (Rieder, 2015). Networked, Big Data-driven digital-guidance technologies thus operate as self-contained cybernetic systems, with the entire tripartite regulatory cycle continuously implemented via a recursive feedback loop which allows dynamic adjustment of both the standard-setting and behaviour modification phases of the regulatory cycle, enabling an individual's choice architecture to be continuously reconfigured in real time in three directions:

(a) refinement of the *individual's choice environment* in response to changes in the target's behaviour and the broader environment, identified by the algorithm designer as relevant to the target's decision-making, based on the analysis of the target's constantly expanding data profile;

(b) *data feedback* to the choice architect, which can itself be collected, stored and repurposed for other Big Data applications; and

(c) monitoring and refinement of the individual's choice environment in light of *population-wide* trends identified via population-wide Big Data surveillance and analysis.

Big Data-driven nudging is therefore nimble, unobtrusive and highly potent, providing the data subject with a highly personalised choice environment – hence I refer to these techniques as 'hypernudge'. Hypernudging relies on highlighting algorithmically determined correlations between data items within data sets that would not otherwise be observable through human cognition alone (or even with standard computing support [Shaw, 2014]), thereby conferring 'salience' on the highlighted data patterns, operating through the technique of 'priming', dynamically configuring the user's informational choice context in ways intentionally designed to influence her decisions.

3. Are Big Data-driven 'hypernudge' techniques legitimate?

Although hypernudging entails the use of 'soft' power, it is extraordinarily strong (i.e., 'soft' power need not be 'weak': Nye, 2004). And, where power lies, there also lies the potential for overreaching, exploitation and abuse. How then should the legitimacy of hypernudge be assessed, if legitimacy is understood primarily in terms of conformity with liberal democratic principles and values rooted in respect for individual autonomy? Before proceeding, two considerations should be borne in mind. Firstly, the massive power asymmetry between global digital service providers, particularly Google and Facebook, and individual service users cannot be ignored (Zuboff, 2015), especially given that the scale of corporate economic surveillance via Big Data tracking dwarfs the surveillance conducted by national intelligence agencies (Harcourt, 2014), particularly as the Internet of Things devices continue to spread their tentacles into every area of daily life (Peppet, 2014). Secondly, Big Data hypernudging operates on a one-to-many basis. Unlike the speed hump which directly affects only one or two vehicles at any moment in time when proceeding over it, a single algorithmic hypernudge initiated by Facebook can directly affect millions of users simultaneously. Hence Facebook's soft algorithmic power is many orders of magnitude greater than those wishing to install speed humps to reduce vehicle speeds and is therefore considerably more troubling.

3.1. The liberal manipulation critique of nudge

Despite enthusiastic embrace by policy-makers in the U.S. and U.K., Thaler and Sunstein's nudge proposals have been extensively criticised. Leaving aside criticisms of the idea of 'libertarian paternalism' which Thaler and Sunstein claim provides the philosophical underpinnings of nudge, two lines of critique have emerged: those doubting their effectiveness, and those which highlight their covert, manipulative quality. My analysis focuses on the second cluster of criticisms (the 'liberal manipulation' critique).

(a) **The illegitimate motive critique** (the 'active' manipulation critique): Firstly, several critics fear that nudges may be used for illegitimate purposes. Consider the so-called Facebook experiments undertaken by social media giant Facebook by manipulating nearly 700,000 users' News Feeds (i.e., the flow of comments, videos, pictures and weblinks posted by other people in their social network) to test whether exposure to emotions led people to change their own Facebook posting-behaviours through a process of 'emotional contagion' (Kramer, Guillory, & Hancock, 2014) provoking a storm of protest. Critics called it a mass experiment in emotional manipulation, accusing Facebook of violating ethical and legal guidelines by failing to notify affected users that they were being manipulated in the experiment (cf. Meyer, 2015). Facebook defended its actions as legitimately attempting 'to improve our services and to make the content people see on Facebook as relevant and engaging as possible' (Booth, 2014). But five months after the experiments became public, Facebook Chief Technology Officer Mike Schroepfer acknowledged that it had mishandled the study, announcing that a new internal 'enhanced review process' for handling internal experiments and research that may later be published would be instituted (Lukerson, 2014).

(b) **The nudge as deception critique** (the 'passive' manipulation critique): Secondly, even if utilised to pursue legitimate purposes, others argue that nudges that deliberately seek to exploit cognitive weaknesses to provoke desired behaviours entail a form of deception (Bovens, 2008; Yeung, 2012). The paradigmatic autonomous decision is that of a mentally competent, fully informed individual, arrived at through a process of rational self-deliberation, so that the individual's chosen outcome can be justified and explained by reference to reasons which the agent has identified and endorsed (Berlin, 1969, p. 131). Yet the causal mechanism through which many nudges are intended to work deliberately seeks to by-pass the individuals' rational decision-making process, exploiting their cognitive irrationalities and thus entailing illegitimate manipulation, expressing contempt and disrespect for individuals as autonomous, rational beings capable of reasoned decision-making concerning their own affairs (Yeung, 2012, p. 137). These concerns resonate with legal critiques which highlight how powerful Internet intermediaries (such as Google) act as critical gatekeepers, with Pasquale and Bracha observing that search engines filter and rank websites based on criteria that will inevitably be structurally biased (designed to satisfy users and maintain a competitive edge over rivals), thus generating systematically skewed results aimed at promoting the underlying interests of the gatekeeper, thus distorting the capacity of individuals to make informed, meaningful choices and undermining individual autonomy (Pasquale & Bracha, 2015).

(c) **The lack of transparency critique:** Pasquale and Bracha's concerns reflect growing calls for institutional mechanisms that can effectively secure 'algorithmic accountability', given that sophisticated algorithms are increasingly utilised to render decisions, or intentionally to influence the decisions of others, yet operate as 'black boxes', tightly shielded from external scrutiny despite their immense influence over flows of information and power (Diakopoulos, 2013; Pasquale, 2015; Rauhofer, 2015). Critics of nudge also highlight their lack of transparency, drawing analogies with subliminal advertising which are widely regarded as unethical and illegitimate (cf. Thaler & Sunstein 244). Although traditional nudge techniques vary in their level of transparency (Bovens, 2008), the critical mechanisms of influence utilised by hypernudging are embedded into the design of complex, machine-learning algorithms, which are highly opaque (and typically protected by trade secrets: Pasquale, 2006; Rauhofer, 2015), thus exacerbating concerns of abuse.

3.2. Can these concerns be overcome via notice and consent?

Can these objections to the opacity and manipulative quality of hypernudging be overcome, either through individual consent to their use or because substantive considerations are sufficiently weighty to override them?[2] I will focus on the first of these possibilities, employing a rights-based approach viewed through the lens of liberal political theory (Dworkin, 1977; Raz, 1986) before interrogating this approach by drawing on insights from STS and surveillance studies. The right most clearly implicated by Big Data-driven hypernudging is the right to informational privacy, given the continuous monitoring of individuals and the collection and algorithmic processing of personal digital data which hypernudging entails. Legal critiques of Big Data processing techniques (and their antecedents) have, therefore, largely centred on whether the systematic collection, storage, processing and re-purposing of personal digital data collected via the Internet have been authorised by affected individuals, thereby waiving their right to informational privacy.

Contemporary data protection laws rest on what Daniel Solove calls a model of 'privacy self-management' in which the law provides individuals with a set of rights aimed at enabling them to exercise control over the use of their personal data, with individuals deciding for themselves how to weigh the costs and benefits of personal data sharing, storage and processing (Solove, 2013). This approach ultimately rests on the paradigm of 'notice and consent', which contemporary data protection scholars have strenuously criticised. Critics argue that individuals are highly unlikely to give meaningful, voluntary consent to the data sharing and processing activities entailed by Big Data analytic techniques, highlighting insuperable challenges faced by individuals navigating a rapidly evolving technological landscape in which they are invited to share their personal data in return for access to digital services (Acquisti, Brandimarte, & Loewenstein, 2015). Firstly, there is overwhelming evidence that most people neither read nor understand online privacy policies which users must 'accept' before accessing digital services, with one oft-cited study estimating that if an individual actually read them, this would consume 244 hours per year (McDonald & Cranor, 2008). Various studies, including those of Lorrie Crannor, have sought to devise creative, practical solutions that will enable online mechanisms to provide helpful and informative notice to networked users, yet all have been found to be inadequate: either because they were not widely used, easily circumvented or misunderstood (Cranor, Frischmann, Harkins, & Nissenbaum, 2013–2014). Secondly, people struggle to make informed decisions about their informational privacy due to problems of bounded rationality and problems of aggregation: struggling to manage their privacy relations with the hundreds of digital service providers that they interact with online (Solove, 2013, p. 1890) and finding it difficult, if not impossible, adequately to assess the risk of harm in a series of isolated transactions given that many privacy harms are cumulative in nature (Solove, 2013, p. 1891). Thirdly, individuals' privacy preferences are highly malleable and context dependent. An impressive array of empirical privacy studies demonstrate that people experience considerable uncertainty about the importance of privacy owing to difficulties in ascertaining the potential consequences of privacy behaviour, often exacerbated by the intangible nature of many privacy harms (e.g., how harmful is it if a stranger becomes aware of one's life history?) and given that privacy is rarely an unalloyed good but typically involves trade-offs (Acquisti et al., 2015). Empirical studies demonstrate that individuals' privacy behaviours are easily influenced through environmental cues, such as defaults, and the design of web environments owing to pervasive reliance on heuristics and social norms. Because people are often 'at sea' when it comes to the consequences of their feelings about privacy, they typically cast around for cues in their environment to guide their behaviour, including the behaviour of others and their past experiences, so that one's privacy preferences are highly context dependent rather than stable and generalisable to a wide range of settings (Acquisti et al., 2015). According to Acquisti and his colleagues, this extensive uncertainty and context dependence imply that people *cannot* be counted on to navigate the complex trade-offs involving privacy in a self-interested fashion (Acquisti et al., 2015). Thus, many information law scholars seriously doubt that individual acceptance of the 'terms and conditions' offered by digital service providers (including Google, Facebook, Twitter and Amazon), typically indicated by clicking on a web page link, constitutes meaningful waiver of one's underlying rights to informational privacy (Solove, 2013, pp. 1880–1903), which even the industry itself acknowledges is a serious problem.[3]

The adequacy of a privacy self-management model is further undermined in the Big Data environment.[4] Firstly, the 'transparency paradox', identified by Helen Nissenbaum, emphasises that in the complex and highly dynamic information network ecology that now characterises the Internet, individuals must be informed about the types of information being collected, with whom it is shared and for what purpose, in order to give meaningful consent. But providing the level of detail needed to enable users to provide genuinely informed consent would overwhelm even savvy users because the practices themselves are volatile and indeterminate, as new providers, parties and practices emerge, all constantly augmenting existing data flows (Barocas & Nissenbaum, 2014, p. 59). Yet to avoid information overload, reliance on simplified, plain language notices is also inadequate, failing to provide sufficiently detailed information to enable people make informed decisions (Nissenbaum, 2011). Secondly, the right to informational privacy includes the 'purpose specification principle', requiring data collectors to state clearly the explicit purpose of collecting and processing that data *at the time of collection*.[5] Yet, as Ryan Harkins, Microsoft's privacy lawyer, observes, this principle is largely antiethical to the concept of Big Data, which is all about collecting more and more data in the hope that you might subsequently be able to use it in unexpected ways (Cranor et al. 2013–2014). The public furore surrounding the Facebook experiments is instructive. Although Facebook claimed that all 700,000 individuals who were subjected to the experiment had provided informed consent by accepting Facebook's terms of service, critics claim that this fell well short of the 'informed consent' that underpins universally accepted ethical principles governing research on human subjects exemplified in the Helsinki Declaration (World Medical Association, 2013). The affected Facebook users could not reasonably have expected that they would be subjected to systematic emotional experimentation when they accepted Facebook's terms of service, but nor is Facebook likely to have contemplated that possibility either, so it could not have specified this proposed purpose in its terms and conditions at that time (although Facebook could have notified affected users of its intention prior to conducting the experiment and offered them an opportunity to opt out).

Thirdly, the primary business model through which Big Data is being monetised preys directly upon the susceptibility of individuals' privacy behaviour to subconscious external influence, particularly the powerful heuristics associated with ostensibly 'free' services. The predominant business model for contemporary digital services is one of 'barter', with users agreeing to disclose their personal data to firms in return for services (van Dijck, 2014, p. 2000) under a 'free' rather than 'fee' for services revenue model, thereby eliminating an important barrier to adoption faced by firms seeking to attract new customers with initially high uncertainty about their valuation of the service offered (Lambrecht, 2013). Yet, as behavioural economist Dan Ariely demonstrates, 'the power of free can get us to make many foolish decisions' (Ariely, 2009). Accordingly, in a Big Data environment, existing notice and consent model *cannot* be relied upon to protect the right to informational privacy, given that individuals are typically asked to consent to the processing of their personal data at some future time, for purposes they could not reasonably have contemplated.

3.3. Authorising deception?

Although digital privacy policies are often drafted in breathtakingly broad, open-ended terms that could be literally interpreted to include Big Data-driven hypernudging techniques, these policies are inadequate to authorise their *deceptive* qualities. Deception is a prima facie moral wrong because it violates the autonomy of the person deceived, involving the control of another without that person's consent (Wendler, 1996, p. 91). Thus in addition to the right to informational privacy, online digital users have a separate and distinct right not to be deceived, rooted in a moral agent's basic right to be treated with dignity and respect. Thus, even assuming that routine acceptance of online privacy notices constitutes valid consent by a user to the sharing and processing of her personal data online, this consent does not *thereby* constitute a concomitant waiver of her right to not to be deceived. For this, specific consent to the use of techniques of deception is needed. Consider, for example, a cafeteria manager who, wishing to encourage healthier food choices, places the following sign at the cafeteria entrance:

> Many patrons want to eat healthy food but often have difficulty choosing the healthier items when selecting from the food on display. In order to assist then, we have arranged the food items on display with the healthier items displayed more prominently, making it more likely that customers will choose those items.

Although such a notice may overcome the manipulative, opaque qualities of the nudge in question (particularly if customers may leave the cafeteria and dine elsewhere), it is likely to distort the effectiveness of the nudge in eliciting the desired behavioural response. As Bovens puts it, the psychological mechanisms that are exploited by nudge techniques 'work best in the dark' (Bovens, 2008, p. 3).

It is also doubtful whether disclosure by digital service providers that they are *withholding* material information is sufficient to overcome these objections, particularly if fundamental rights are implicated. Consider the practice of 'digital gerrymandering', a term coined by leading American cyberscholar Jonthan Zittrain following the Facebook experiments to describe how easily social media platforms could utilise Big Data analytics actively to manipulate the voting behaviour of individuals during an election campaign. For Zittrain, digital gerrymandering 'clearly seem wrong', yet he struggles to articulate the nature of the wrong, suggesting it might constitute an 'abuse of a powerful platform' (Zittrain, 2014). Might such a practice be acceptable if Facebook's terms and conditions included the following?

> The content of your news feeds is determined by an algorithm that has been constructed in ways intended to foster Facebook's success as a commercial enterprise.

This notice seems inadequate to authorise digital gerrymandering, because it fails to provide users with sufficient notice of the *deceptive* nature of the technique involved. Consider then the following more detailed statement:

> The content of your newsfeeds is determined by an algorithm that has been constructed in ways intended to encourage you to favour the views of political candidates favoured by Facebook.

By notifying users that relevant information of a certain kind will be omitted from their news feeds, users who are unhappy with this policy can stop using the service, while those who are content to proceed might be regarded as providing 'second order consent', thereby waiving their right not to be deceived (Wendler, 1996) and their underlying democratic and constitutional rights to freedom of information and political participation. But second-order consent processes would not overcome the objection that in practice, people do not read digital privacy notices, let alone properly comprehend their consequences. Furthermore, as Zuboff observes, the tools Google offers 'respond to the needs of beleaguered second modernity individuals – like the apple in the garden – once tasted, they are impossible to live without' (Zuboff, 2015, p. 83).

Digital gerrymandering is an extreme example, but it nevertheless highlights how Big Data hypernudging techniques could be employed in ways that undermine individual autonomy and the quality of democratic participation. But what of techniques that are not so obviously deceptive nor directly implicate democratic participation – the kinds of practices that might be regarded as more akin to conventionally accepted marketing techniques used by firms to peddle their wares? What of the algorithmic design of Facebook functions aimed at keeping users logged in to Facebook, since the longer they linger, the more advertising they are exposed to, thereby enhancing the commercial value of Facebook? As Bernard Rieder argues, Big Data-driven algorithmic models are being used by institutions as a form of 'accounting realism' to 'sniff out patterns or differentiations in data and, by optimising for a target variable, transform them into (economic) opportunity' in pursuit of self-serving purposes (Rieder, 2015). Yet liberal political theory has little to say about such techniques – if their use is adequately disclosed and duly consented to, there is nothing further of concern: individual autonomy is respected, while the market mechanism fosters innovation in the digital services industry.

4. Post-liberal critiques: selective insights from STS and surveillance studies

The inability of the liberal political tradition to grasp how commercial applications of Big Data-driven hypernudging implicate deeper societal, democratic and ethical concerns is ultimately traceable to its understanding of the self and the self-society relation. As Julie Cohen observes, within the liberal tradition, the 'self' as a legal subject has three principal attributes: (1) the self is a definitionally autonomous being possessed of liberty rights that are presumed capable of exercise regardless of context; (2) the legal subject possesses the capacity for rational deliberation and this capacity too is detached from contexts, situated within the tradition of Enlightenment rationalism in which the existence of universal truths amenable to rational discourse and analysis is presumed; and (3) the selfhood that the legal subject possesses is transcendent and immaterial – it is distinct from the body in which the legal subject resides (Cohen, 2012). This, she argues, results is an emphasis on individual consent and a conception of privacy harm that is both economic and individualised so that the 'distress' associated with interference attracts little monetary compensation (Cohen, 2012; Rauhofer, 2015). Cohen laments U.S. law's response to concerns about the genuineness of consent in networked environments by seeking to correct information asymmetries faced by the liberal consumer when consenting to data collection for profiling purposes (Cohen, 2015). For Cohen, by looking to economics rather than sociology, which is more congenial to law's conventional grounding in philosophical commitments associated with liberal political theory (rather than political theory more generally), and to analytic philosophy rather than the sociology of knowledge, the centrality of consent in the liberal paradigm is reinforced, conveying the impression that there is nothing more at stake individually or collectively (Cohen, 2015).

The liberal account's emphasis on consent flows naturally from the special significance of individual choice. My self-regarding choices are imbued with moral and political significance simply because they are *mine*, and it is presumed in liberal societies that they are worthy of respect, however foolish or unwise, for that reason alone (Feinberg, 1989). The core liberal idea of personality articulated in terms of personal autonomy demands that individuals be allowed to choose and pursue their different plans or paths of life for themselves *without interference from others* (Kleing, 1983). But what, exactly, constitutes an 'interference' with an agent's choice (Yeung, 2016)? While coercive choice architectures (evident in the design of prisons, for example, or the gunman who offers his victim 'your money or your life?') clearly constitute interferences, what of the rearrangement of the informational choice architecture intended to nudge the agent's choices in particular directions? Choices cannot be made abstracted from their context: they are always made from a limited choice set or options and, so long as we interact with others, the actions of others will affect the range of options open to us at any time (Wertheimer, 1988). Yet from the liberal viewpoint, except in relation to pervasive choices (Raz, 1986), one cannot object simply on the basis that the actions of another have reduced the scope of one's choices. As White reminds us, when I take the last seat at the bar, you have to stand or go find somewhere else to drink and, from the liberal perspective, there is nothing problematic about this (White, 2010).

But conventional liberal accounts of individual autonomy are criticised by those who highlight their problematic divergence from aspects of identity through which most of us define ourselves.[6] These critics point out that we are deeply enmeshed in identity-constituting relations, cultural and other connections, and that we have little or no choice over some aspects of the self (such as our embodiment) and which conventional liberal accounts fail to take seriously (Christman, 2009). One strand of STS scholarship can be understood as taking these critiques even further, rejecting conventional liberal conceptions of the autonomous self by emphasising the nature of human selfhood as both embodied and subjectively experienced (Rey and Boesel, 2014), and thus offer a more realistic account of the actual, embodied experience of individuals and human decision-making. Rather than decontextualise and abstract the self from her environment, these inquiries focus on how individual self-understanding and self-development are pervasively shaped by the surrounding environment, including technological artefacts. Networked information communications technologies, like other artefacts, shape and mediate our relationship with the world around us and, over time, we come to perceive the world through the lenses that our artefacts create (Verbeek, 2006). As a result, networked information technologies directly configure citizens themselves, actively shaping the relationship between humans and their world, and the way in which they perceive and understand themselves (Cohen, 2012).

So understood, Big Data hypernudging constitutes a 'soft' mechanism of surveillant control. But, unlike the disciplinary control emphasised by Foucault and epitomised by Bentham's Panopticon (Lyon, 2014, p. 6), Big Data's algorithmic control operates in a more subtle yet 'seductive' manner (Boyne, 2000) via continuous feedback loops based on an online user's interactions, configuring individuals online by 'tailoring their conditions of possibility' (Cheney-Lippold, 2011, p. 169). The resulting form of control is both more potent and powerful than the kind of disciplinary control typically associated with pre-digital forms of surveillance which rely upon the coercive experience of living with the uncertainty of being seen (Lyon, 2007, p. 59). Yet this process is essential to an emerging form of information capitalism which Shoshana Zuboff dubs 'surveillance capitalism', dominated by powerful transnational corporations ('surveillance capitalists') (Zuboff, 2015). Unlike industrial capitalism, in which power was identified with the ownership of the means of production and which prevailed from the early to late twentieth century, the surveillance capitalism emerging at the dawn of the twenty-first century produces a new form of power, constituting a new kind of invisible hand in which power is now identified with ownership of the means of behavioural modification (Zuboff, 2015, p. 82). It rests on a default business model that depends upon 'eyeballs' rather than revenue as a predictor of remunerative surveillance assets (Zuboff, 2015, p. 81).

While Zuboff regards Google's products and practices as the leading exemplar of surveillance capitalism at work, Facebook's News Feed algorithm vividly illustrates the role of algorithms in this emerging 'logic of accumulation' (Zuboff, 2015). Victor Lukerson has recently described how News Feed's controversial emergence in 2006 has evolved into 'the most valuable billboard on Earth', tracing its evolution from a fairly crude algorithm based on essentially arbitrary judgements by software engineers assigning point scores to different features of Facebook posts to determine their ranking, into a complex machine-learning system that provides a much more individualised user experience, in which the algorithm adapts to users' behaviour – for example, people who click on more photos see more pictures, and those who do not see fewer (Lukerson, 2015). Because the average Facebook user has access to about 1500 posts per day but only looks at 300, most see only a sliver of the potential posts in their network each day: hence algorithmic ranking critically determines how these posts are filtered and highlighted in users' News Feed (Lukerson, 2015). Facebook therefore invests substantially in developing its News Feed algorithm, claiming to use thousands of factors to determine what shows up in any individual's news feed, and typically making two to three changes to the algorithm weekly. This is Zuboff's surveillance capitalism in operation, undertaken by Facebook for purposes that are portrayed as offering customers a highly personalised, 'meaningful' informational environment that is dynamically and efficiently updated in ways ultimately designed to foster and entrench Facebook as the leading global provider of social networking services, thus securing and expanding its revenue base.

5. Conclusion

I have demonstrated how Big Data-driven decision-guidance techniques can be understood as a design-based instrument of control, operating as a potent form of 'nudge'. The algorithmic analysis of data patterns dynamically configures the targeted individual's choice environment in highly personalised ways, affecting individual users' behaviour and perceptions by subtly moulding the networked user's understanding of the surrounding world. Their distinctly manipulative, if not straightforwardly deceptive, qualities arise from deliberately exploiting systematic cognitive weaknesses which pervade human decision-making to channel behaviour in directions preferred by the choice architect. Yet for liberals, except in clear cases of deception and provided that the targeted individual consents to the deliberate configuration of her informational choice environment, having been duly notified of the choice architect's purpose, there is nothing especially troubling about them (Ford, 2000). It is this largely liberal perspective that informs the work of many privacy law scholars, who highlight the inadequacy of notice and consent procedures in digital, networked environments, emphasising the systematic failure of users to either read or properly understand the significance of digital privacy policies so that the action of clicking on a website to indicate user acceptance typically falls well short of the informed consent required to authorise interference with fundamental rights.

Yet the liberal focus on notice and consent fails to grapple with the particular *way* in which Big Data algorithmic techniques exert behavioural influence through the hyperpersonalisation of individuals' informational choice environments. Optimists, such as Eric Goldman, argue that the algorithmic manipulation of general search engine results need not concern us because the efficient functioning of markets will ensure that alternative search engines will emerge to provide algorithmic evaluations that better meet individual needs (Goldman, 2006). But this fails to recognise that the selective omission of relevant information can be deceptive, yet is virtually impossible for affected users to detect. Moreover, such naïve faith in the market as a vehicle for securing algorithmic accountability seems completely misplaced, given the opacity of the underlying algorithms and the lack of awareness or understanding by many digital service users of their significance and operation (Eslami et al., 2015) and the dominance of a handful of extraordinarily powerful transnational companies in a global networked market for digital services.

Big Data digital-guidance technologies are proving difficult for individuals to resist, operating through subtle persuasion rather than blunt coercion (Ford, 2000). Supported by the prevailing neo-liberal ideology that has fuelled the rapid growth of the Big Data industry, these applications 'beckon with seductive allure' (Cohen, 2012) offering myriad modern conveniences that offer bespoke, highly personalised services that are algorithmically designed to respond rapidly, dynamically and as unobtrusively and seamlessly as possible. By willingly and actively allowing ourselves to be continuously, pervasively and increasingly subjected to Big Data hypernudging strategies, our relationship with the emerging commercial Big Data Barons takes the form of what Natasha Dow Schull refers to as 'asymmetric collusion'. Dow Schull's observations refer to the relationship between gambling addicts and the U.S. gambling industry, in which the latter maximises its returns by successfully harnessing the power of algorithmic analytics to adapt the design of both casino layouts and the gambling machines which they house, in order to 'give players what they want'(Dow Schull, 2012). The relationship between commercial Big Data-driven service providers and individuals is similarly structured: through our increasing willingness to submit ourselves to continuous algorithmic surveillance in return for the highly tailored convenience and efficiency which their selection optimisation tools appear to offer, we also engage in a process of asymmetric collusion that threatens ultimately to impoverish us. Like so many addictions, our short-term cravings are likely to be detrimental to our long-term well-being. By allowing ourselves to be surveilled and subtly regulated on a continuous, highly granular and pervasive basis, we may be slowly but surely eroding our capacity for authentic processes of self-creation and development (Cohen, 2012). While lawyers might be tempted to dismiss these concerns on the basis that 'we have given our informed consent', evidenced by our willingness to incorporate these services into our daily lives, this consent is arguably more akin to that of the compulsive gambling addict (Dow Schull, 2012) than that of the liberal ideal of the auton-omous self. The neo-liberal self is primarily a consumer of digital services, rather than a politically active citizen engaged in processes of public deliberation that characterise the deliberative democratic ideal (Gutmann & Thompson, 1996). As Zuboff chillingly observes, Google's tools are not the objects of value exchange, but 'hooks' that 'lure users into extractive operations that turn ordinary life into the daily renewal of a 21st century Faustian pact' (Zuboff, 2015, pp. 83–84). Yet, she points out that, unlike former industrial capitalists, who were dependent upon institutionalised reciprocity between employees and consumer populations in the form of durable employment systems, steady wage increases and affordable access to goods and services for more consumers, surveillance capitalists are structurally independent from their populations, thus allowing them and their practices to escape democratic scrutiny (Zuboff, 2015, p. 80).

To take seriously the implications of the Big Data revolution that we are currently embarking upon, we must lift our eyes beyond the familiar liberal fixation with notice and consent (Brownsword, 2004). Before succumbing to the allures of the convenience and efficiency that Big Data claims to offer, we must be attentive to its regulatory power, operating as a particularly potent, pervasive yet 'soft' form of control, modulating our informational environment according to logics that are ultimately outside our control and which erode our capacity for democratic self-government (Cohen, 2012). As we increasingly retreat into our own algorithmically determined 'filter bubbles' (Pariser, 2012), our exposure to shared, diverse and unexpected experiences that are essential to sustain our capacity for individual flourishing and democratic engagement is correspond-ingly diminished. If we are to avoid narrow and commercially filtered, algorithmically determined lives, we must establish more effective, practically enforceable constraints to tame the excesses of Big Data-driven hypernudging which will secure meaningful account-ability over the algorithms that exert ever more influence on our lives, in ways that allow genuine democratic participation and input into the design of the networked digital tech-nologies which we increasingly find so irresistible.

Notes

1. This definition amalgamates various refinements to the definition of regulation which Julia Black has offered over time: see Black (2001), Black (2008, p. 139) and Black (2014, p. 2).
2. In relation to Big Data surveillance techniques by government intelligence agencies, con-siderable discussion has focused on the extent to which interests of public and national secur-ity override fundamental rights, such as rights to liberty and privacy: in the U.S., see for example, the President's Review Group on Intelligence and Communications Technologies (2013).
3. To quote Microsoft's privacy lawyer, Ryan Harkins,

   the informed consent edifice is cracking, because it places much of the burden on indi-viduals who are expected to read privacy notices ... while the notice and consent edifice may have been cracking before, I think it's fair to say that big data threatens to obliterate it altogether because big data will mean that there will be even more data collected. It'll be overwhelming and it will make it extremely hard for individuals to provide effective consent or make informed decisions about all of the data that's being collected about them and about all of the prospective uses of the data ... and this challenge will be compounded by the rise of the internet of things. (cited in Cranor et al. 2013–2014, pp. 795–786)

4. In the U.S.A. and Canada, this right is protected primarily through the Fair Information Principles through specific legislation in particular contexts, while in the EU, it is primarily protected via the EU Data Protection Directive and the European Convention on Human Rights, Article 8 (right to privacy).

5. In the EU Data Protection Directive, this is expressed in Art 6(1)(b) which provides that

> Member States shall provide that personal data must be … (b) collected for specified, explicit and legitimate purposes and not further processed in a way incompatible with those purposes. Further processing of data for historical, statistical or scientific purposes shall not be considered as incompatible provided that Member States provide appropriate safeguards. (EU Directive 95/46/EC)

The Organisation for Economic Co-operation and Development Fair Information Practice Principles includes the 'Purpose Specification Principle', which provides that

> [t]he purposes for which personal data are collected should be specified not later than at the time of data collection and the subsequent use limited to the fulfilment of those purposes or such others as are not incompatible with those purposes and as are specified on each occasion of change of purpose. (http://oecdprivacy.org/)

6. The concept of 'relational autonomy' offers a potentially fruitful approach: see Nedelsky (1990); Mackenzie and Stoljar (2000). I am indebted to Barbara Prainsack for drawing my attention to this literature.

Acknowledgements

I am grateful to Joris van Hoboken and Helen Nissenbaum for hosting my visit to NYU to attend NYU's *Algorithms and Accountability* conference, and providing me with an opportunity to discuss my ideas at such an immensely stimulating forum. I am also indebted to Barbara Prainsack, Roger Brownsword, Lyria Bennett Moses, John Coggan, Alessandro Spina and Chris Townley for comments on earlier drafts and to Florian Gamper for excellent research assistance. All errors remain my own.

Disclosure statement

No potential conflict of interest was reported by the author.

References

Acquisti, A., Brandimarte, L., & Loewenstein, G. (2015). Privacy and human behavior in the age of information. *Science, 347*, 509–514.

Ariely, D. (2009). *Predictably irrational: The hidden forces that shape our decisions*. London: Harper Collins.

Barocas, S., & Nissenbaum, H. (2014). Big Data's end run around anonymity and consent. In J. Lane, V. Stodder, S. Bender, & H. Nissenbaum (Eds.), *Privacy, Big Data and the public good* (pp. 44–75). New York, NY: Cambridge University Press.

Berlin, I. (1969). Two concepts of liberty. In I. Berlin (Ed.), *Four essays on liberty* (pp. 118–172). London: Oxford University Press.

Black, J. (2001). Decentring regulation: Understanding the role of regulation and self-regulation in a 'post-regulatory' world. *Current Legal Problems, 54,* 103–146.

Black, J. (2008). Constructing and contesting legitimacy and accountability in polycentric regulatory regimes. *Regulation & Governance, 2,* 137–164.

Black, J. (2014). Learning from regulatory disasters, Sir Frank Holmes Memorial Lecture. Retrieved from http://www.ssrn.com/en/

Booth, R. (2014, June 30). Facebook reveals news feed experiment to control emotions. *The Guardian.* Retrieved from http://www.theguardian.com

Bovens, L. (2008). The ethics of *nudge.* In T. Grune-Yanoff and S. O. Hansson (Eds.), *Preference change: Approaches from philosophy, economics and psychology* (pp. 207–219). Dordrecht: Springer.

boyd, d., & Crawford, K. (2012). Critical questions for Big Data. *Information, Communication and Society, 15,* 662–679.

Boyne, R. (2000). Post-panopticism. *Economy and Society, 29,* 285–307.

Brownsword, R. (2004). The cult of consent: Fixation and fallacy. *Kings College Law Journal, 15,* 223–251.

Brownsword, R. (2005). Code, control, and choice: Why east is east and west is west. *Legal Studies, 25,* 1–21.

Cheney-Lippold, J. (2011). A new algorithmic identity: Soft biopolitics and the modulation of control. *Theory, Culture & Society, 28,* 164–181.

Christman, J. (2009). Autonomy in moral and political philosophy. *Stanford Encyclopedia of Philosophy.* Retrieved from http://plato.stanford.edu/entries/autonomy-moral/

Citron, D. K. (2008). Technological due process. *Washington University Law Review, 85,* 1249–1313.

Citron, D. K., & Pasquale, F. (2014). The scored society: Due process for automated predictions. *Washington Law Review, 89,* 1–33.

Clarke, R. V., & Newman, G. R. (Eds.). (2005). *Designing out crime from products and systems.* Monsey, NY: Criminal Justice Press.

Cohen, J. E. (2012). *Configuring the networked self.* New Haven, CT: Yale University Press.

Cohen, J. E. (2015). Studying law studying surveillance. *Surveillance & Society, 13,* 191–101.

Cranor, L., Frischmann, B. M., Harkins, R., & Nissenbaum, H. (2013–2014). Panel I: Disclosure and notice practices in private data collection. *Cardozo Arts & Entertainment Law Journal, 32,* 781–812.

Degli Esposti, S. (2014). When Big Data meets dataveillance: The hidden side of analytics. *Surveillance & Society, 12,* 209–225.

Diakopoulos, N. (2013, October 3). Race against the algorithms. *The Atlantic.* Retrieved from http://www.theatlantic.com/world/

van Dijck, J. (2014). Datafication, dataism and dataveillance: Big Data between scientific paradigm and ideology. *Surveillance & Society, 12*(2), 199–208.

Dow Schull, N. (2012). *Addiction by design.* New Jersey, NJ: Princeton University Press.

Dworkin, R. (1977). *Taking rights seriously.* London: Duckworth.

Eslami, M., Rickmany, A., Vaccaro, K., Aleyasen, A., Vuong, A., Karahalios, K., Hamilton, K. & Sandvig, C. (2015) "I Always Assumed That I Wasn't Really That Close to [Her]": Reasoning about invisible algorithms in the news feed. In *Proceeding CHI '15 Proceedings of the 33rd Annual ACM Conference on Human Factors in Computing Systems* (pp. 153–162), ACM New York, NY, USA. Retrieved from http://social.cs.uiuc.edu/papers/pdfs/Eslami_Algorithms_CHI15.pdf.

Feinberg, J. (1989). *The moral limits of the criminal law volume 3: Harm to self.* Oxford: Oxford University Press.

Ford, R. T. (2000). Save the robots: Cyber profiling and your so-called life. *Stanford Law Review, 52,* 1573–1584.

Goldman, E. (2006). Search engine bias and the demise of search engine utopianism. *Yale Journal of Law & Technology, 8,* 188–200.

Gutmann, A., & Thompson, D. (1996). *Democracy and disagreement.* Cambridge, MA: Harvard University Press.

Harcourt, B. E. (2014). *Governing, exchanging, securing: Big Data and the production of digital knowledge.* (Columbia Public Law Research Paper No 14-390). Retrieved from http://www.ssrn.com/en/

Hood, C., Rothstein, H., & Baldwin, R. (2001). *The government of risk.* Oxford: Oxford University Press.

Kahneman, D. (2013). *Thinking, fast and slow.* New York, NY: Farrer, Strauss and Giroux.

Kleing, J. (1983). *Paternalism.* Manchester: Manchester University Press.

Kramer, A. D. I., Guillory, J. E., & Hancock, J. T. (2014). Experimental evidence of massive-scale emotional contagion through social networks. *Proceedings of the National Academy of Sciences, 111,* 8788–8790.

Lambrecht, A. (2013). Pricing services online, economics of. In S. N. Surlauf & L. E. Blume (Eds.), *The New palgrave dictionary of economics.* Palgrave Macmillan. Retrieved May 12, 2016, from http://www.dictionaryofeconomics.com/article?id=pde2013_P000380

Latour, B. (1994). On technical mediation - Philosophy, sociology, genealogy. *Common Knowledge, 3*(2), 29–64.

Lessig, L. (1999). *Code and other laws of cyberspace.* New York, NY: Basic Books.

Lukerson, V. (2014, October 2). Facebook changing research methods after controversial mood study. *Time Magazine.* Retrieved from http://time.com/

Lukerson, V. (2015, July 9). Here's how Facebook's news feed actually works. *Time Magazine.* Retrieved from http://time.com/

Lyon, D. (2007). *Surveillance studies.* Cambridge: Polity Press.

Lyon, D. (2014). Surveillance, Snowden, and Big Data: Capacities, consequences, critique. *Big Data & Society, 1*(2), 1–13.

Mackenzie, C., & Stoljar, N. (2000). *Relational autonomy: Feminist perspectives on autonomy, agency and the social self.* Oxford: Oxford University Press.

Mayer-Schonberger, V., & Cukier, K. (2013). *Big Data.* London: John Murray.

McDonald, A. M., & Cranor, L. F. (2008). The cost of Reading privacy policies. *A Journal of Law and Policy for the Information Society, 4,* 540–565.

Meyer, M. N. (2015). Two cheers for corporate experimentation: The A/B illusion and the virtues of data-driven innovation. *Colorado Technology Law Journal, 13,* 273–332.

Morgan, B., & Yeung, K. (2007). *An introduction to law and regulation.* Cambridge: Cambridge University Press.

Nedelsky, J. (1990). Law, boundaries and the bounded self. *Representations, 30,* 162–189.

Nissenbaum, H. (2011). A contextual approach to privacy online. *Daedalus, 140*(4), 32–48.

Nye Jr., J. (2004). *Soft power.* New York, NY: Public Affairs.

Pariser, E. (2012). *The filter bubble.* London: Penguin Books.

Pasquale, F. (2006). Rankings, reductionism, and responsibility. *Cleveland State Law Review, 54,* 115–138.

Pasquale, F. (2015). *The black box society.* Cambridge, MA: Harvard University Press.

Pasquale, F., & Bracha, O. (2015). Federal search commission? Access, fairness and accountability in the law of search. *Cornell Law Review, 93,* 1149–1191.

Peppet, S. R. (2014). Regulating the Internet of things: First steps towards managing discrimination, privacy, security and consent. *Texas Law Review, 93,* 85–176.

President's Review Group on Intelligence and Communications Technologies. (2013). *Liberty and security in a changing world.* Washington, DC: Office of the Whitehouse.

Rauhofer, J. (2015). Of men and mice: Should the EU data protection authorities' reaction to Google's new privacy policy raise concern for the future of the purpose limitation principle. *European Data Protection Law Review, 1,* 5–15.

Raz, J. (1986). *The morality of freedom*. Oxford: Clarendon Press.

Rey, P. J. & Boesel, E. (2014). The web, digital prostheses and augmented subjectivity. In D. L. Kleinman, & K. P. Moore (Eds.), *Routledge handbook of science, technology and society* (pp. 173–188). Whitney: Routledge.

Rieder, B. (2015, February). *On the diversity of the accountability problem - Machine learning and knowledge capitalism*. Paper presented at the meeting of NYU Information Law Institute, Algorithms and Accountability Conference, New York, NY.

Selinger, E., & Seager, T. (2012). *Digital jiminy crickets: Do apps that promote ethical behavior diminish our ability to make just decisions?* Slate. Retrieved from www.slate.com.

Shaw, J. (2014). Why "Big Data" is a big deal. *Harvard Magazine, 116*(4), 30–35.

Solove, D. J. (2013). Privacy self management and the consent dilemma. *Harvard Law Review, 126*, 1880–1893.

Thaler, R., & Sunstein, C. (2008). *Nudge*. London: Penguin Books.

Tversky, A., & Kahneman, D. (1974). Judgment under uncertainty: Heuristics and biases. *Science, 185*, 1124–1131.

Tversky, A., & Kahneman, D. (1981). The framing of decisions and the psychology of choice. *Science, 211*, 453–458.

Verbeek, P.-P. (2006). Materializing morality: Design ethics and technological mediation. *Science, Technology & Human Values, 31*, 361–380.

von Hirsch, A., Garland, D., & Wakefield, A. (Eds.). (2000). *Ethical and social perspectives on situational crime prevention*. Portland, OR: Hart Publishing.

Wendler, D. (1996). Deception in medical and behavioral research: Is it ever acceptable? *The Milbank Quarterly, 74*(1), 87–114.

Wertheimer, A. (1988). *Coercion*. Princeton: Princeton University Press.

White, S. J. (2010, May). *What's wrong with coercion?* Paper presented at the meeting of the Society for Ethical Theory and Political Philosophy, Northwestern University.

World Medical Association. (2013). World Medical Association declaration of Helsinki: Ethical principles for medical research involving human subjects. *JAMA, 310*, 2191–2194.

Yeung, K. (2008). Towards an understanding of regulation by design. In R. Brownsword & K. Yeung (Eds.), *Regulating technologies* (pp. 79–94). Portland, OR: Hart Publishing.

Yeung, K. (2012). Nudge as fudge. *The Modern Law Review, 75*(1), 122–148.

Yeung, K. (2016). The forms and limits of choice architecture. *Law and Policy, 38*(3). doi:10.1111/lapo.12057

Yeung, K., & Dixon-Woods, M. (2010). Design-based regulation and patient safety: A regulatory studies perspective. *Social Science and Medicine, 71*, 502–509.

Zittrain, J. (2014). Engineering an election. *Harvard Law Review Forum, 127*, 335.

Zittrain, J. (2008) Tethered appliances, software as service, and perfect enforcement. In R. Brownsword & K. Yeung (Eds.), *Regulating technologies* (pp. 125–156). Portland, OR: Hart Publishing.

Zuboff, S. (2015). Big other: Surveillance capitalism and the prospects of an information civilization. *Journal of Information Technology, 30*, 75–89.

Algorithms (and the) everyday

Michele Willson ⓘ

ABSTRACT

Our everyday practices are increasingly mediated through online technologies, entailing the navigation and also oft-simultaneous creation of large quantities of information and communication data. The scale and types of activities being undertaken, the data that are being created and engaged with, and the possibilities for analysis, archiving and distribution are now so extensive that technical constructs are necessarily required as a way to manage, interpret and distribute these. These constructs include the platforms, the software, the codes and the algorithms. This paper explores the place of the algorithm in shaping and engaging with the contemporary everyday. It does this via an exploration of some particular instances of algorithmic sorting and presentation as well as considering some of the ways these contribute to shaping our everyday practices and understandings. In doing so, it raises questions about understandings of agency and power, shifting world views and our complex relationship with technologies.

Our everyday practices are increasingly mediated through online technologies, entailing the navigation and also oft-simultaneous creation of large quantities of information and communication data. The scale and types of activities being undertaken, the data that are being created and engaged with, and the possibilities for analysis, archiving and distribution are now so extensive that technical constructs are necessarily required as a way to manage, interpret and distribute these. These constructs include the platforms, the software, the codes and the algorithms. This paper explores the place of the algorithm in shaping and engaging with the contemporary everyday.

Algorithms are ubiquitous and pervasive, employed in many ways. For example, the work of algorithms can be seen in the generation of Twitter Trends or in Twitter follow recommendations; in Google personalised search results or Facebook newsfeeds; or in suggested Google map directions, just to note a few. These seemingly banal and mundane though multiple and often intersecting interactions online are becoming increasingly prevalent and extensive as more and more of our everyday activities are conducted in online spaces and through online processes (Figure 1).

This article considers why algorithms are matters of concern when considering questions of the everyday. It does this via an exploration of particular instances of algorithmic sorting and presentation as well as exploring ways these contribute to shaping our everyday practices and understandings. In doing so, it raises questions about understandings of agency and power, shifting world views and our complex relationship with technologies.

The everyday

Everyday practices constitute the habitus (Bourdieu, 1997) or background within which people operate. They are the seemingly mundane or banal, recurrent and multiple activities and routines that we all engage with and that shape the form and flow of our individual and social lives in space and time. These activities and routines are replicated in countless ways by many people on a daily or regular basis. Through this process, practices become normalised or naturalised, usually enacted with minimal thought and often rendered invisible or in the background (or at the very least as largely unquestioned). Studies of the everyday are, therefore, partly concerned with rendering the seemingly invisible visible and thereby open to critique and the examination of power relations and practices that are in play. These studies are also concerned with understanding how everyday practices are also performative – not only being situated in, but also giving shape to the form/s of time and space.

The shaping of the everyday, at least for de Certeau (1988), is partly the result of the intersection of social, cultural, political and economic strategies enacted by powerful

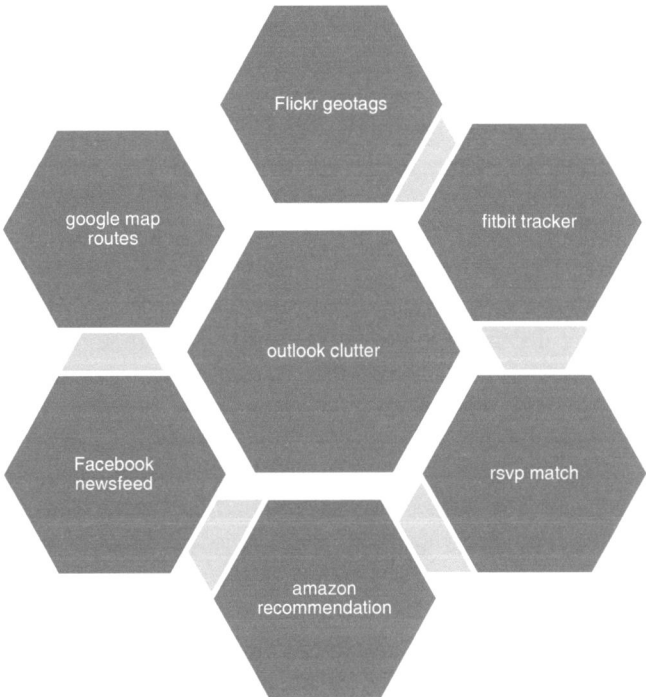

Figure 1. Examples of algorithmic output encountered in our everyday.

systems and actors with the tactics of those who are the consumers or users of these systems and the ways of operating that are employed as a result. For example,

> the street geometrically defined by urban planning is transformed into a space by walkers. In the same way, an act of reading is the space produced by the practice of a particular place: a written text, i.e. a place constituted by a system of signs. (de Certeau, 1988, p. 117)

If we extend these ideas to understanding the online as being spatialised and navigable, those who design and construct, navigate and use define the online (as well as its intersection or melding with the offline).

The Internet is a series of systems within which many people navigate and, therefore, must devise 'ways of operating or doing' the everyday (de Certeau, 1988, p. xi). Indeed, in many societies, Internet connectivity and associated digital literacies are increasingly necessary for the enactment of activities and functions that could be readily classed as everyday practices. By extension, then, we should consider the ways the online systems and practices – of searching, communicating, purchasing or other activities – enabled by code, software and algorithms work to constitute and enact the everyday: an everyday that straddles the on- and offline (the awkwardness of simply trying to demarcate these as 'different' spaces is evident in this phrasing, pointing to the intertwining and interrelationship of both spaces already perceived as commonplace). This translation of everyday activities (through delegation) into actions performed in online spaces is enabled by a range of strategies that include the use of algorithms to sort, manipulate, analyse and predict.

One of the things that render algorithms online interesting in any discussion of the everyday is the ways they can operate semi-autonomously, without the need for interaction with, or knowledge of, human users or operators. Latour (1998) would refer to this as delegation. An algorithm is delegated a task or process and the way it is instantiated and engaged with in turn impacts upon those things, people and processes that it interacts with – with varying consequences.

Latour uses the example of a door groom (or door closer) to illustrate the ways the delegation of an activity or process to a technology (or nonhuman) has broad and differing outcomes and responses according to design and interactions. The automatic door groom does not require a salary or to have working hours allotted; however, the way in which it is designed means that there are influences upon particular human interactions with the door and the passing-through-the-door process. For example, Latour (1988, p. 302) notes that the design of the particular automatic or technical version of his door groom means that 'neither my little nephews nor my grand-mother could get in unaided because our groom needed the force of an able-bodied person to accumulate enough energy to close the door'. The assumptions built into the door groom design along with its implementation presume a certain type and capacity of person who will be using the door. The replacement of a human door groom with an automatic closer also impacts upon labour relations and opportunities through changing the types of work available, operating hours and so forth.

Similarly, the delegation of an everyday practice such as the searching for and evaluation of information by a human agent/actor to an algorithmic equation/process also assumes certain parameters or values. In developed nations with high end computing capacities, the delegation of a range of everyday practices to technologies, and to algorithmic processes is extensive and ever-expanding. As noted above, search, communication, information analysis, decision-making, navigation and route determination are all routine and mundane functions that are increasingly delegated to and through software, code and algorithmic functions. Google is not only the name of a corporation, but it has also become a verb. Comments such as 'Why don't you google it?' or 'I googled x,' for example, has slipped into the vernacular in a way that denotes the commonplace conflation of corporate service provision enabled by algorithms with the activity itself.

This fits nicely into de Certeau's (1988) discussion of strategies. Strategies refer to:

> the calculation (or manipulation) of power relationships that becomes possible as soon as a subject with will and power (a business, an army, a city, a scientific institution) can be isolated. It postulates a *place* that can be delimited as its own and serve as the base from which relations with an *exteriority* composed of targets or threats (customers of competitors, enemies, the country surrounding the city, objectives and objects of research etc) can be managed. (pp. 35–36)

By extension, the delegation and management of everyday practices within online places by powerful actors (such as Google) demonstrate the application of complex strategies of control and manipulation of users and data. However, it is also important to note that de Certeau did not see those upon whom such strategies were directed as passive or lacking in power. He refers to the use of tactics by such targets – users and consumers, for example – to describe the ways that the seemingly less powerful appropriate (poach) and subvert through their ways of doing or making things happen. It is the intersection of strategies and tactics that lends shape to everyday life.

Algorithms

Many of the algorithms we encounter daily are proprietary owned – and thus opaque and inaccessible to outside critique; and their parameters, intent and assumptions indiscernible. And yet the working of algorithms has wide-ranging consequences for the shape and direction of our everyday. As researchers are increasingly able to demonstrate, the ways algorithms are designed and implemented (and their resultant outcomes) help to influence the ways we conduct our friendships (Bucher, 2013), shape our identities (Cheney-Lippold, 2011) and navigate our lives more generally (Beer, 2009).

Tarleton Gillespie notes, 'in the broadest sense, they [algorithms] are encoded procedures for transforming input data into a desired output, based on specified calculations' (2014, p. 167). Algorithms make things happen – they are designed to be executed and to bring about particular outcomes according to certain desires, needs and possibilities. In online spaces, algorithms are central to the ways communication and information (including the relational) are located, retrieved, filtered, presented and/or prevented.

To describe algorithmic processes, the analogy of a recipe is often employed. A recipe has a particular identified end point – a meal, or a cake, for example. What the recipe provides is a list of ingredients (contributing items or variables), but more importantly, it also contains a step-by-step description of a process that outlines what needs to happen and when, what needs to be combined or separated and when, following a very specific, detailed order. It also needs to be written in a way that the user will understand and be able to follow. Similarly, an algorithm considers particular variables or items that need to be included or excluded, particular steps to be followed in a particular order and a number of decision or action points to be identified and negotiated eventually to result in a desired outcome or end point. The algorithm is formulaic with an identified function or role that determines the steps and the processes that are employed. It is also relational in that it needs to communicate with other systems and structures with which it interacts; it needs to be able to speak to or be read by other systems and entities. In that sense, it articulates a particular operating logic.

Constantiou and Kallinikos (2015, p. 54) note that,

> Although certainly important, algorithms are the last step in a complex chain of data operations, data structures and architectures that harvest and make data available for aggregation and computation … . Algorithms without data are just a mathematical fiction.

Their point is well made; algorithms cannot be adequately studied as stand-alone processes if we are to start understanding the roles they now play. But they are also more than technical infrastructures – algorithms also need to be recognised more broadly as both situated artefacts and generative processes that engage in complex ways with their surrounding ecosystems. This is an ecosystem that involves technical – software, code, platforms and infrastructure – and human designs, intents, audiences and uses more broadly.

In many arenas (amongst public, corporate and increasingly academic entities), there is a tendency to see online-generated data and algorithmic output as being a simple resource able to guide consumer behaviour, encourage particular choices and change the ways we live and see our lives. Yet as those who critique this understanding of data as able to simply and cleanly collect and analyse note, there is no such thing as 'raw data' (Gitelman, 2011). There is also no such thing as a raw algorithm in terms of it being seen as an uncomplicated and objective instruction. Algorithms are embedded in complex amalgams of political, technical, cultural and social interactions. As Roberge and Melançon (2015, p. 3) note, 'They [algorithms] construct meanings as much as they are shaped by meanings and thus exhibit a form of double agency'. As a result, algorithms help to bring about particular ways of seeing the world, reproduce stereotypes, reify practices (Postigo, 2014) and world views, restrict choices or open possibilities previously unidentified.

When we talk about algorithms and the delegation of tasks and processes to them, we therefore need to take into account the ways their designs and their actions interact with their human counterparts, their relations, systems and structures (social, technical, cultural and political). We also need to consider who designs and implements them and what intended and unintended outcomes result. The question of who designs and implements them is often intimately bound up with questions of power and control, particularly (though not exclusively) in the case of large corporate online entities such as Google.

The power of Google

When organisations have the technical skills and the data resources readily at hand, the consequences of their algorithmic practices can be far-reaching. Google is a vast multinational company that has a long (and seemingly ever-expanding) list of product and capabilities that it offers to companies, shareholders and consumers. As a result of these extensive engagements through online systems and human and technical users, Google has access to ever-increasing quantities of data drawn from across these platforms, alongside the technical ability to aggregate, combine, manipulate and process these in ways that are not open to those outside of its corporate system: granting them considerable power to shape lives and outcomes as a consequence.

In its efforts to maximise its profits and thereby satisfy its shareholders, Google needs to meet a number of objectives: ensuring viable and attractive consumer products (e.g. Search, Maps, Gmail, YouTube, Android and Google Play), facilitating and providing compelling industry products (data analytics, targeted advertising and platform for app purchase and distribution) and in the process generating growth and income. This means the plethora of algorithms being designed and enacted similarly are required to meet differing needs and functions, sometimes simultaneously. These requirements necessitate the incorporation of an iterative process of feedback and change to accommodate the shifting environments upon which the algorithms operate.

Google's chief economist Hal Varian has publicly noted that Google runs continual experiments on its users to try to identify causality and consequence: what might drive changes in user behaviour, changes in the way in which information is found and displayed, the list is endless. The online environment is a perfect test site for trying new things, monitoring what happens and playing with variations. In a paper given at the National Association for Business Economics annual meeting in 2013, Varian wrote,

> Experiments. … . This is pretty easy to do on the web. You can assign treatment and control groups based on traffic, cookies, usernames, geographic areas, and so on.
> Google runs about 10,000 experiments a year in search and ads. There are about 1,000 running at any one time, and when you access Google you are in dozens of experiments. (Varian, 2013, p. 27)

A decision by Google to privilege mobile-optimised sites in its mobile technology search results required the implementation of an algorithm that would push those sites better suited to mobile screen views and navigation to the top of a user's search results. Google explained the reasons for its decision as their effort at enhancing user experience in accessing search results in an environment of increasing mobile use. While this change obviously makes sense in terms of optimising the user's viewing and navigation experience, the display algorithm makes its decisions on this basis in conjunction with other parameters around the usefulness of the search information retrieved. The mobile friendliness design of the site becomes one of the indicators of 'quality' for this type of search purpose. Google discussed the algorithm update in its *Webmaster Central Blog*:

> As we noted earlier this year, today's the day we begin globally rolling out our mobile-friendly update. We're boosting the ranking of mobile-friendly pages on mobile search results. Now searchers can more easily find high-quality and relevant results where text is readable without tapping or zooming, tap targets are spaced appropriately, and the page avoids unplayable content or horizontal scrolling.
> While the mobile-friendly change is important, we still use a variety of signals to rank search results. The intent of the search query is still a very strong signal – so even if a page with high quality content is not mobile-friendly, it could still rank high if it has great content for the query. (http://googlewebmastercentral.blogspot.com.au/2015/02/finding-more-mobile-friendly-search.html)

Google's Panda, Penguin and Hummingbird algorithms and recurrent updates are other examples where changes are made in order to encourage some outcomes, shift priorities: technical and social. These possibilities to shape, direct and reflect outcomes and behaviour on the basis of algorithmic sorting of large data sets gleaned from everyday activities alongside the ability to test or experiment with these and to be able to track and identify resultant changes place enormous power in the hands of organisations such as Google, whose products are fundamentally entwined in the everyday lives of its users.

However, these possibilities also raise questions as to how we can conceptualise the delegated agency of the algorithms themselves and as to how we can analyse and position their place in the everyday. While the strategies of corporations such as Google work to shape the environment and practices of its users, for example, the tactics users employ when engaging in these practices and in these spaces intersect and iteratively shape the ways in which the everyday is manifest and experienced. Relationships and understandings of technology are inferred: These relationships are complex with many descriptions connoting an interpersonal or anthropomorphic framing of everyday algorithmic output. This is evident when exploring the language used by technology researchers. For example, in the following quotation, despite the use of scare quotes around terms indicating a certain appropriation of language and actions being applied to technological process, the choice to include such language is interesting, indicating the complex relationship between human and algorithm and also the lack of an appropriate language to describe these complex processes.

> Search engines 'learn' about our preferences and desires as they endlessly concatenate information about the potential quests of searchers. As algorithms come to 'know' more about our search activities, search and targeted advertisements become more effective, which leads to better understanding of searchers' supposedly 'inner' selves, and so on in a recursive circle of adaptation and modulation driven by the algorithms as much as searchers and their desires. (Hillis, Petit, & Jarrett, 2013, p. 16)

Increasing everyday dependence on and engagement with and through the online, and extending out to our engagement with other objects (Internet of things, driverless cars or with robots, e.g.) render these relationships and the 'algorithmisation' of everyday practices as commonplace and unremarkable and yet relatedly, worthy of closer critical attention.

Unlikely or unintended relationships

> Larry Page used to say that the trouble with Google was that you had to ask it questions. It should know what you want and tell it to you before you ask the question. Well, that vision has now been realized by Google Now, an application that runs on Android phones. One day my phone buzzed and I looked at a message from Google Now. It said: 'Your meeting at Stanford starts in 45 minutes and the traffic is heavy, so you better leave now.' The kicker is that I had never told Google Now about my meeting. It just looked at my Google Calendar, saw where I was going, sent my current location and destination to Google Maps, and figured out how long it would take me to get to my appointment. (Varian, 2013, p. 28)

The extract above points to the increasing reliance and almost interpersonal engagement that we are beginning to have with our devices and our desire to delegate many of our everyday needs, decisions and actions into a synergistic melding of human and machine. Individual user responses to a technology anticipating their movements might invoke mixed feelings: for some users such as Hal Varian, this is uncritically accepted as a helpful and obvious relationship, whereas others, as Varian notes, may feel uncomfortable with the obvious surveillance and data monitoring of everyday routines that this interaction infers. Yet, this continual expansion in delegation and prediction is likely to become increasingly normalised and even expected. The increase in the number of personal assistants such as Apple's Siri or Microsoft's Cortana, and the continual extension of 'their' personal assistant capabilities, encapsulates this desire within its very expression and intent. The attempts to render the interface between the user, the device and the software and algorithms, and the activity itself seamless and ubiquitous, also work to obscure the range of powerful strategies and interests involved.

These potentials accentuate the drive to design ever more sophisticated and extensive algorithmic processes that can analyse, manipulate and predict on the basis of broader and more complex data sets enabled by the relocation of everyday practices online. Yet hidden away behind the screen and from the everyday user's ability to unpack and understand the specific practices, programming choices of these algorithms (even more difficult with machine learning possibilities and multiple algorithm interactions), what they do and do not do, are less transparent or able to be critiqued. Unintended and unanticipated consequences are an obvious, and will be an increasingly common, outcome. It is, therefore, the outcomes that signal issues or problems that need to be addressed and that we need to be alert to. These issues may be a result of internal programming or interactions, but they can also be a result of the algorithmic outcomes and interactions with other social systems and practices – as a result of their engagement with people.

Recommender systems, for example, employ algorithms to identify and present recommendations on the basis of a user's preferences and online practices. The Amazon website will appear to 'recommend' particular purchases according to the assumption of shared associative interests – if you are interested in a book on algorithmic processes, then it is likely there might be other relevant books that you might be interested in around this topic. This assumption is translated into the system then presenting to you, the algorithm interested user, the search or purchase results of other people who also searched or purchased that book along with other books that they have purchased, books that possibly have similar search terms in their metadata, on the assumption that a shared interest will result in an increased likelihood of purchase. This results in not only varyingly useful, but also at times strange or unanticipated associations.

McKelvey (2014, p. 589) points to the ways a recommender system's inference of a relationship or association between users and users' interests can be translated into troubling or unexpected connotations more broadly. He recounts an article by Mike Ananny that noted an associative relationship inferred on the basis of recommendation and placement on Google Play Store between Grindr (self-described as a gay guy finder) and a sex offender search app. The title and byline of Ananny's (2011) article makes the connections and consequences clear: 'The Curious Connection between Apps for Gay Men and Sex Offenders: Reckless associations can do very real harm when they appear in supposedly neutral environments like online stores'. By the very coupling of these two apps on an online store website – linked by the tag, related and relevant applications – an association is made raising questions about the algorithms and programming that are being used in order to generate such results, but also highlighting the possibilities for human associative interpretations of these recommendations that are problematic socially, ethically and politically. The algorithm/s involved would not distinguish between the data they have been instructed to analyse and manipulate in terms of its political or social values explicitly. Yet the outcomes point to the lack of nuance or contextual understanding that such processes often do not accommodate, and the impact they may have when being addressed to complex, socially embedded human users and systems. They are also not open to outside scrutiny that might enable underpinning assumptions to be interrogated: it is only their products or outputs that can be addressed. In this instance, a direct inference could be drawn between sex offenders and gay men.

Bias

This combination of delegated everyday practices and algorithmic functions within social, cultural and political systems inescapably results in biases being enacted. In 1996, Friedman and Nissenbaum categorised the range of biases evident in computer systems at that time.

These biases derived from a range of inputs, social, technical and emergent, as time, technology and social influences impacted on outcomes. Bias could be beneficial or detrimental or both, similarly they could be intentional or unintentional. Friedman and Nissenbaum use the example of travel airline operator listings as demonstrating bias. In their example, they noted the way in which airlines operators were listed on a screen, whether ordered by alphabet or by preferred supplier, had an impact on which airlines were used or referred to by the travel agents. As agents were more likely to refer to those operators listed on the top page, this meant that decisions as to ordering criteria benefitted some airlines and disadvantaged others. This is not a dissimilar practice and outcome to the one that has been noted with Google search results and the fact that users rarely refer to listings after the first or second page of search results. More recently, in relation to algorithms and social media, Bozdag (2013) noted how Facebook prioritises popularity of posts or particular types of interactions in its ordering and inclusion of items in a user's newsfeed, and the ways Twitter prioritises currency as an important ranking value: these choices and actions demonstrate particular biases and in the process, particular practices of power.

Friedman and Nissenbaums' (1996) categories of bias as well as their origins are listed below.

- Pre-existing: from social institutions, practices and attitudes
  – Individual
  – Societal
- Technical: technical constraints and considerations
  – Computer tools
  – Decontextualised algorithms
  – Random number generation
  – Formalisation of human constructs
- Emergent: arises in context of use
  – New societal knowledge
  – Mismatch between users and system design (differing expertise or values)

This delineation of different types of bias reveals the multitude of factors that come into play when technical, social, cultural and political elements are engaged. Bias is generated and enacted through the ways the technology is designed, the ways that the data are encoded into various relationships and actions, and the ways people and broader society engage with one another and with the various systems that they have put in place in order to navigate and control their lives. Twitter Trends analysis, for example, highlights the technical and emergent biases embedded in algorithms that value particular types of activity and push these to the forefront. Gillespie (2011) notes the process by which a Twitter topic is prioritised up the list according to the value given to certain criteria, and also the possible human/social bias displayed in the categorising of content in Amazon filtering processes. As Mackenzie (2006, p. 44) notes, '[an algorithm] naturalizes certain orders and animates certain movements. An algorithm naturalizes who does what to whom by subsuming existing patterns and orderings of cognition, communication and movement'.

The challenge for many researchers who are trying to understand the role of algorithms and the ways they intersect with and influence the everyday is trying to understand the origin of such bias when the origin, outcomes, instructions and implementation of many algorithms are not open to scrutiny and are multidirectional. This is not only partly due to the proprietory nature of many algorithms, their multiplicity and complexity, their embeddedness in many online processes and the mundane nature of much of what they do, but also by the requirement for technical knowledge or literacy that many people lack when dealing with often complex mathematical and technical systems.

Different frames: ways of seeing

Mackenzie (2006, p. 43) notes that 'algorithms carry, fold, frame and redistribute actions in different environments'. The suggestion being made in this article is that algorithms are being increasingly delegated the function of performing or enabling everyday practices enacted through technologies. And in turn, the practice of delegation of functions to algorithms is itself becoming an everyday practice, that is, increasingly mundane and normalised. In this delegation process, data (actions, relations, and objects) of the everyday are translated, framed and reconfigured.

From algorithms telling us what we are seeing or the filtering and curation of what we are seeing online, we have also framings that tell us what we, the user, *should* be seeing. A random selection of news headlines on algorithm-related topics searched (using Google search functions) for this paper brings forth the following titles: Algorithm spots beauty that humans overlook; The algorithm that can spot the 'beauty' in your holiday snaps – and tell you which selfies to delete; The shortest path to happiness. There are many, many others.

While these news headings tell us much about human belief in the capacity of technology, the stories themselves also detail the ways we – human users – can use (or delegate capacity to) these technologies to enact everyday practices with the inclusion of certain assumptions and parameters as a result. The algorithm that spots beauty carries within it assumptions and definitions of beauty represented as though they are universal and timeless and easily reduced to a particular combination of data; the one that edits your selfies implies you are less than capable and that you should trust the technology more than yourself to make these aesthetic choices; the shortest path to happiness suggests various routes to travel depending upon what the algorithm determines is the quietest, the most peaceful or the most beautiful route (without sacrificing too much time).

The goal of the travel algorithm was to 'suggest routes that are not only short but also emotionally pleasant' (Quercia, Schifanella, & Aiello, 2014, p. 1). According to the researchers,

> To date, there has not been any work that considers people's emotional perceptions of urban spaces when recommending routes to them. We thus set out to do such a work by collecting reliable perceptions of urban scenes, incorporating them into algorithmic solutions, and quantitatively and qualitatively evaluating those solutions.

When the development process is investigated further, the interplay of human emotions, decisions and inputs alongside the sorting, analytical and manipulative capacity of the technologies becomes more complex and reveals an iterative, multilayered exchange that takes place between human process and technical process. In the travel algorithm, input data were drawn from combining the analysis of data from a crowd-sourcing platform that shows two street scenes in London, and inputted user votes selecting which scene looked more beautiful, quiet or happy. This information was then analysed to form a model of the characteristics of beautiful, quiet and happy travel.

Then, to test for generalisability, the developers investigated whether their algorithm model would also work to predict beauty scores on Flickr by first analysing Flickr user votes, and then holding interviews directly with users about the choices that were suggested to validate their findings. As a result of this analysis, the developers of the algorithm claim that their algorithm can suggest, with reasonably accurate results, a number of possible travel routes able to meet the traveller's requirements in order to make a journey more pleasurable, while still accommodating the need for time considerations.

While it is not clear whether this algorithmic model was applied or developed further, it is clear that it could be monetised and offered within services such as Yahoo maps (it was developed in conjunction with Yahoo) or other GPS-based services. Zuboff (2015, 2016) makes this link quite explicit in her description of the rise of surveillance capitalism and the capture and commodification of users' behavioural data for persuasive and predictive application.

Capitalism, modularisation, quantification and the everyday

Algorithms are able to function as a result of the translation of items, actions and processes into calculable and malleable units or data points – rendering all (objects, actions and relations) in some senses as equivalent regardless of the actual content or context, and in turn these renderings are attributed value, meaning and relationships through the very design and operation of the algorithm itself and its interaction with its broader environment. In some ways, this rendering process is indiscriminate and without judgement: time, bodies, friendships, transactions, sexual preferences, ethnicity, places and spaces are all translated into data for manipulation and storage within a technical system or systems. On that basis alone, questions can be posed as to the broader philosophical issues raised around ontological understandings and experiences of the world that are engaged with and developed when the everyday is increasingly algorithmically articulated, or more simply, to ask how this might affect how people see and understand their environment and their relations (when all is reducible to malleable discrete but combinable units).

An illustration of this reduction and increasing fragmentation of every *thing* including the everyday can be seen in the growth of the quantified self and self-tracking movement and the ways various aspects of human activity and individual biological and health data are identified, tracked, captured by wearable technologies and then analysed and relayed back to the individual, the provider of the various monitoring service providers, and other interested parties (such as health services). These reductive manoeuvres are necessary to be able to capture and manipulate biological items and actions into data and processes; yet the very act of translation is also transformative: the process from biology (heart) and practice (walking) to data becomes unquestioned, normalised and invisible.

This reduction to singular data or units is, however, only one aspect of the process. The use of algorithms requires this reduction but then introduces, defines and creates relations between these varying units through the processes they are instructed or designed to implement. Therefore, algorithms are also incredibly relational – it is the relation that defines, describes and shapes how that data are then (re)presented. These relations are defined and designed by the architects of the algorithm according to a design brief, a particular desire or identified output, and shaped by technical specificity, commercial incentive and social predispositions, bias and cultural understandings.

The delegation (and resultant commodification that often results) of everyday practices such as information search and analysis functions or of communication between friends to algorithmic processes and software coding forms part of the fabric of the everyday (or habitus). Here, the strategies of actors (such as Facebook) to enframe, shape and capture user practices and desires intersect and engage with the tactics of users in making operational their everyday.

Conclusion

Algorithms invoke questions about how to conceptualise issues such as agency and power within a technologised everyday. Algorithms are dynamic processes designed and implemented by humans in conjunction with technical affordances and within broader political, social and cultural environments that are shaped by the continual interactions of strategies, structures and tactics. As a result, they are in a constant flux – think about the continual updates that we see with Google search algorithms, for example – with changes made by humans and by machines. We cannot ignore their actions, or fail to deal with their consequences. Science and Technology Studies, software studies and actor network theory all provide some fruitful insights and methods particularly in relation to the specificity of particular algorithms, yet largely fail to address many of the broader issues and questions of the everyday that are raised.

Some of the questions raised in this article relate to the relationship we have with our machines and the broader inability to critique and guide many of the algorithmic processes enacted by large corporations with which we increasingly interact. Another relates to something that Zuboff refers to with her term *surveillance capitalism*, though there is more involved in this process than increased commodification alone. As de Certeau made clear, consumers and users are not passive – they work within the systems in which they find themselves and appropriate, and subvert through various tactics of making do (something that Zuboff fails to acknowledge). Yet this still does not completely encapsulate what I am pointing to.

I suggest that by delegating everyday practices to technological processes, with the resultant need to break down and reduce complex actions into a series of steps and data decision points, algorithms epitomise and encapsulate a growing tendency towards atomisation and fragmentation that resonates more broadly with an increasing emphasis on singularity, quantification and classification evident in the everyday. Algorithms, and the delegation of human behaviour to algorithmic processes, also become part of the (technologised) everyday as a result. What this might mean for broader social and ethical relations with one another, our technologies and our understanding of the everyday itself is a question worthy of further consideration.

Disclosure statement

No potential conflict of interest was reported by the authors.

ORCiD

Michele Willson ⓘ http://orcid.org/0000-0002-3703-3020

References

Ananny, M. (2011, April). *The curious connection between apps for gay men and sex offenders*. The Atlantic. Retrieved from http://www.theatlantic.com/technology/archive/2011/04/the-curiousconnection-between-apps-for-gay-men-and-sex-offenders/237340/

Beer, D. (2009). Power through the algorithm? Participatory web cultures and the technological unconscious. *New Media & Society, 11* (6), 985–1002.

Bourdieu, P. (1997). *Outline of a theory of practice* (R. Nice, Trans.). Cambridge, NY: Cambridge University Press.

Bozdag, E. (2013). Bias in algorithmic filtering and personalization. *Ethics and Information Technology, 15*, 209–227.

Bucher, T. (2013). The friendship assemblage: Investigating programmed sociality on Facebook. *Television & New Media, 14*(6), 479–493.

Cheney-Lippold, J. (2011). A new algorithmic identity: Soft biopolitics and the modulation of control. *Theory, Culture & Society, 28*(6), 164–181.

Constantiou, I. D., & Kallinikos, J. (2015). New games, new rules: Big data and the changing context of strategy. *Journal of Information Technology, 30*, 44–57.

de Certeau, M. (1988). *The Practice of Everyday Life* (S. Rendall, Trans.). Berkeley: University of California Press.

Friedman, B., & Nissenbaum, H. (1996). Bias in computer systems. *ACM Transactions on Information Systems, 14* (3), 330–347.

Gillespie, T. (2011, October). Can an algorithm be wrong? Twitter trends, the spectre of censorship, and our faith in the algorithms around us. *Culture Digitally*. Retrieved from http://culturedigitally.org/2011/10/can-an-algorithm-be-wrong/

Gillespie, T. (2014). The relevance of algorithms. In T. Gillespie, P. J. Boczkowski, & K. A. Foot (Eds.), *Media technologies: Essays on communication, materiality, and society* (pp. 167–93). Cambridge, MA: The MIT Press.

Gitelman, L. (Ed.). (2011). *Raw data is an oxymoron*. Cambridge, MA: The MIT Press.

Hillis, K., Petit, M., & Jarrett, K. (2013). *Google and the culture of search*. New York: Routledge.

Latour, B. [J. Johnson] (1998). Mixing humans and nonhumans together: The sociology of a door-closer. *Social Problems, 35*(3), 298–310.

Mackenzie, A. (2006). *Cutting code: Software and sociality*. Digital Formations Series, Vol. 30. New York: Peter Lang.

McKelvey, F. (2014). Algorithmic media needs democratic methods: Why publics matter. *Canadian Journal of Communication, 39*, 597–613.

Postigo, H. (2014, April). Capture, fixation and conversation: How the matrix has you and will sell you, part 3/3. *Culture Digitally*, [blog post]. Retrieved from http://culturedigitally.org/2014/04/capture-fixation-and-conversation-how-the-matrix-has-you-and-will-sell-you-part-33/#sthash.6sGBTcmy.mXWelSyy.dpuf

Quercia, D., Schifanella, R., & Aiello, L. M. (2014, September 1–4). The shortest path to happiness: Recommending beautiful, quiet, and happy routes in the city. *HT'14*, Santiago, Chile. Retrieved from http://researchswinger.org/publications/quercia14_shortest.pdf

Roberge, J., & Melançon, L. (2015, July 1–19). Being the King Kong of algorithmic culture is a tough job after all: Google's regimes of justification and the meanings of Glass. *Convergence: The International Journal of Research into New Media Technologies*. Published online before print. doi:10.1177/1354856515592506

Varian, H. R. (2013, September 10). *Beyond big data*. Presented at the NABE annual meeting, San Franciso, CA. Retrieved from http://people.ischool.berkeley.edu/~hal/Papers/2013/BeyondBigDataPaperFINAL.pdf

Zuboff, S. (2015). Big other: Surveillance capitalism and the prospects of an information civilization. *Journal of Information Technology, 30*, 75–89.

Zuboff, S. (2016, March). Google as fortune teller: The secrets of surveillance capitalism. *Frankfurter Allgemeine*, Feuilleton. Retrieved from http://www.faz.net/aktuell/feuilleton/debatten/the-digital-debate/shoshana-zuboff-secrets-of-surveillance-capitalism-14103616.html

Index

INDEX